Deb Hunt was born in England, whe[...] teacher, event manager, PR executive, [...] She self-published her first book, *Dream Wheeler*, in 2013. She has worked with Shakespeare in the Park in London, *Australian House & Garden* magazine in Sydney and with the Royal Flying Doctor Service. She has lived in France, Spain, Saudi Arabia, London, Broken Hill and a small village in Gloucestershire. Deb now lives in Sydney with her partner and their dog.

love
in the outback

love
in the outback

deb hunt

MACMILLAN
Pan Macmillan Australia

In memory of Mum and Dad

prologue

Forty-five degrees, that's what they're forecasting for today. There's a total fire ban and Maggie has left her kennel and retreated indoors. I'm freezing bottles of water so I can wrap them in towels and slip them into bed tonight. The curtains are drawn, the blinds are closed and the evaporative air cooler is struggling to cope. It might bring the temperature down a few degrees but only if I leave the doors and windows open so the air can circulate. That seems like madness on a day like today. Open windows are a sure invitation for blowflies – hateful creatures that settle in ugly clusters on furniture and countertops. At least we've still got power. A main transformer blew yesterday and half the town was cut off for five hours.

The sparkling waters of Sydney Harbour are twelve hundred kilometres away from this dusty outback town. It's a place of regular dust storms; plagues of mice and crickets; hordes of red-back spiders, snakes, moths, locusts, cockroaches and small black beetle things no one seems able to identify. It's also a place of sunsets that take your breath away, until the next morning when you realise sunset was simply the prelude.

Heritage-listed buildings of majestic beauty tower over crumbling miners' cottages, modern bungalows stand next to ancient shacks seemingly built entirely out of scrap metal. The road I live on dribbles to a stop when it reaches the edge of town, as if the original road gang simply lost interest, turned around and gave up, leaving the desert to reclaim its territory. Sharp sand nibbles at broken bitumen. Pavements are optional.

It's an odd place for a middle-aged English woman to live, a vegetarian with a lifetime of failed relationships behind her, but life has a strange way of sending you in the right direction when you finally stop fighting the tide. When I gave up on love and concentrated on like, this is where it led me.

I dreaded the thought of living in such an isolated place. How would I fill my time? Who would I socialise with? It was only when I let go of my preconceived ideas and prejudices that I learnt to appreciate life in such a remote spot. This town didn't expect me to be smart or funny or engaging, it simply accepted me. The welcome was unconditional, friends easy to find and the sense of community tangible. It was like stepping back in time, to an age when shops shut for the weekend by Saturday lunchtime, when jars of homemade jam appear unexpectedly on your doorstep and kindly neighbours offer to put out your bins.

Saturday nights no longer involve tickets to Sydney Theatre Company or expensive restaurants in Balmain. We throw camping chairs into the car, pack an esky with steak and eggs and drive out to an empty creek bed, where fallen branches from the Coolabah tree form the basis of a roaring campfire. When the fire dies down, we settle a battered frying pan onto a bed of glowing charcoal and brew a billy for tea. Some nights there can be a dozen of us out there, surrounded by silence and empty space, the roof of our theatre a million stars, the walls a line of majestic trees.

Love turned up too, much to my surprise. There was no spectacular electrical storm, no bolt of lightning or clap of thunder. Love simply stood beside me and waited, with infinite patience, for me to notice it was there. Having spent years chasing the wrong men, pursuing a romantic notion of love based on fairytales and fiction, when the right man turned up I was convinced he couldn't possibly be the man of my dreams. He wasn't. (And boy am I lucky he wasn't, the man of my dreams would have made a rubbish partner!) Sometimes it's hard to recognise the value of a real man until it's almost too late.

I've found a level of contentment I didn't know existed and I've never been happier.

Five years ago it was a different story.

chapter one

Framley Coddrington is a picturesque English village. Church bells ring on Sunday mornings, the Live and Let Live pub serves award-winning real ale and the fields are full of dairy cows. In autumn, blackberries ripe for the picking cluster in ragged hedgerows.

The cottage I lived in had climbing roses in the back garden, productive fruit trees and a flourishing vegetable patch. I had a well-paid job, several close friends, five adorable nieces and nephews, three loving sisters, two caring brothers-in-law, one kindly partner-in-law and dear old Dad in the next village along.

I was also, to put it mildly, throat-chokingly miserable. There was no partridge in my pear tree and there hadn't been for many, many years.

I was the odd one out in the family when it came to relationships. My parents got engaged within three weeks of meeting each other and they'd enjoyed a long, happy, stable marriage. My three sisters – Wendy, Elizabeth and Rachel – all married their childhood sweethearts, men they'd met when they were still at school, and they'd raised happy, well-adjusted children.

Rachel's marriage to her first (and I suspect only) boyfriend may have ended in divorce but she was on good terms with him and happily resettled with a stable, long-term, committed partner. Relationships seemed to happen naturally and easily, for other people that is. If I'm perfectly honest, they also seemed a tad boring. Where was the passion? Where was the romance? I was holding out for perfection, which probably explained why I was still single (the only person who seemed surprised about that fact was me). I lived alone, I had no children and no pets (not since the demise of the last cat) and the longest proper relationship I'd ever had was way back in 1984. It had lasted less than two years. There had been a series of short-term flings and even two short-lived engagements, embarked upon not because I was in love but because I wanted to fit in and get married like most of my peers. On both occasions I broke the engagements off, causing untold hurt and confusion. I was terrified of commitment and utterly confused by love.

As a gullible young child, curled up in a corner of the local library on wet Saturday afternoons, I consumed an endless diet of fairytales. I gulped down a succession of stories in *The Red Fairy Story Book*, *The Blue Fairy Story Book*, as well as the yellow, pink, green and all colours in-between books. I believed the world was a magical place, full of knights in shining armour, damsels in distress, beautiful princesses and handsome princes ready to ride to the rescue.

A combination of burning curiosity, crippling shyness and hopeless naivety was always destined to get me into trouble. At twelve I was old enough to catch a bus to visit a friend in the next village but too shy to speak to the man sitting next to me. 'I'm getting off at the next stop, could I please reach across you and ring the bell?' The words stuck in my throat and I missed my stop. I missed several stops. In fact, rather than speak to the man or stand up to encourage him to move, I stayed on the bus until he finally got up and hopped off, forcing me to walk five miles home in the dark.

At fifteen I attended a local youth club and met sixteen-year-old Sandra, whose brash self-confidence seemed the perfect antidote to my blushing shyness.

'My parents force me to stay in at night so I pretend to go to sleep then I climb out the bedroom window,' she boasted. What she did after she had climbed through the window wasn't clear, but it sounded like a great adventure.

'Can I come too?' I asked.

So I followed her through the village one night to a house where two men were waiting upstairs. I was mutely compliant in what followed and washed off the shame when I got home. I told no one and never saw Sandra again.

I moved on to romantic fiction – Georgette Heyer, Catherine Cookson, Daphne du Maurier. In these books the only thing that mattered was meeting the man of your dreams, and the destiny of star-crossed lovers was hampered by cruel fate in the form of wicked stepmothers, scheming employers, shipwrecks, thunder, lightning, fire and flood. No matter what the obstacle, the ending was always the same – lovers who fell into each other's arms and lived happily ever after.

The world of romantic fiction offered an escape from the shameful secret that I carried inside like a petri dish full of spores, multiplying in the dark. Secrets don't like company. A secret forces you to keep to yourself, even in the midst of a happy family, so I withdrew from my sisters and left them to the sweet innocence of first boyfriends; I needed something more ambitious to erase the memory of that false start.

One hot Saturday afternoon at the end of June, several months short of my sixteenth birthday, with the exams over and the school holidays stretching ahead of us, I went to my friend Anne's house for tea. Her music promoter dad introduced us to Stavros, a short chunky musician in his late twenties who was booked to play the summer season on the island of Guernsey. Stavros handed me a cup of tea and smiled at me. Whoosh. I fell off a cliff I hadn't even known was there. Our eyes met, the teacup rattled and I was his, whether he wanted me or not. Here was the romantic love I'd read about, the absolution I craved to erase the guilty memory of grubby sex with a stranger in a back bedroom.

The foreignness of Stavros reminded me of the swashbuckling heroes I'd read about. Here was my dashing, handsome prince. I didn't think beyond the desire to be with him, to fall into his outstretched arms and be swept off my feet. I found out where Stavros lived and wrote to him, emboldened beyond measure by this new feeling. 'I'm planning a week's holiday in Guernsey,' I lied. 'Could I visit you?' I added my phone number at the end of the letter. A few days later he rang. 'When you come over?'

I told my unsuspecting parents that I'd been invited to stay with Rebecca, a school friend, and her aunt in Somerset during the school holidays.

'How lovely, I'll write to Mrs Jackson and thank her.'

'Shall I post it for you, Mum?'

I walked up to the local post office and threw the letter in the bin, suffering a stab of conscience that wasn't strong enough to make me come clean.

The money I'd earned working weekends on the bacon counter in the local Tesco supermarket was enough for a bus from Bristol to Weymouth, then a ferry from Weymouth to Guernsey. 'I've booked a bus to visit Rebecca, will you be able to drop me off at the station please, Dad?'

On the day of departure my skittish teenage nerves were cloaked in flared jeans that featured a lampshade fringe sewn on the hem, a simple white t-shirt and a yellow jacket casually tossed over my shoulder. Dad dropped me at the station as requested.

'Say hello to Rebecca from us. Have a good holiday, love. See you in a week.'

I watched his familiar Ford Cortina pull away with an unexpected lump in my throat then I picked up my bag and presented myself at the ticket office.

'You're too late,' said the man in the ticket booth, glancing up at the clock. 'You've missed the ten thirty. Be another three hours before the next bus to Weymouth.' He went back to the paper he'd been reading.

It took a moment for his words to sink in. If I waited three hours for the next bus I would miss the ferry from Weymouth to Guernsey.

'You could get a bus to Bath, maybe pick up a train from there,' he added, turning the page.

'One-way ticket to Bath please.'

I arrived in Bath four minutes after the train to Weymouth left. At that point I wavered, tearfully wondering if I should give up, go home and admit the lie. I pictured my kindly parents' shocked faces as they listened to the story, imagined their incredulity slowly giving way to anger and disappointment as the depth of my deception unfolded and I knew I couldn't do it. I walked to the road in front of the station and stuck out my thumb.

The first driver to offer me a lift was an elderly woman who had to be reassured that, yes, my parents knew exactly where I was and, no, she didn't need to call them. I fretted when the lorry driver who picked me up next had a dirty cab; I didn't want oil staining my treasured yellow jacket. The third lift was from a middle-aged salesman driving a Ford Cortina. Surely I would be safe with him?

We drove through open countryside. On the last stretch of motorway before Weymouth he offered me a cigarette.

'No thank you, I don't smoke,' I lied.

He put a cigarette to his lips and there was an awkward fumble with a box of matches that somehow dropped into his lap. I glanced across to see sweat marks spreading from under his arms.

'Would you like to stop for a bit? Get out and stretch your legs?' he asked, fumbling with some intensity between his legs for the fallen matches that were proving difficult to pick up. I stared straight ahead. 'No thank you, I'm in a bit of a hurry,' I said, primly. 'I've got a ferry to catch.'

Guardian angels do exist. That sweaty travelling salesman kept driving and dropped me in Weymouth without another word.

I walked off the ferry in Guernsey to find Stavros waiting for me. He kissed my cheek – oh, what a sweet, romantic thing to do – and sent my heart swooping through the clouds, where it floated for the next seven days. During the day I would sit trance-like for hours, watching Stavros chain-smoke or strum the guitar, and at night I would accompany him to the venue and watch him perform, nodding sagely so any girls in the audience would realise he was taken. I even feigned a wince, as if I'd spotted a wrong note (this from someone who doesn't have a musical bone in her body). It was a blissful week of sweet sex and gentle music and we were destined to be together, no question. When it was time to leave, Stavros put me on the ferry home and he kissed me again, this time far more passionately.

'I love you,' I whispered, my arms wrapped around his neck.

'I am married,' he whispered back. 'But we still meet, yes? Stay close to the wires of distant freedom,' he added, cryptically. 'I call you.'

I cried all the way home. Who could I tell? Not my parents, certainly, and not my older sister either, or she might have told my parents. And if Anne found out, she would have told her father and he might have called the police.

'Hello, love. How was your holiday?' Mum said when I got back.

'It was good, thanks, but Rebecca wasn't well. I think I caught the flu from her.'

I went to bed and stayed there all week, grieving for lost love. How could such powerful feelings be evoked then denied? Was I meant to just go back to school and forget him? Nothing I'd read had prepared me for such misery.

We met a couple more times, clandestinely of course, but I hated knowing that he went home to someone else afterwards. In the end I stopped seeing him. I kept the whole escapade to myself, confided in no one and took long, sobbing walks through the village before drying my eyes then going home to sulk in my bedroom, nursing another shameful secret that couldn't be shared. I fanned the flames of my tragic existence by writing truly awful poetry.

After that, it was easy to lurch from one instant fix to another, throwing myself at men in a series of encounters that proved as unsatisfying as packet mash potato. In a desperate bid to recapture the bliss I'd lost and erase yet another painful memory I asked out my French teacher, my bank manager and my economics lecturer. The French teacher stood me up, the bank manager turned out to be a transvestite who wanted to wear my clothes and the economics lecturer had not one but *two* wives.

'We live in the same house, everyone is happy with the arrangement,' he said, leading me upstairs to the attic room of a student house that he owned. It was the middle of the day and he was armed with fish and chips and a bottle of vodka. 'Of course, I'm only married to one of the women, but I think of them both as my wives,' he added, taking off his trousers.

He must have assumed the tenants would be out. Moments later the attic door burst open and the startled face of a nice young man (with all his clothes on) appeared. 'Who the hell are you?' he asked.

'Your landlord,' said my lecturer, not bothering to reach for his trousers.

I even asked my doctor out one day. I was in my early twenties and he was a young registrar, filling in for a few weeks. He seemed like a nice young man, for once almost the right age for me, so I rang the surgery and asked to speak to him.

'Are you allowed to see patients socially?' I asked. 'Because if you are maybe we could have dinner?' I added, not waiting for a reply to the first question.

'I'm so sorry,' he said quietly, 'I'm afraid that's not ethical.'

Two weeks later I was forced to go back and see him about a pimple under my arm that had developed into a festering boil. By the time I plucked up the courage to do something about it I was nursing a raging fever and the boil was the size of a lemon.

'That looks angry,' he said, as I lay on the examination table with my arm above my head.

'I hope you're not.'

He shook his head. 'No hard feelings,' he said, reaching for a scalpel.

'I suppose this is divine retribution?' I said, trying to make light of the situation.

'I'm not divine,' he replied.

I disagreed, oh how I disagreed, but somehow it didn't seem the right time to tell him. We both focused our attention on my sweaty armpit and I watched pus drain from the boil he'd just lanced.

After a dwindling number of depressingly similar encounters in my twenties and early thirties I punished myself for all that meaningless sex and gave up on men altogether. I'd given up on a few jobs by then as well, from librarianship to event management and public relations. I was a quitter.

'Give sorrow words', isn't that what Shakespeare once said? 'The grief that does not speak whispers the o'er-fraught heart and bids it break.' How true. I'd kept my feelings hidden for so long I couldn't speak of anything that involved emotion without my throat constricting. An overflow of emotion, like a body of water pressing against the sides of a dam, would push at the back of my throat and tears would quickly follow. I could cry at the drop of a hat onstage; offstage I battened down the hatches, tightened the screws and let no one in. Intimacy was a foreign concept.

Five shrivelling years of celibacy followed and I aged into the original Miss Prissy Knickers, in sensible shoes, big pants and no make-up. Sex became a dirty word. My favourite word was no. Don't, won't, can't, shan't and mustn't were all up there, but nothing beat the simplicity of no; the absoluteness of it; the sound of a door slammed in your face.

Eventually I plucked up the courage to start again, at the beginning of the alphabet.

chapter two

The party was at Margaret's flat, in a housing estate in South East London. A was stretched out on the floor, a self-confident bear of a man in his mid-thirties, with Nordic features and a clipped beard. He lay there, claiming the carpet, his rugby player thighs encased in child-like dungarees while he absent-mindedly stroked a girl's ankle. I knew Jenny wasn't his girlfriend; we were both anxiously single. She looked at me as if to say, 'Is this guy for real?' I watched him caress her ankle, much as you might fondly stroke a dog's head when your attention is focused elsewhere, and I listened to him talk about live theatre in Prague and the plays of Václav Havel (a playwright I'd never heard of). What hands, what thighs, what ideas! Later that evening I stood on the brick-covered balcony with Jenny and we talked about A.

'He looks keen on you,' I said.

She shook her head. 'Not interested, not my type. What about you?'

'No.'

We were both lying.

A was casting a production of A *Christmas Carol*, destined for a short European tour, and he wanted performers who could sing. Jenny had the voice of an angel, as effortless and clear as sunlight shining on water.

Since I couldn't sing I helped at the audition. Jenny was cast. She was an obvious choice. The surprise came later, when I went to the pub with A to discuss the auditions. We talked, we laughed and (this was the clincher) he cried. I've always been a sucker for a sad puppy. Weakness in a man melts my heart, not strength. Two pints of lager and a single unexpected kiss later my long drought was over. A was relaxed, easygoing, good company and the best kisser. But was he the right man for me? Would he measure up to the exacting standards set by Miss Prissy Knickers?

On an early date at a pub on Waterloo Road, after a teenage overdose of lip-smackingly good kissing, Miss Prissy Knickers took the floor.

'Have you been married? Have you got any children? How do you earn a living?'

He scraped through those questions so Miss PK brought out the big guns.

'How old are you?'

'Seven.'

'Pardon?'

'Seven is the perfect age. I never want to be older than seven.'

Miss PK processed this alarming news, passing information back to the troops, never taking her eyes off the target. *Did you hear that? He thinks he's seven years old. How irresponsible is that? How can a seven-year-old be relied on? That's not even legal.*

She went in for the kill. 'Are you looking for a fling or a full-time commitment?'

'A fling.'

'Do you believe in monogamy?'

'No. I want to go through life having as many sexual partners as I can.'

The possibility that he might have been teasing in response to the barrage of questions didn't occur to Miss Prissy Knickers.

OK, that's it, get your coat, we're leaving.

What about the kissing? I murmured, even as Miss Prissy Knickers bundled me out the door.

At thirty-five, after a lifetime of failed relationships, I wasn't interested in having fun; I was looking for long-term commitment. I wanted to cut to the chase and get married before it was too late. Based on those parameters, A could have no place in my life. Never mind the intense attraction, never mind the laughter, the tears and the shared interests, my life was all about moral certitude, answers rather than questions. There was no place for ambiguity. Convinced we had no future, I told A we couldn't get involved. He promptly took up with Jenny. Now that, dear reader, was the point when I should have walked away and wished them well; I should have stuck to my moral guns and looked elsewhere. I didn't. Jealousy got the better of me (the kissing was hard to resist as well) and over the next two years Jenny and I engaged in an ugly tug of war that could have no winners.

At one point A dumped Jenny, definitively and decisively, and he moved in with me. He was tender, loving and emotionally open. I was suspicious, wary and in control. He did his best to defrost the block of ice that encased my heart but Miss PK could only be persuaded to take a back seat for a limited time (weeks, not months). Pretty soon she was back to worrying about his lack of a steady job, his childlike approach to life and his sexual proclivities. It was obvious there was no future for us. Walking along the seafront at Dover one afternoon with A, on a dull drizzle of a day with not much conversation and even less kissing, we passed a buoy with the name Jolene etched on it. That line from Dolly Parton, about not taking some guy just because you can, played in my head all afternoon.

That is precisely what I had done.

I believe in retribution and, after that sorry episode, I deserved a bucket-load. My comeuppance wasn't long coming. On a brief visit to Australia, during a lull in the tug of war with Jenny over A1, I met A2. The two men couldn't have been more different. A2 was a dependable, professional family man with two young children. He owned a house, drove a convertible sports car and sailed a yacht. His wife had recently left him and his suffering and vulnerability were deeply attractive. He also offered financial security and a ready-made family that saved me the bother of having to create one of my own. I should have been ashamed of myself but I lacked the self-awareness for that. I still hadn't worked out that the instant fix of fairytales, when lovers meet and what happens next takes care of itself, was just that – a fairytale. A friend suggested we go to the theatre one night and that first date was followed two nights later by dinner and a moonlit sail on Sydney Harbour. It didn't take much for me to convince myself that A2 was the one. I went back to England, disentangled myself from the sad mess with A1 and set my sights on A2.

Over the next three years I used all my savings travelling back and forth to Australia. A2 liked me, that much was clear from his letters and phone calls, but I craved certainty. I was looking for a passionate outpouring to reassure me we had a future together. Distance sharpened my desire. I sent notes and gifts to his children; I ordered flowers and sent him poetry. He sent the poems to his ex-wife in an attempt to win her back but I didn't care – understanding flowed through me in a river of compassion; we were meant for each other, he was simply pining for what he could no longer have. He'd get over it and, in the end, as long as I was nice, he'd be mine. In the months that followed I tried in vain to read some kind of commitment into his letters. I refused to see that he was blatantly still in love with his ex-wife.

Sitting at home in England I grew impatient for an outcome, convinced that if only we were together I could heal A2's broken heart. One Saturday afternoon I closed the curtains, switched off *Lighthouse Family* and settled down at the kitchen table, a deck of Tarot cards in front of me. I found it so much easier to consult a deck of cards than attempt the messy business of speaking directly to someone. When you live through dreams and fantasies, as I did, you do anything to avoid conflict and reality. I shuffled the pack, spread the cards face down on the kitchen table and selected ten, mentally asking what would happen if I moved to Australia.

The reading was inconclusive, with conflicting cards that made no sense, so I picked up the deck and reshuffled. Why waste time on a full reading? I decided to pick a single card, one solitary image that would decide my destiny. I spread the deck out, scanned the cards and picked one. The Hanged Man: wrong card. I was looking for The Lovers or the Ace of Cups, something that signified love and new beginnings, not a card that suggested I might have to let go of something unattainable.

I slowed my breathing, collected the cards and reshuffled, eyes closed this time. Show me a sign, I whispered, just one card that will decide my fate and future with A2 if I move to Australia. I ran my fingers along the pack, waited until it felt right then picked another card. The Hanged Man stared back at me. When it happened a third time I packed the cards away, sold my flat in London and applied for permanent residency in Australia.

I rang A2 when I arrived. 'Surprise!' A short time later I was dumped in favour of someone more stable. 'If any part of your decision to come back to Australia involved the hope that you and I might one day be together (he did have a lovely turn of phrase) you must now let go of that. I have met and fallen in love with someone else.' (Any part? It was the only reason!) The comeuppance I so richly deserved was sharpened in two exquisitely painful ways. I was dumped by email and the 'someone' was a friend I had confided in.

I took anti-depressants and invested in wailing therapy sessions. 'Of course you're upset, you gave up everything, moved to the other side of the world and the man you love dumped you. And your friend betrayed you. Your reaction is perfectly normal. Anyone in your position would be upset.' The therapist was a kind soul who didn't want to see me waste what little money I had.

I stayed in Australia, hoping A2 would change his mind (the fact that I had nowhere else to go played no small part in my decision). I had staked my future on A2. I had sold a beautiful Edwardian ground-floor flat in West London that had a flourishing garden and was within walking distance of the tube and squandered most of the proceeds flying back and forth to Australia. The end result was a small rented apartment in Leichhardt, on the top floor of a building that imprisoned the sticky Sydney heat under a flat roof, trapping it inside with me. I ate TV dinners from a badly chipped formica-topped table, my bare legs glued to a sweaty plastic sofa marooned in the centre of a shag-pile carpet. Planes on final approach to Mascot lined up with a beacon at the end of the street; every fifteen minutes they would roar overhead, rattling the windows and sending the six-metre span of vertical blinds into a tangled spin. I felt much the same way.

I lived on a diet of gin, chocolate and cigarettes, bursting into tears on the bus during the day and howling at the moon at night. It was like a rerun of my teenage years, only now I was forty-one. Life is so unfair, I wailed, grieving for the happiness that had been so cruelly snatched from my grasp – it would have been perfect if only it had worked. The irony was lost on me.

Eventually I stopped crying. I gave up smoking, found free-lance work as a journalist with *Australian House & Garden* magazine, lost weight, saved money, even thought about putting a deposit on a small flat in Balmain. Then one fine day, about four years later, I was sent on a travel assignment to Canada. It was the kind of assignment most journalists dream of. In return for writing an article on eco-tourism, I got to spend a week at an exclusive resort on Vancouver Island. That was where I met A3.

A3 was a university lecturer from England. He was spending a week of his summer break teaching environmental studies to the group of committed eco-warriors who'd all signed up to spend a week in the wilderness. When he got up to speak on the first morning his voice wobbled uncontrollably. That show of nerves was enough for me to experience a rush of sympathy.

A3 was childlike in his enthusiasm for mushroom hunting in the forest, beach combing and hiking in the woods. 'Nature's a wonderful thing; isn't it marvellous?' he gushed, grabbing my hand to point out a patch of moss.

'Did you two know each other before you came here?' asked one of the participants as we sat peeling garlic for lentil salad at lunch one day. A3 was standing at the sink, chopping onions and shedding mock tears.

'No,' I said.

'Everyone seems to think you're an item.'

In less than a week we became inseparable. 'Wouldn't it be wonderful to live here,' he said one afternoon as we sat beside the clear spring that circled the camp. 'You could build a hut in the forest, grow vegetables, make your own wine.'

'That would be my idea of heaven,' I said.

On the last night he opened up.

'It won't last,' he said, gloomily.

'What won't?'

'I've got a girlfriend, back in England. It's bound to fail eventually. We argue all the time. I wish I didn't have to go. I wish I could stay here.'

Nothing much happened – Miss PK saw to that – but I held his soft hand as we listened to the sound of horses gently sighing in the darkness, and believe it or not (even I find it hard to believe when I look back on it) that was all the encouragement I needed to start making plans.

Once again I had set my sights on an impossible dream, an unattainable fantasy of life elsewhere. We can make this happen, I thought. I can rescue you from a relationship that's not working and we can create the perfect life together, we just have to work out a way of making it happen. The challenge and the distance spurred me on. If I'd shared such bizarre thinking with any of my girlfriends they would have (quite rightly) told me to stop being such a crazy fool, so naturally I didn't tell them. I didn't tell A3 what I was planning either since anyone with an ounce of sense would have seen that he had simply enjoyed a wonderful holiday and he wasn't looking forward to going home. I had no such sense and I was a long way from learning my lesson.

We stayed in touch by email and it wasn't long before I decided it was time to move back to the other side of the world.

My good friend Kate, a touchstone since university days and happily married to James with two young children, spotted the pattern long before I did.

'You're not moving back to England because of that guy you met?'

'What guy?'

She raised her eyebrows.

'Oh you mean the guy in Vancouver? Hah! No.'

'Because that would be a big mistake, wouldn't it?'

'The biggest!'

'You've got a good job here, and you love living in Sydney.'

'I know, I know!' I lowered my voice an octave. 'Don't worry, I'll be back. I just want to reconnect with family, that's all.'

I was lying, as usual.

I gave up the best job I'd ever had and moved to Framley Coddrington, back to the village where I'd grown up. When A3 learnt what I'd done we met for dinner.

'It's so good to *see* you,' he said, bouncing on his feet like a small child as we hugged hello. 'Wasn't that a great holiday?'

'The best,' I said. 'How's life?'

He pulled a face. 'Not good. White or red?'

I drank enough to silence Miss PK and later that evening, with his girlfriend conveniently away, we ended up at his flat in Hammersmith. I woke up the next morning elated, convinced this was the start of a new life for us both. He woke up with a hangover. 'What have we done?' he groaned.

Over the months that followed we saw each other a few times. Each time he told me how bad things were with his girlfriend before insisting he couldn't possibly break up with her. Eventually, to his credit, he said it would have to stop. By now I was hooked. What is it about something you can't have that makes it so attractive?

I feigned friendship and developed an interest in caving, his main hobby. I joined the local Frenchay and Region Troglodyte Society, bought a hard hat with FART written across the front of it and went caving in the Mendips. I sent him newspaper cuttings on underground caving expeditions and joined a group of singers performing in Cheddar Gorge. None of it made a jot of difference.

A3 tried patiently, and frequently, to explain that the fling we'd had was just that – a fling – and would I please stop being silly; he valued my friendship but he didn't want anything more.

I didn't believe him. If I'd been worried about time running out in my thirties, now, in my late forties, I was desperate – desperate enough to convince myself we had a future; if only he would leave Melanie, his 'she's part-time for heaven's sake' girlfriend, and fall into my outstretched arms, all would be well.

All was far from well.

Don't get me wrong, I wasn't crazy. I've never hung around the gates of Buckingham Palace thinking Prince Charles was in love with me, and I've never driven halfway across America wearing a nappy so I didn't have to stop for a toilet break in my bid to reach the man I loved as quickly as possible (I wasn't *that* desperate), but I did hound him with the occasional text message now and then . . .

How are you?
Are you OK?
Haven't heard from you, I'm worried. Please call or text.
Just need to know you're OK, that's all.
Are you depressed? What's the problem?
Please call me.
What's the bloody problem?
Sorry, ignore that last message.
Seriously though, are you OK?

. . . sent over the course of, oh, twenty minutes?

It reached the point where I decided I would have to stake everything on an outright declaration of love; maybe I'd been too subtle, maybe he didn't realise how I felt?

A3's house was 120 miles away from mine, in West London. I would sometimes turn up unannounced. *Hey, how are you? No, I just fancied a day in London, happened to be passing, thought I'd set off early to miss the traffic. Before dawn is best, don't you think?*

So one cold winter's morning, with rain teeming down, I got up at five and drove to London. I parked the car in Ealing, outside my old flat where I knew I could get free parking for the day, then I hopped on a tube to Hammersmith and by eight o'clock I was in Starbucks, paying for a bag of croissants.

With the paper bag tucked inside my coat, I waited impatiently for the lights to change on Hammersmith Road then sprinted across the pedestrian crossing, dashed down Bute Gardens and stood for a moment outside his front door, trying to catch my breath. I rang the doorbell, clutching the still-warm croissants, and suddenly there he was, the man of my dreams, a look of weary resignation on his beautiful, crumpled, sleep-creased face. Clutching the sweaty bag, I hoisted it into the air. 'Surprise!'

He pulled the cord of his dressing gown tighter around his waist, turned his back and padded down the corridor. I followed, staring at his calves.

We reached the living room and I attempted a clumsy, affectionate, 'we're just friends and this is what friends do' kind of hug. He sidestepped the hug and turned away. 'Sit down,' he said. 'I've got something to tell you.' I sat on the sofa, hoping he'd sit next to me but he sat on a wooden chair at the table under the window and gave me an equally hard, wooden stare.

'I'm getting married,' he said.

'Wow,' I replied, mentally cursing the fact that I'd run out of time. 'You've waited long enough.'

'It's not Melanie.'

For a heart-stopping moment I thought he was about to propose. He must have seen the look on my face because he rushed to explain.

'I met someone, someone else! Someone new.'

'You met –? You didn't . . . why didn't you . . .?' I was so confused I couldn't form a complete sentence. In the end I just said, 'When?'

'About a year ago.'

Twelve months of courtship. A whole year of dinners and sex and flowers and all the sweetness of new love, culminating in an engagement to be married, and I hadn't known anything about it. 'Congratulations,' I managed.

I drove home along a dismal stretch of the M4 motorway, sobbing all the way. We were meant for each other, why couldn't he see that? What more could I have done to convince him? Symbolism stalked me in single magpies, frozen ponds and signs of bleak misfortune. A white van I followed had the words *I've gone* scrawled in dirt on the back and Amy Winehouse came on the radio singing about trouble and being no good. I sobbed some more.

Of course, somewhere deep in my subconscious I knew A3 and I weren't right for each other, and I'd known it from the beginning. If I had told him what was on my mind – *I want to be with you, leave your girlfriend and run away with me instead* – I knew what the answer would have been. So I said nothing and concentrated on the fantasy life I'd built in my head. Four long years had passed since then.

Reality sank in on the drive home and a stark, inescapable truth cut through all my romantic fantasies: I was nothing but a silly, middle-aged fool who should have learnt her lesson long ago. At forty-nine I may as well have been in kindergarten when it came to men.

If I had been a man I could have run away to join the Foreign Legion so no one would have seen me cry.

But I wasn't a man; I was a stalking middle-aged spinster with a resume that would stand up in court as confirmation of multiple personality disorder.

So I applied for a job with the Royal Flying Doctor Service (RFDS) instead.

chapter three

I have no medical qualifications and I can't fly a plane but, since the Flying Doctor job didn't involve sucking the venom out of a farmer's leg or landing a plane on a dirt strip in the middle of a dust storm (am I the only one who remembers that old TV series?), that didn't matter.

The Flying Doctor wanted a junior in their Sydney marketing office, someone who could draft a press release, organise events, update the website and produce their quarterly newsletter. I wasn't actually qualified to do many of those things either (and by no stretch of the imagination could you call me a junior, even stuck in a stationery cupboard with the lights off) but I was desperate to get away. It was only an eight-month maternity post, just long enough to make sure I'd be on the other side of the world when A2 and his fiancée got married. I didn't want to embarrass myself (or the happy couple) by turning up for the ceremony in dark glasses and sobbing loudly.

I liked the idea of a short-term job. I was a serial monogamist when it came to jobs, totally committed in the short term but always ready to move on. I'd lost count of the jobs I'd had – telephonist, receptionist, librarian, PR executive, English teacher, writer, actor, workshop co-ordinator, theatre producer, event manager, journalist – to say nothing of the failed attempts at speech therapy and primary school teaching. But there was another reason to be away for less than a year, and that was family. After four years of pining for A3 I'd begun to feel settled in England; it was the longest I'd lived anywhere since child-hood. Village life was slow and measured and I was enjoying getting to know my sisters. I'd spent so much time obsessing over men I'd failed to appreciate how valuable female friends could be. In many cases I'd seen them as rivals, not friends. I had three sisters, one older and two younger yet I knew little about sisterhood. Growing up, I had shut myself off from them and escaped into a world of fiction. Wendy, Elizabeth and Rachel were wise, funny, understanding and supportive. I knew I would miss them and their families.

I made a mental pledge.

If I get this job I promise to stop stalking and start living; I pledge to have fun. I will embrace life before the cellulite that spans the troubled seas of my dimpled thighs drops as far as my knees. I will drink mint julep (whatever that might be), wear matching under-wear and stop feeling like the last piece of mouldy old cheddar left on the cheeseboard.

I thought back over the four years I'd spent in a damp stone cottage buried deep in the English countryside, much of it waiting in vain for the phone to ring, when my only excitement had been checking the number of worms in the compost bin (if you've never tried it, don't mock it). Here was an opportunity to head back to the sunshine of Sydney, and this time I wouldn't be chasing a man. I would be going on my own, to make my own way.

Determined not to ask the Tarot cards if it was the right thing to do, I trudged up to the top of the garden instead, squelching through fallen leaves. Brushing aside cobwebs, I wrenched open the shed door and settled into an old green armchair with broken springs and velour cushions that once took pride of place in my aunt and uncle's house. It still had a comforting smell of cigar smoke.

I reached for a talisman I'd told no one about. My little voodoo doll was mounted on a bamboo cane about twelve inches high, with worn trousers, a ragged straw hat and a lopsided grin. I'd found the miniature scarecrow in a tangle of brambles when I'd first started digging the garden and I had slowly invested him with all of A3's characteristics. Many was the time I had sat in that armchair, as the evening light faded and the rain teemed down outside, clutching the scarecrow, begging the universe to bring us together. What must I have looked like? Exactly what I was, I suppose: a sad, middle-aged spinster who saved used tea bags, cut her own hair and normally had dirt lodged under her fingernails, crooning to a stuffed scarecrow in the shed at the top of the garden. My tears were unhurried and unstoppable, like rain set in for the afternoon.

I had made a pledge to move on so I took the scarecrow into the fading light of that gloomy afternoon, intending to plant him in one of the garden beds where he belonged. As I lifted his tattered jacket I saw the clear outline of a heart, traced in mould on the back of his pants. The discovery made me waver, tears falling freely, and I forced myself to ignore the sign. 'I love you,' I whispered and thrust my little scarecrow into the mud, leaving him to the vagaries of a harsh English winter.

Back inside I banked up the wood-burning stove and couldn't resist a quick Tarot card reading, not for me but for the man I loved and his bride to be. Will they be happy? Are they an ideal couple, meant for each other? Will their love last? The cards were unequivocal, topped by the Ten of Cups depicting Psyche hand in hand with Eros. There was no finer card when it came to happiness and family life. I pictured them at their wedding, the sun setting behind the trees as they exchanged their vows, sparkling lovers in diaphanous chiffon and crumpled linen, champagne flowing, baby-making to follow. Bugger.

I put the cards away and turned my attention to the application form for the Flying Doctor, downloaded from the *Sydney Morning Herald* website. With the time difference between England and Australia, I had just three hours to submit, so there was no time to waver or prevaricate. I erased several years of intermittent work experience as a librarian, a telephonist, a secretary, a workshop co-ordinator and an English teacher (five years as a struggling actor wasn't going to impress anyone either) and said nothing about my age. Instead I focused on public relations. Years ago, back in my early twenties, I'd had a stint with a PR company in London, pitching lame story ideas on industrial shelving to Fleet Street journalists who were far too busy to listen. They had glamorous product launches to attend, some of which I had to organise. The editor of *Industrial Shelving Weekly* could always be relied on to turn up but he normally had the canapés to himself. I hated PR, frequently went home in tears and couldn't wait to leave. No matter now, I needed this job.

The job spec also asked for someone to help organise events. Freelance event management was one of those jobs I had fallen into in my thirties, during a lull in theatre work. (Apologies to any professionals who've worked their butts off getting a foothold in the industry but that's the way it goes. I bet you're married and I'm an ageing spinster, remember?)

When it came to event management I had made it up as I went along: handing out badges, directing people to breakfast in five-star hotels, making sure luggage got to the right room

('Porter!'), I'd greet guests with a flourish ('Bonjour', 'Buenos dias', 'Ciao') and was often in charge of counting them on and off coaches – that was until the day I lost someone in the souks of Marrakesh. I miscounted, told the driver to leave and the poor sod I'd forgotten had to make his own way back from the teeming madness of Jemaa el-Fna. When he eventually turned up at the hotel several hours later, a sweaty, gibbering wreck, I made him swear not to tell anyone. I reckon he blabbed, though, because they never gave me the coach counting job again.

My colleagues in event management were consummate professionals and I was waiting for the day they would finally work out I didn't know what I was doing. One of the best was Lilian, a blonde Swedish bundle of energy, who rang one day to check my availability.

'We're taking a group to Puerto Rico. Are you interested?'

Seriously, that's what she would say. Are you interested? As if I might have something better to do.

'When is it?' I said. It didn't do to sound too eager.

'In three weeks; we need you for eight days.'

Eight days in Puerto Rico, all expenses paid, staying in a top-class resort. Sometimes I couldn't go through the whole 'let me check my diary' nonsense in case I snorted and blew my cover. I took a deep breath. 'That looks OK,' I said.

'Book your flight and we'll reimburse you,' Lilian said.

A few days later I joined a conference call to confirm the final details.

'Who are you flying with?' Lilian asked.

'BA.'

'Great, so are the rest of us. Let's meet at Heathrow around noon.'

It wasn't often I got the chance to show how professional I was so I grabbed the opportunity whenever I could. This one was too good to miss, especially with six other event managers on the call.

'Isn't that cutting it a bit fine?' I said. 'The flight's at 12.45.'

'No it's not, it's at 2.30,' said Lilian.

'Oh. I must be on an earlier flight.'

'There isn't an earlier BA flight from London to Puerto Rico.'

What Lilian didn't know about airlines wasn't worth knowing. In this case, though, I knew she was wrong.

'Hang on. I'll check my ticket. Yep, here we go, Heathrow to San Jose, leaving Heathrow Terminal 2 at 12.45.'

There was a pause on the other end of the phone.

'Why are you flying to San Jose?'

I wondered if it was a trick question. The pause stretched into silence, giving me the sinking sense it wasn't.

'The job's in Puerto Rico,' she reminded me.

'That's right, Puerto Rico,' I said, weakly.

'San Jose is the capital of Costa Rica,' said Lilian, a little too sternly for my liking.

Unbelievably they continued to employ me after that, but my days at the glamorous end of event management were numbered.

In the Flying Doctor application, I glossed over my lack of website management skills – there was no way they'd find someone who could do everything – and concentrated on my writing experience instead, which was harder than I expected. No amount of imagination could make articles on kitchen benchtops for *House & Garden* magazine relate to the world of emergency medicine. Then I remembered I had once edited a newsletter for Wimpy, the UK hamburger chain. There was a nutritional angle there, surely.

Desperation underpinned the stream of words that filled the page. I was hoping this job would save me; from what, I wasn't sure. Myself perhaps. I lodged the form online with examples of work and slumped into a chair by the fire, clutching a mess of soggy tissues.

Two days later I received an email.

'The marketing manager of the Royal Flying Doctor Service would like to interview you, do you have Skype?'

I immediately hit reply. Yes! I was no slouch when it came to modern forms of communication. Surely that would have to count for something in a marketing department.

Excitement faded to insecurity as I considered the implications of a video interview at seven o'clock the next morning. They were looking for an office junior, not an ageing spinster whose face betrayed the fact that she'd been dumped once too often. Crap. I rearranged the furniture in the living room, set up soft lighting, added flowers to distract their attention and balanced my laptop on a pile of books so the camera wouldn't focus on my double chin. It would have to do.

The alarm went off at five o'clock the next morning, while it was still dark outside. An overnight frost had blanketed the lawn in shards of white and it was shimmering under the moonlight. I pictured Sydney, hot and sunny, at the end of another perfect summer's day.

My experience of Australians told me they were friendly, open, welcoming and overwhelmingly youthful, so my task was to appear happy, professional and at least ten years younger. I washed and blow-dried my hair (not something I had much practice with) then logged on to Skype to check the result. The image of a 65-year-old Soviet dissident recently released from a five-year stretch in a remote Gulag, but who'd somehow managed to get to a hairdresser, popped up on screen. I reworked the lighting, changed the angle and tried again. The Soviet dissident stared back.

I knew there was some old make-up in a shoebox under the stairs but a frantic scrabble past scraps of carpet, pots of paint

and bags of compost produced nothing more useful than a
bottle of orange nail polish. I felt vulnerable and tearful, cursing
myself for such ridiculous optimism. What made me think they
would ever want to employ a heartbroken, middle-aged woman?
The marketing department of the Royal Flying Doctor Service
(RFDS) was probably run by the equivalent of Kylie Minogue.
I shrank like a slug exposed to sunlight, desperate to admit defeat
and crawl back to bed, but it was too late. I averted my eyes from
the startled crone staring out of a small square in a corner of
the screen.

Then the phone rang.

'G'day. Sorry about this. We can't get the technology to work.
Can we do a phone interview instead?'

Can we? Oh yes, yes, YES! I was so relieved, I sparkled. There
was more razzle-dazzle in me than a New Year's Eve firework
display over Sydney Harbour Bridge. I was witty, clever and upbeat.
I answered all their questions more or less truthfully, never mind
that the job involved PR which I hated, or event management which
I'd proved I was crap at, or updating a website which I knew nothing
about. It was a job with purpose, a reason to dry my self-pitying eyes,
stop stalking and start living. They were too polite to ask how old I
was and by the end of the interview I knew I'd impressed them.

'You do know what the salary is?'

'Yes.'

'It's not much.'

'It doesn't matter.'

Yes it does.

'Shut up, PK.'

'Pardon?'

'Sorry, I was talking to the dog.'

'What will happen to your dog if you get the job?'

What now, Clever Clogs?

'He's not mine, I'm just minding him.'

'The job starts in five weeks, is that a problem?'

'Gosh no, I was planning to move back to Australia anyway.'

There was no stopping me. When I came off the call I danced around the dining room because, improbable as it seemed, I was convinced I'd got the job.

No chance.

Two days later they offered me the job.

'Stick that up your arse, Miss Prissy Knickers.'

No need to be crude.

To all those people who were better qualified, I'm sorry. Your turn will come.

*

With five weeks to get to Australia, I abandoned stalking and started packing. My sisters and their partners helped me pile books into cardboard boxes, clean the house, fill the shed with packing crates and sell my battered second-hand car. Dad offered to drive me over a hundred miles to the airport, which was a sweet and lovely gesture given that he was eighty-three years old and not the world's best driver. But I knew I'd fall apart if I had to say goodbye at Heathrow, so I bought a train ticket, booked a taxi to take me to the station and said my goodbyes in the village. Most people weren't surprised by the choking sobs I couldn't hold back; my secret obsession with A3 hadn't been that secret after all.

'We'll see you at the end of the year,' my brother-in-law Don said, crushing me in a hug that threatened to burst the dam on my pent-up emotions.

'You can always come back,' said Wendy, my older sister who saw through most things and worried quietly in the background about all of us.

*

Two hours before the taxi was due to arrive I was still touching up paintwork on the windowsill in the front sitting room, a last-minute job that had been overlooked. The windows were clean, the paths were swept and the smell of wet paint mingled with disinfectant and floor polish. I could see early daffodils beginning to poke their heads above the frozen earth in the front garden. Spring would bring tulips; lavender, roses and honeysuckle would follow in summer.

I dabbed at worn patches of timber with a stiff brush that held layers of old paint trapped between the bristles. My suitcase was standing in the hall. Once I'd finished painting, I would empty the bin, drop the keys off with the agent, take the taxi to Parkway station, then a train to Heathrow . . . next stop: Australia. The phone rang, and I wondered which one of my sisters it might be.

'Hello.'

I held my breath at the unexpected sound of A3's voice.

'What am I doing? I must be MAD! Why do I want to get married?' I listened to his familiar rising wail, the phone tucked under one ear as I held the paintbrush above the windowsill, watching a single drop of glossy white paint slowly form into a thickening teardrop. It glistened in the winter sunlight.

I did my best to keep my voice steady. 'Don't do it,' I said. 'Call it off.' The smell of acrylic paint grew stronger and I could feel my heart thudding against my ribs.

'That's easy for you to say, you've never been married.'

The drop of white paint trembled and my throat tightened, words trapped in a glue of unspoken grief. The blob lengthened, hesitated then slowly released its sticky hold, disappearing into the silence.

'No,' I said eventually. 'I haven't.'

I lowered the brush and balanced it on the edge of the pot with a trembling hand.

'Haven't you ever wanted to?'

Oh sure, I felt like saying, I wanted to marry you and isn't that the funniest thing you've ever heard? And then I wondered if he was trying to tell me something. Was he suggesting there might still be a chance?

Don't be ridiculous he adores his fiancée. He's got cold feet, that's all. It's perfectly normal behaviour.

For once I thought PK was right. Maybe he missed all the attention I used to lavish on him. He would never have asked me to marry him anyway, not in a million years. If he had asked, would I have said yes? I suspected the answer to that question lay at the heart of my problem with men. I don't think I would have. I just wanted what I couldn't have; what I'd known all along I could never have.

'No,' I said quietly. 'I've never wanted get married.'

'Oh well, have a safe flight.'

And he hung up.

I boarded the flight to Australia on Thursday 28 February. We were due to land in Sydney on Saturday 1 March and, since it was a leap year, I was going to miss 29 February altogether – the one day every four years when a girl could supposedly ask a man to marry her. I reached for my phone but we were taxiing down the runway and the woman in the next seat shot me a warning glare.

chapter four

Bleary-eyed with lack of sleep, I stood in Sydney airport and waited for my luggage to appear on the carousel. We should have landed in Sydney at seven o'clock in the morning but delays in Singapore threw the schedule; it was nine o'clock before we touched down. By the time we'd disembarked and made our way through passport control it was 10 am on Saturday 1 March; back in England it was eleven o'clock at night. With a sickening lurch I realised it wasn't too late – with the time difference it was still 29 February in England. I could call, tell him I'd changed my mind, ask him not to marry her, beg him to marry me instead. The phone was in my hand, I was scrolling frantically through the address book, his number was backlit on the screen in front of me . . . then I pictured his shocked face as he received a late-night marriage proposal from someone he thought of as only a friend, an amusing part of his past, his future decided elsewhere. I pictured her lying next to him, 'Who's calling at this time of night?' Did I really want to ruin someone else's chance of happiness, especially someone I professed to love? No. I suppressed the destructive, irrational impulse, closed my phone and waited for my familiar blue suit-case to trundle towards me.

There was no point speculating; the past was over, I was in Sydney, and in two days I would start a new job with the RFDS.

I collected my suitcase, passed unheeded through customs and stepped into the early morning sunshine. In spite of my misgivings and the ache in my heart, it felt good to be back.

*

The suburbs of Balmain and Birchgrove are crowded onto a skinny finger of land that stretches into Sydney Harbour, tanta-lisingly close to the city. The streets are filled with weatherboard houses and terraced cottages, originally built to house workers on the nearby dockyards. Glimpses of Sydney Harbour are never far away. Impossibly narrow in places, the streets are lined with towering gum trees; jasmine tumbles over white picket fences and frangipani trees bloom overhead. Much of the peninsula has been gentrified but the suburb still has a village feel and a whiff of original character.

My friend Kate lived in Birchgrove and we'd been friends since university. I was 'Aunty' to her two children, Ben and Hanne. When Kate and her husband James moved to Australia she gave up a successful PR business to retrain as a social worker. She took a job as a grief counsellor in the department of forensic medicine at the city morgue, a demanding job few people could cope with. She nurtured her marriage, raised two children and forged a worthwhile career while I grizzled my way through a series of shallow obsessions and mediocre jobs. Somehow we had stayed friends, good friends, and until I could find a place of my own I would be staying with them.

Anny, Kate's sister, met me at the airport and drove me straight to Birchgrove in time for an open viewing of an apartment I'd spotted on the internet before I'd left England. I was keen to find somewhere as close to Kate and her family as I could. Anny parked the car opposite an old apartment block and I was astonished to see Kate waiting on the steps outside. 'Welcome back!' Kate shouted, waving from across the road. She rose to her feet, carefully and slowly, hiding the fact that she was in pain. Three months earlier Kate had been diagnosed with breast cancer and two weeks before my arrival she'd undergone a double mastectomy with reconstructive surgery, taking fat from her stomach to create new breasts. My beautiful brave friend, whose hair had turned prematurely grey, was hunched over like an old woman.

I ran across the road, gave her a tentative hug and, not for the first time, felt blessed that I had the good fortune to call such a loving and gracious woman my friend.

Feeling like a leaky tap I wept as Kate's son Ben, a budding lawyer, gave me a huge hug, followed by Hanne, now a sports science student at Wollongong uni. Even their Danish Granny Inga was there as well. I squeezed the kids, hugged Inga and grinned at Kate, who'd been camped on the steps of the apartment building for the past twenty minutes. Thanks to her, we were first in the queue.

'Sign on the spot if you can,' said Kate. 'Tenants are desperate; they're offering to pay more rent, putting down huge deposits and signing leases that lock them in for years. If it's any good, grab it.'

Within minutes another forty people had arrived, some of them clutching coffees, others checking their mobiles or scanning copies of the local paper, fingers blackened by heat-smudged newsprint.

Kate and the others waited downstairs while I trudged upstairs. Being first in the queue gave me a five-second advantage before the others swarmed in, and that was enough.

The chipped paintwork and stained floors could be overlooked because there were two large rooms with high ceilings and stained-glass windows, a small bathroom and an even smaller kitchen. I craned my head out of the window to peer across Birchgrove Oval; somewhere out there was the Harbour Bridge. The flat looked old and tired – like me – but it was affordable. Having given up a well-paid corporate job for a junior position in a charity, I couldn't afford to be choosy, not if I wanted to live in the same suburb as Kate. The only downside was an open stairwell between the living room and the kitchen, but since I wouldn't be able to afford to drink there was no danger of falling down it.

'I'll take it,' I said to the agent.

He looked at me strangely and handed me an application form.

'The deadline's Monday morning,' he said, liberally passing out application forms to other people. They swarmed behind him like a flock of pigeons at Trafalgar Square, swooping and grabbing at the fluttering paper.

'I'm not sure you understand,' I said, pushing my way past the pigeons as he headed downstairs. 'I was first in the queue. I'm happy to take the apartment.'

'Fill out the form. Nine o'clock Monday morning,' he repeated.

'Could you please make a note that I was first in the queue?' I called to his retreating back. I doubt if he heard me; he was already out the door.

Back at Kate and James's house I examined the form and was dismayed to find I needed references, bank account details, contact details of previous landlords, confirmation of employment, plus a photocopy of my passport, driving licence and medical card.

'Don't worry,' said James. 'I'll write you a reference.'

I walked up to the newsagent's on Darling Street to photo-copy the few documents I did have and then I completed the rental application form, in triplicate, with the requisite photo-copies and references. I added a note to explain about not having a bank account then I scribbled on the front 'I was first in the queue' before slipping it under the door of the real estate agent's on Sunday evening.

The weekend passed in a fuzzy blur of jet lag and comforting, familiar faces. Ben spent Sunday afternoon taking part in a game of pub golf and we spotted him wandering the streets of Balmain with a scorecard tied around his neck. Some of his friends looked like they already had massive handicaps and I had to suppress an automatic sneer of disapproval from Miss Prissy Knickers. They were having fun and where was the harm in that? It's what I had pledged to do.

*

I slept in Hanne's old bedroom, surrounded by pictures of horses and dogs, trophies lining the shelves and pennants pinned to the wall. 'Don't give up,' one said. 'Reach for the stars,' said another. 'Only begin and the rest will follow.' I lay awake on Sunday night, preparing to start my new job the next day, reading the advice and vowing to stay strong.

Come Monday morning I was a bag of nerves. For the past four years I'd worn black, navy, grey or brown – mostly brown. As I lost confidence, my wardrobe lost colour and I gradually put away anything vibrant and replaced it with dark brown. When I heard I'd got the job with the RFDS I made sure there wasn't a single item of brown clothing in my suitcase. What I wouldn't have given that morning for an article of brown clothing. I was begging for it, craving the security and anonymity of it, and all I had was a rainbow of colour. I had packed hoping the clothes would make me look younger but I felt like an ageing *Play School* presenter. I pulled on a green flowered blouse and (large) white trousers.

'You look lovely,' said Kate, lying in bed, massaging rose oil into an ugly scar that stretched from one side of her stomach to the other. I wondered what I'd ever done to deserve such a generous friend and I dug my nails into the palm of my hands. Her whole family was a touchstone, a reminder that love, commitment and kindness were the bedrock of any successful long-term relationship.

'Good luck. You'll be fab,' said Kate. 'And remember how talented you are. They're lucky to have you,' she added, correctly reading the anxious expression on my face.

chapter five

The 441 chugged up Rowntree Street, past the All India restaurant and across Darling Street, stopping to fill up with passengers outside the Town Hall Hotel, then cramming in more on Mullens Street before speeding across Anzac Bridge, circling Darling Harbour and depositing me on Sussex Street; a journey of just eighteen minutes, from start to finish. With no way to access the office at eight o'clock in the morning I wandered down to Sydney Aquarium and sat on the wharf, watching seagulls bob on the water and noisy myna birds peck at discarded flecks of pastry. A ferry pulled in, churning up water as the engines slammed into reverse sending a fine salty spray drifting past. Office workers in white shirts and (I couldn't help noticing) black, brown, grey or navy trousers and skirts poured down the gangplank. I followed them back up to Sussex Street, feeling like a tourist.

The Slip Inn on the corner was made famous when a young unknown Tasmanian met a Danish prince; next thing she knew, people were calling her 'Your Royal Highness'. Falling for a prince is the stuff of fairytales and I couldn't help thinking my childhood overdose of fairy stories and romantic fiction probably helped get me into trouble in the first place. I banished thoughts of romance as I passed the pub and kept my eyes open for the Flying Doctor office.

It turned out to be an unassuming building with a concrete grey front and glass doors that slid open to reveal an empty lobby. There was no doorman and no receptionist, just an old display board on the wall, individual white letters pegged behind glass: ROYAL FLYING DOCTOR SERVICE, SE SECTION, FLOOR NINE.

To her credit, if the marketing manager was surprised at how old I was she hid it well. More Janis Joplin than Kylie Minogue, she was a tall woman in her mid-thirties, with fine curly hair falling to her waist, a patterned swishy skirt and an air of distraction that I hoped might come in handy – it could delay the discovery that I didn't know what I was doing.

'This is Rachel,' said Janis with a dreamy smile, introducing me to a twenty-something who was sitting cross-legged on a typing chair, dark grey leggings stretched across her pregnant belly, black hair held in a neat ponytail. I marvelled at her agility and wondered if my thighs would squeeze between the armrests.

'Shall I make a pot of tea?' asked Janis, addressing the air around her and then drifting away without waiting for a reply.

Rachel raised her eyebrows. 'Come and sit down,' she said. 'This is where the real work gets done.'

She ran through a program of morning teas, school awareness days, base openings, volunteer speaker events, photographic shoots, press visits, the annual report, the quarterly newsletter, the weekly e-news bulletin, fundraising booklets, marketing leaflets and the back end of a website that looked like the control panel of a heat-seeking guided missile.

'That's pretty much it,' she said.

'Wow, the marketing department does all that? Sounds like a busy place.'

She looked at me with what I can only describe as tenderness and spoke with quiet patience. 'Those are my responsibilities,' she said.

'You do *all* of it?'

Sweat prickled the neckline of my green silk blouse as the enormity of what I'd taken on began to sink in. I would be covering for Rachel during her maternity leave.

Superwoman unfolded herself from the typing chair and smiled. 'It's not too bad if you're organised, you just have to shut the door and get on with it.' She glanced towards the closed door of the marketing manager's office. 'And ignore half the things she asks you to do.'

Ignore what someone asks me to do? I'd always been a people pleaser, doing things to win approval, from cleaning a friend's oven to having sex when I didn't want to. I once took a part-time job at the back end of event management that involved input-ting data about hotel bookings onto multiple spreadsheets. By mid-morning on the first day I knew I'd made a terrible mistake. I'd somehow managed to cancel a perfectly legitimate booking for the Head of Finance and I'd booked Mrs Peabody into a smoking room with Mr Blackstone, when what she (quite reasonably) wanted was a non-smoking room with her husband. He'd disap-peared off the sheet altogether.

At eleven o'clock I rang Julie, who had hired me. 'I'm so sorry, I've made a terrible mistake. I shouldn't have applied for this job. I'm the wrong person. You've got the wrong person!'

'Calm down,' said the lovely Julie, who never panicked about anything. 'It just takes some getting used to.'

'I'm not a numbers person, I never have been!'

'You'll cope,' said Julie.

'I don't think so. Can you please look for someone else?'

'All right, but would you just stay until the end of the week? Please?'

'OK.'

It took four years for me to leave; saying no wasn't my strong point.

Rachel took me on a tour of the ninth floor, through a suite of offices that were reassuringly old and untidy, while a radio played in the background. There were people opening post, inputting data and typing at speed. Bonnie was a friendly ex-New Yorker responsible for major donors and (thankfully) almost as old as I was; Nicole knew most of the donors by their first name and radiated serenity; and Jude, the database manager, revealed she had relatives who grew up in England.

'Where?' I asked.

'In a small village in the West Country.'

'What's it called?'

'You won't have heard of it.'

'Try me.'

'Framley Coddrington.'

On the other side of the world, in a city of several million people, I was working with someone who knew the small village in Gloucestershire where I grew up. The coincidence helped me feel more at home.

'Why don't you spend the morning reading,' said Rachel. 'It might help you get a feel for what we do.' It was a generous offer when they were all clearly so busy and I felt an overwhelming urge to do a good job for the RFDS. They'd taken a chance on me, given me the escape I needed and I was determined to repay that trust.

I took refuge in a corner of the archive room, a dusty sanctuary where the stacks held gems of historical interest, to read about the Reverend John Flynn who started it all. He embarked on his missionary work in the early 1900s, when half of all Australians – around two million people in those days – lived in rural areas, battling the harsh conditions of the Australian outback. Access to medical assistance was sporadic at best, and in most cases meant travelling huge distances at great personal cost to reach help.

I found a dog-eared pamphlet Flynn co-wrote in 1910, *The Bushman's Companion*, a slender book with a blue cardboard cover, small enough to slip into a trouser pocket. The fragile pages contained first-aid tips, extracts from scriptures and snatches of poetry. The page on snakebite was crinkled and worn, as if it had been read and re-read many times.

> Without delaying a fraction of a second, in the case of a leg or arm, put a twitch on upper arm or thigh . . . if finger, put twitch on joint against hand. Don't chop it off. If bite is of a poisonous snake, stab in with a knife all round bite. Quarter of an inch will be deep enough. Suck for dear life. Do not swallow any blood.

Extracts from Flynn's magazine *The Inlander* made more sobering reading. I sat quietly in a corner of the dimly lit archive room and read his description of the predicament of a ten-year-old boy, with four younger siblings, who discovered his mother had died while their father was away prospecting for gold. The ten-year-old had no option but to gather the younger children together and set off to fetch help.

> He first fed the poultry, gave them water, turned the wind-mill off and gave each of the children a piece of bread and butter and a drink of water, taking a big drink himself to see

him through the journey. He filled the water bag and got a bottle for the baby to drink from, put the baby into a go-cart and, for fear it would perish, took a young puppy with them.

Between one thirty and 2 p.m. the sad little procession started out for the Empress mine, over five miles away, bare-footed and through sand, with the thermometer registering 110 degrees in the shade. This little band consisted of Vincent, aged ten, Robert eight, Isabel five, Arthur three and the baby, seven months old.

The puppy was the first to knock up and had to be carried; then Arthur, whose feet were badly blistered. Vincent, with his young brother on his back, pushing the go-cart through the sand, became greatly distressed, but pushed manfully on. With the extreme heat the baby required every attention and a sip of water every few hundred yards. Vincent's great anxiety was that the water bag would give out before they reached the Empress Mine but he brought his little expedition safely through, and they arrived at about 5 p.m., when he reported the sad news and obtained assistance.

I was left with a sense of shame that so much of my life had been spent doing something as silly as chasing men, flitting from one job to another, always ready to give up at the first hint of trouble. I turned the page and it was as if the ghost of John Flynn was standing beside me.

'Said a young man to his old minister, "It's no use. It's all up. I'm a damned fool!" But the gentle answer came: "No. You've been a fool, but you're not a damned fool yet."'

I'm not sure why I cried; maybe it was the thought that redemption might still be possible. Whatever the reason, I was glad to be sitting in that dusty archive room alone.

*

Towards the end of the day I phoned the real estate agent and he ran through a speech he must have made many times before. I knew as soon as he started that I didn't get the apartment.

'Forty people saw it, twenty people applied to rent it and we narrowed the field down to six,' he said. 'You made it to the last six,' he added, as if that was some kind of consolation. The sense of disappointment was acute.

'So why didn't I get it? I was first in line. Doesn't that count for anything?'

'There's always someone who's disappointed.'

'But why me? What could I have done differently?'

'It was the landlord's decision,' he said. Ignoring the irritation I could hear in his voice, I pressed on. 'How did the landlord decide? What was his decision based on?'

'I'm afraid you'd have to ask the landlord that.'

'Can I speak to the landlord?'

'No, you can only deal through the agency.'

'So why didn't I get the apartment?'

We went round and round in circles but he wouldn't be drawn. In the end I was forced to accept that no amount of pleading or arguing would get me that beautiful apartment overlooking Birchgrove Oval, just as no amount of obsessive pursuit will ever get me a man who doesn't want to be with me.

'Think positive,' said Kate when I broke the news to her that night. 'There'll be another one and at least now you've got all your references in place, ready to pounce when the next one comes up.'

Her response was simple, straightforward and adult. Let it go, it wasn't meant to be. It was behaviour I needed to emulate.

*

By the end of the first week I had established a routine of catching the bus to work and the ferry back. The terminal at

Darling Harbour was a five-minute walk from the office and the salty breeze of an open deck was a great way to end the day. From the terminal at East Balmain the 442 offered an easy climb up Darling Street but I badly needed the exercise so I walked instead, feeling the sun on my face, strolling past open door-ways as the heady scent of gardenia drifted in the warm autumn air. Pavement cafes crowded with chattering diners lined the restaurant strip on Darling Street but I preferred to walk in silence so I cut behind St Andrew's church, welcoming the cool shade offered by towering gum trees.

Finding somewhere to live wasn't easy and thoughts of A3 were never far from my mind. What was he doing? How was he feeling? Would he really go through with the wedding? Did he ever think about me? I tried to banish such pointless thoughts and concentrate on the task of finding a flat. News reports suggested vacancy rates had dropped to one per cent, tenants were offering twelve months rent up-front and tiny Balmain apartments advertised at $400 a week were fetching $450. Every Saturday morning I joined dozens of people chasing the same short supply, armed with copies of documents in case I could push my way to the front and sign on the spot. I saw shoeboxes with floor areas no bigger than a single garage advertised at $400 a week; a two-bedroom terrace for $720 a week, the living room barely large enough for a sofa and the bedrooms so small it was a choice of what to include – a bed or a wardrobe. You wanted both? Forget it. I trudged away.

Three weeks later I was ready to give up on Balmain, convinced I would never be able to afford to live there, when I spotted a miniscule two-bedroom terrace advertised at $500 a week. It had no pictures of the inside so it was bound to be a hovel, especially at that price. Kate bucked me up.

'It's just around the corner,' she said. 'We'll go together.'

The woman standing at the front door was heavily pregnant and we assumed that she was waiting outside to leave room for people to get in. I'd never seen such a skinny house.

'Not many people have turned up,' she said, wistfully.

We smiled and walked in, down a narrow corridor that ran past a small study on the left. The corridor opened onto a slim living room in the centre of the house; beyond that was a sunroom. Standing at the window we could see glimpses of Mort Bay and the skyscrapers of the city beyond. Kate pinched me and I said nothing. From the living room, one set of stairs led up, another down, so we explored upstairs, finding an open-plan double bedroom with attic windows on one side and a picture window on the other, offering unobstructed views across the water. I spotted the Harbour Bridge and now I was the one pinching Kate.

Downstairs was a subterranean dining room painted bright red, another step down brought us to the kitchen and bathroom, down again to a laundry and finally, at the bottom of yet another flight of steps, was a small, sunny patio.

The house was dark, damp and musty. Plaster bubbled off the walls, the bathroom taps were peeling, the kitchen cabinets were warped and the linoleum on the floor was cracked. I felt like I'd stepped into the Armistead Maupin novel series, *Tales of the City*. It was perfect, the kind of place I could picture myself in, mixing a mint julep.

'There's got to be a mistake,' whispered Kate, dashing my hopes. 'They must have the price wrong.'

We climbed back upstairs and found a young couple deep in conversation with the pregnant woman.

'I wanted to meet potential renters myself, that's why I didn't go through an agent,' she said. Another couple was waiting in line to speak to her, no doubt ready to paint themselves as the perfect couple ready and able to look after her gorgeous home.

'Excuse me, could I just confirm how much the rent is?' I asked politely.

'Five hundred dollars a week.'

Kate and I huddled outside to confer. 'How can it be that price? It's lovely,' I hissed.

'She must be a Balmain Basket Weaver.'

'A what?'

Kate explained about the flaky creative types who get drawn to the inner west. That's me! I wanted to shout. I'm a flaky creative type, only I've never had the courage to admit it, and the owner could be my new best friend if I could just get close enough to buddy up to her. Kate's not flaky at all and I didn't want to alarm her (nor did I really want to trade my BF for a BBW, even if it did get me the house) so I said nothing.

'We need a plan,' Kate said.

'I know. Follow her home, camp on the doorstep and refuse to leave until she agrees I can have the house.'

There was a pause and the look on Kate's face made me back-pedal from the stalker approach.

'Or maybe . . .'

'Wait until the other couples have gone, then go back in,' said Kate. 'Tell her you'll sign a two-year lease, offer her more money and get her to sign on the spot if you can.'

'But I was only planning to stay until the end of the year.'

'Don't worry, if that happens you'll find someone else to take the lease on.'

I may be drawn to creative types but at that precise moment I was so glad Kate wasn't a Balmain Basket Weaver. She's a strategic thinker, organised, clear-sighted and a demon nego-tiator. I should have paid more attention when we were at university instead of chasing men. I could have learnt a thing or two from her.

I lurked on the street corner to count the number of people leaving and slipped back in when the coast was clear. The owner was in the sunroom, sitting on the couch making notes.

'Sorry to bother you, I just thought I may as well give you my references now.'

I handed the sheaf of papers over and she gave me a tired smile as she glanced through them.

'Oh, the Royal Flying Doctor Service?'

'Yes,' I said, hoping I looked like a doctor. 'I love your house,' I added meekly.

'Do you? Would you be happy to sign a two-year lease?' she asked.

'Of course.'

'Would you mind if we had builders in for a short while? We want to lay new flagstones on the patio.'

'That wouldn't bother me.'

'And we thought of building a deck out towards the water.' She waved her hand towards the sunroom. 'It might improve on the views.'

She had my absolute, undivided attention.

'Not a problem,' I said.

'I suppose it would be good to have a single person living here, instead of a couple. Less wear and tear,' she mused.

I said nothing about the dinner parties I hoped to throw, or the lodger I might have to get in order to pay the rent and instead I burst into tears, unexpectedly, like a true-blue Balmain Basket Weaver.

'I love this house,' I sobbed. 'I really want to live here.'

She melted and gave me a big smile. 'Do you? I'd like you to live here too.'

I dried my eyes. 'Would you like me to sign now?'

'I just need to check with my husband,' she said. 'I'm sure it will be fine, though. I'll call you on Monday.'

I tore back to Kate's house and we spent the next twenty minutes discussing strategy over a coffee.

'Should I call? Offer to pay more?'

'No. See what happens on Monday.'

'What, just wait?

'Yes.'

'Do nothing?'

'Yes.'

*

For someone like me, doing nothing was a near-impossible ask. Over the weekend I swung from elation to despair, from hope to self-pity, agonising over the frustration of having to step back and let the universe take over. The weather reflected my mood, with relentless, soaking rain that overflowed gutters, poured through gaps in closed windows and thundered onto concrete pavements, only for the sun to break through and drench the world with dazzling colour moments later.

More rain on Monday morning seemed an ominous sign and the bus was crowded with passengers emitting puffs of steam. I didn't want to seem unpatriotic; I knew Australia's dams needed filling and the crops needed watering and we were all being urged to think about saving the country's precious water resources but I sat on that bus and I wished it would STOP RAINING FOR FIVE MINUTES. If I wasn't going to get that sodding house, at least let the bloody sun come out, I thought miserably, slumped into a soggy mess of steaming self-pity, rain dripping from the umbrella jammed between my knees.

When I got to work the phone rang.

'We'd like to offer you the house.'

I choked back tears of gratitude and arranged to send a deposit. So let's hear it for Balmain Basket Weavers and Best

Friends! Thanks to Kate's wise counsel and her wait-and-see strategy, I was going to be living in a quirky terrace in Birchgrove, with friends just around the corner. What's more, having done the sums I realised I could scrape by without getting a lodger as long as I went everywhere by public transport. Or got a bicycle. And stopped drinking.

chapter six

The tarmac shimmered in bright sunlight and I offered a silent thank you to the gods as Friday lunchtime's Rex flight from Sydney taxied towards the terminal in Broken Hill. The propellers fell silent, the plane door swung open and heat rushed in.

It was mid-April and I'd been in Australia just six weeks. Work had been frantic since Rachel had left and oddly I wasn't complaining; it helped distract me from thinking about A3's impending wedding. We'd stayed in touch since I left, just the odd email now and then: *How are you? Fine thanks, how are you?* Nothing deep and meaningful, just enough to keep hope alive. And that was the problem. I'd nurtured hope for so long that the acute sense of loss I felt now threatened to overwhelm me. How silly that losing something I didn't ever have should have caused me such grief. But there it was, that old familiar sadness, settling in like a weather pattern of looming depression. What an irrational thing love is. I had to put A3 out of my mind and move on.

I had flown to Broken Hill to oversee a photo shoot for the annual report. All I knew about the place (from a quick Google search) was that Charles Sturt – the first European to pass through – thought it the most desolate land he'd ever seen. Having viewed it from the air, I had to agree. The town was surrounded by scrub and red earth and was seemingly empty for miles around. Menindee Lakes were out there somewhere but I must have been sitting on the wrong side of the plane because all I saw was a barren landscape. What Sturt missed was a lucrative seam of silver, lead and zinc that led to an explosion of growth; after its eventual discovery it took just eight years for Broken Hill to become the third largest city in New South Wales.

It didn't look so hip and happening now. A short walk across the tarmac brought us to a sleepy terminal with a single check-in desk, a snack bar and an unmanned car-rental counter. The blue electric bug zapper on the ceiling was working overtime. Bags from the hold were loaded onto a cart, driven a few metres to the terminal and left outside for passengers to drift across and help themselves.

I collected my case and walked the few metres to an adjacent hangar, Head Office of the Royal Flying Doctor Service, South Eastern Section. I entered through the visitor centre and looked around. I'd spent most of the past three weeks researching the history of the RFDS for an upcoming issue of the newsletter. All the information I needed for the anniversary issue – history, timeline, quotations, every type of aircraft they'd ever flown, contents of the medical chest, pioneering surgical instruments, dental equipment – was all here. I could have saved myself hours of painstaking research if only Queen Bee, as I had mentally dubbed the Janis Joplin lookalike marketing manager, had told me about it.

The hangar was disappointingly empty. I had pictured noise and energy, planes revving their engines, doctors and nurses racing to jump on board a plane before it climbed into the skies on a dangerous yet daring rescue mission to swoop into the desert, land on a patch of barren earth and scoop up a child bitten by a king brown. I was hoping for a cross between Heathrow Terminal 4 and *Grey's Anatomy*. Maybe I'd watched too many episodes of the original RFDS TV series. I consoled myself by thinking that the 'swoop and scoop' must have been going on right at that moment somewhere out in the bush.

There was a relaxed, laid-back atmosphere in the hangar, with a radio playing in the background and groups of engineers bent over dismantled engines. I wandered unchallenged until a petite woman with blonde hair and twinkly eyes spotted me and led me to the main office. Barb introduced me to her boss, the CEO, and I tried not to stare. The accident must have been a bad one. His face had been reconstructed, his hands too. I could see where his fingers had fused together and new knuckles had been put in. The scar tissue ran under the sleeve of his shirt on both hands and I wondered how far up his arms it went.

Barb ran through the itinerary she'd organised for the next few days then she handed me a map of Broken Hill and the keys to a car. 'You can use one of the base vehicles parked by the chain link fence,' she said. 'If you'll follow me into town, I'll show you where you're staying.'

'What are you wearing tonight?' I asked. In my role as PR co-ordinator I was attending the Broken Hill Women's Auxiliary Ball that night. I was hoping I might sit at Barb's table.

'Didn't they tell you?' she said. 'I can't be there tonight, but whatever you wear will be fine,' she added, leading me out to the car park. 'It's always a good night, I'm sure you'll enjoy it.'

I wasn't so sure. Gardening gloves and rubber boots were more my style than high heels and a ball gown.

Mid-afternoon heat bounced off the bitumen as I scanned the car park, squinting towards a line of cars parked under a shade cloth. I pointed the keys, pressed the unlock button and a Toyota Landcruiser lit up. Pretty soon I was bouncing along the road from the airport into town, feeling like a bus driver, tooling the streets of Broken Hill to get my bearings. You wouldn't tool the streets in a Ford Focus, or a Mitsubishi Mirage, but perched above the suspension in a Toyota Landcruiser I was definitely tooling. And loving it.

Barb made sure I had everything I needed then she left me to explore. This was a mining town, no doubt about it. The streets I explored were named after metals and minerals – Argent, Silver, Bromide, Cobalt, Oxide, Tin, Bismuth, Silica. Overshadowing them all was a giant slagheap, the tailings left from decades of mining. I drove up to have a look and a fearsome hot wind skittered and sheared along the rocks, wrenching the car door from my hand as I opened it.

Head down, buffeted by the wind, I made my way to the Miners Memorial, a quiet place paying tribute to the hundreds of men and boys (some as young as twelve) who lost their lives in the late 1800s and early 1900s, poisoned by lead or killed in explosions and rock falls.

In cheerful contrast to the sombre grey moonscape and the Miner's Memorial was an outsize bench painted the colour of a London bus. I looked around. No one was watching. Why not?

The concrete breeze blocks piled at the side of the bench wobbled as I stepped on them.

What do you think you're doing?

Having fun, PK, you should try it some time.

I pushed the hair out of my eyes, tucked it behind my ears to stop it being whipped into a tangled frenzy, grabbed the red timber slats and hauled myself up, laughing at how ridiculous I must have looked, clambering over the four-metre-high structure. It was an ungainly ascent but what a view. I could see the whole town from up there, right to the edge of the desert that closed in on all sides. I could see Mario's Palace Hotel, with its wide verandas and ornate wrought-iron balustrades, where they filmed *The Adventures of Priscilla, Queen of the Desert*, and the equally impressive post office. Argent Street had a surprising number of beautiful buildings that must have taken years to construct.

It was easy to imagine Broken Hill in its early days when settlers put down roots and civic-minded citizens would have set up local councils and started building a community in this remote, out-of-the-way place. Just as easy to imagine scores of pioneering prospectors and lawless gunslingers strutting down the main streets, rich beyond their wildest imaginings.

I climbed off the bench, dusted myself down and drove on. Boarded-up shops and derelict houses on the edge of town, some even closer to the centre, suggested the locals had been doing it tough. The town had a solid, settled appearance but it looked like the glory days were long gone. Broken Hill felt like a town holding its breath, and not just because of the heat.

*

The Miss Australia Runner-Up was guest of honour at the Broken Hill Women's Auxiliary Ball, accompanied by Miss Australia 'Made it to the Final'. The two beauties went gliding around the civic centre in exquisite gowns dripping with jewels; I hadn't realised how grand the ball would be. My little black dress looked out of place among the full-length gowns and tuxedos, and I tugged at the hem, desperate to cover my fat knees. All that did was expose more cleavage. I covered my cleavage in a shawl and made polite conversation with the person sitting next to me, secretly wishing I was at home in front of the television with a bottle of wine instead. There must have been 450 people there and they all seemed to know one another.

'Do you live locally?' I asked.

'Nope.'

'Did you come far?'

'Few hours' drive.'

'What's it called?'

The man on my left named a place I'd never heard of.

'I don't think I know where that is.' I probably sounded snooty; nerves make me come over all British.

'It's a station.'

'A station? I thought you said you drove?'

The man I was attempting to have a conversation with looked bored.

'A station is what we call a farm.'

Ah. I see. 'And how big is your farm? Sorry, station.'

'About 400 by 300.'

'Kilometres?'

He nodded. Geography and maths have never been my strong point but that sounded bigger than Devon and Cornwall, with maybe a bit of Somerset and Dorset thrown in.

I left the table as the conversation turned to light aircraft and motorbikes, and wandered across to watch the auction of a live pig.

'Who'll give me $600? In the corner, yes, you sir. Do I hear $700? And $800, thank you. The man on my left, $900.'

Quickfire bidding sent the total well beyond $1000 and, as soon as the hammer fell, the winning bidder donated the pig back to the RFDS.

'Here we go again. Who'll give me $500? How about $550? . . .'

'Enjoying yourself?'

The battle-scarred CEO appeared beside me, in dinner jacket and bow tie.

'Yes!' I had to shout above the noise of a band that had started up.

'What are your plans for the weekend?'

'Not sure. Probably explore town some more, drive around a bit.'

'A few of us go cycling on a Sunday. You're welcome to join us.'

It had been years since I'd ridden a bicycle. I had fond memories of the occasional weekend spent cycling in the Cotswolds, free-wheeling along country lanes with my good friends, Helen and Louise. I pictured a scenic ride on the outskirts of Broken Hill, meandering through the desert. The CEO looked to be in his early sixties so I figured a Sunday afternoon ride wouldn't be too taxing. It might even be fun and fun was what I'd been asking for.

'Thank you, I'd love to.'

He gave me his address. 'I'll lend you a bicycle,' he said. 'We leave at 7 am.'

That didn't sound quite so laid-back but I was keen to make a good impression, so I wrote down his address and made arrangements to meet the following day.

*

'Haven't you got any cycling shorts?'

I was dressed in sensible trousers and a sleeveless t-shirt with a cardigan tied around my waist in case it got cold. I thought my cycling attire was stylish and entirely suitable, and standing on the CEO's doorstep at ten to seven on that Sunday morning I felt irritation rise. Funnily enough, I thought, no, I don't have any cycling shorts because I hadn't planned to go cycling on my day off. I wasn't at my best that morning; I'd downed half a bottle of wine when I got back from the ball and I was nursing a hangover.

He's the CEO, don't be rude.

'No, I'm afraid I haven't,' I said meekly.

'I've got a spare pair,' he said, disappearing into the back of the house. He came back carrying a small square of black fabric.

'Try those. You'll need them.'

The man had the legs of a greyhound and the torso of an underfed whippet. He handed me the small cycling shorts, the sort of thing you'd wear to the gym, only shorter and tighter, with a padded bum. I popped into the bathroom and did my best to squeeze into them. It looked like I'd stuffed a nappy down a pair of pants already a couple of sizes too small. Suddenly my cycling attire wasn't quite so stylish.

'They're a bit tight,' I shouted. I'd lost weight since I arrived in Australia but I was still more of a labrador than a chihuahua.

'They're meant to be snug; don't worry, they'll stretch.'

I came out of the bathroom and he squinted at me.

'They'll do,' he said. 'We'll just go and pick up David. He lives up the road.'

Outside he introduced me to a bicycle with twenty-one gears and gallantly made sure the saddle was the right height, and then he leapt onto the saddle of his expensive-looking machine and pedalled off, as sprightly as a man twenty years younger. I did my best to keep up.

As I struggled up the first rise I contemplated the name of the town I was staying in. Broken Hill. Not Broken Flat or Broken Level: Broken Hill. It hadn't occurred to me before, I suppose because I was in a car. Now I was on a bike, watching the CEO's tight little arse disappear into the distance, up a bloody great big hill. It took a long time to catch up but he waited.

'Having trouble with the gears?'

I didn't answer, partly because I didn't trust myself to and partly because I couldn't breathe. Was he taking the piss? I was suddenly afraid he might be and I wondered if this was a regular thing. How many other gullible females had worn these shorts? By the time we got to David's house I was feeling sick. David took one look at me and shook his head.

'You can't wear that top,' he said.

'He's right. I should have given you a different top.'

David was head of the University Department of Rural Health and they were clearly mates, two of a kind: sun-tanned, lean sportsmen, not an ounce of fat between them. I wondered if they were in on the joke together.

'If you fall off, you'll scrape the skin on your arms wearing that,' said David.

Why would I fall off? I had no intention of falling off but there was no point protesting. I felt outnumbered so I waited as David rummaged around indoors then reappeared, triumphantly handing me an XXXL lycra cycling top, the sort they wear on the Tour de France. It was a lurid mix of orange and blue, 'Broken Hill Mountain Bike Club' plastered across it. Mountains? No one said anything about mountains.

'Here, try that on,' he said.

It was far too early on a Sunday morning to be anything other than compliant so I ducked into yet another stranger's bathroom, dragged the baggy top over the too-tight nappy and waddled back outside.

'That'll do. Let's go pick up the students. They live on the other side of town.'

Students? No one had said anything about students either. By the time we got to where the students lived (and, what a surprise, they were are all wearing trendy cargo pants and skimpy tops; you wouldn't catch them wearing nappies and lycra) I had peaked. My legs were shaking, my heart was racing, my stomach was churning and I badly needed to vomit or empty my bowels.

'You go ahead,' I said. 'I'll catch up.'

I locked myself into a student toilet and dropped my head between my knees, trying not to be sick. I didn't want to go cycling, I had a hangover. I wanted to lie down on the side of the road in the scorching desert and let a massive eagle chew my head off. Anything rather than go cycling.

*

I stayed in the toilet long enough to make sure they'd gone, then I wiped the sweat from my face and ventured out to find them all still there, dozens of super-fit cyclists, casually leaning on their handlebars, chatting, waiting. I was about to pike out and admit defeat when a woman my age arrived. She looked fit, but not that fit, so I dragged my bike over and begged her to stay at the back of the pack with me.

The real cyclists whizzed off into the bush following a bumpy dirt track but Maureen and I stuck to the bitumen, and if we hadn't kept moving we might have quite literally stuck to it, because even this early in the day it must have been in the mid-thirties.

Moments later we reached the edge of town and I forgot all about my aching muscles. I was in the outback, the real Australian outback, and far from being empty and barren it was full of life. We cycled past balls of tangled scrub, the kind that blows across the screen in American westerns, and kangaroos kept pace with us until they got bored and put on a spurt of speed that made it look like we were standing still. Wedge-tailed eagles gliding the thermals soared overhead and emus clustered at the side of the road in feathery six-foot clumps, their improbable spindle-thin legs sticking out below their fat bodies. Maureen and I cycled past, staying well back so as not to disturb them. The emus stared and there was a moment's silence, a dithering hesitation before panic set in. The emus dashed into the road, bumping into each other as they ran and, before either of us could react, a lump of feathers with floppy legs was running straight for us, feet slapping the hot tarmac. We swerved and somehow managed to stay on our bikes.

Distant hills of scorched red earth folded over the horizon and the clear blue sky stretched in a seemingly endless arc above us. We covered about twenty kilometres all up – not much, I know, but my bum was going to ache for a week, even with the padded shorts.

The CEO invited me in for a coffee at the end of the ride and I peeled off his now sweaty shorts and allowed my constricted cellulite to spread into comfy cargo pants. He made me laugh, recounting how he'd swerved to avoid a kangaroo and fallen headfirst into a bush and I felt oddly at home in his kitchen, morning papers strewn across the table. I wondered where his wife was. There had to be a wife; the house was immaculate. I could see plastic flowers on the dining room table, perched in the exact centre of a white lace doily. Maybe he was gay? We lingered over a second cup of coffee and I decided his wife must be away. That would explain why he seemed so lonely.

chapter seven

'Do you want to sit up front?'

I was strapped into the back of a Beechcraft King Air, cargo door closed, propellers turning and Shane (why are pilots always called Shane or Otto, not Bob or Ben?) looked back at me, peering over the top of his aviators. In spite of his regulation RFDS flight suit and peaked cap, the immaculately attired Captain Shane Brooks barely looked old enough to drive a car, never mind fly a plane.

It had been a desert cold start to the day, chilly enough for engineers in the hangar to be wearing beanies and jumpers as I hurried through to join the seven-thirty clinic flight to Ivanhoe. The strip of light at the edge of the runway had shifted from the colour of sun-ripened nectarines to palest china blue.

'Well?'

Two months earlier, I'd been weeping my way through an English winter, waiting for love to land in my lap. Now I was being invited to sit in the jump seat of a Beechcraft King Air, owned and operated by the RFDS of Australia. Did I want to? You betcha, Baby Face!

Before Miss PK could intervene, I unclipped my shoulder

harness and lap belt and moved to the front of the seven-seat plane. I clambered into an alarmingly small space next to Shane, trying not to knock any instruments as I squeezed my thighs into a snug fur-covered seat.

He handed me a headset. 'Here, put this on. And don't touch any buttons.'

I hadn't planned to, but once he'd mentioned it, it was like saying don't think about elephants. I stared at a bank of dials, buttons, knobs and levers, all of which were crying out to be flicked, twiddled, turned and pushed.

I suppressed a jittery impulse to reach out and press a button that carried my exact initials and jammed my wayward hands under my thighs. Shane looked back at Jacqueline, a child and family health nurse combing her hair at the back of the plane, and she gave him the thumbs up. I think that meant she'd shut the door. Shane looked out the window, checked the runway was clear (this was Broken Hill – you can forget air traffic control) then he pushed the throttle forwards.

We picked up speed, bounced along the runway then kicked into the air, an alarmingly sudden steep climb that saw us soaring over the streets of Broken Hill in moments. As we banked hard left, Shane's window filled with dark smudges, shadows pooling in the early morning light. A line of darker red earth, with a margin of wispy trees and bushes, indicated a creek bed where once there would have been water. Now it was a parched empty landscape, locked into the middle of Australia's worst drought for years.

As we climbed higher the scenery faded into blotchy spots and wavy lines, an Aboriginal dot painting if ever there was one. How would they have known what it looked like from up here?

'QF7 clear to climb to flight level 350.'

'Malaysian 862, clear track direct Sydney.'

'Echo Bravo Charlie, report your position please.'

I glanced at Shane.

'Air traffic control in Melbourne,' he said, and flicked a switch to patch us through, waiting for a break in the chatter before he joined in. 'This is Mike Victor Whisky, airborne Broken Hill, runway two-one, turning left to track one-four-five degrees climbing to flight level two-one-zero,' he declared, sounding like a proper grown-up pilot. The illusion was shattered moments later when a broad Aussie accent sounded in my headphones.

'Hey Shane, how you doing, mate?'

I smiled and looked out of the window, remembering an interview I'd conducted with Nancy Bird Walton before I'd left Sydney. She was the first female pilot to work commercially in Australia and a lifelong supporter of the RFDS.

'When I learnt to fly we navigated by following train lines or riverbeds,' she'd said. 'If I had to make an emergency landing I would try and break a telegraph line, that way someone would be forced to come out and repair the line, discover the ditched plane and rescue me at the same time.'

She'd tilted her head back and smiled. 'And I always kept a pair of shoes and a little black dress in the back of the plane. I never knew when I might need them.' At ninety-two and living in a retirement home, Nancy Bird Walton was an immaculate picture of grace, sitting upright in a wing chair, lipstick the exact shade of her polished nails. She gave me the impression she could slip into her LBD and dance a tango any time she liked. I watched the sparse red desert unfurl beneath us and made a mental note to wear jeans less often.

*

If Broken Hill was remote, Ivanhoe may as well have been on the moon. The town felt like a threadbare pair of trousers, darned too often and ready to be turned into rags.

As we drove into town from the landing strip, I forced myself to forget the march of green fields I was used to – the towns and villages with churches, village greens and bus stops, thriving post offices, well-stocked greengrocers and busy fish and chip shops – and remember this was remote Australia, not rural England. Turning off the wide main street, bordered by sparse gum trees, we drove through an opening in a chain-link fence to park outside a small brick hospital. It was single storey, with two or three beds at most. Twice a week the Flying Doctor held a GP surgery there; local nurses staffed it the rest of the time.

I was there to find stories, and it wasn't hard. A guard from Ivanhoe prison came in for a check-up after a nasty accident with an iron bar weeks before. He'd been repairing the perimeter fence, tensioning steel wire, when the bar slipped, spun back and slammed into his face. Inmates who could have escaped stayed with him and called for help, a nurse radioed the Flying Doctor and Captain Magnus Badger, who was passing overhead on his way back from flying an emergency patient to Orange, did some fast recalculations. He diverted the flight and was on the ground within eight minutes.

Then there was Nicole, a quietly spoken mum from Sydney, anxiously cradling her son, Lachlan. She and her husband had been camping with four-year-old Lachlan and six-year-old Ben in Willandra National Park the night before.

'We were roasting marshmallows over the fire,' she told me. 'The boys were fooling around, just having fun, then Lachlan started crying. Ben had accidentally poked him in the eye with a stick. He didn't mean to,' she added quickly, reassuring the tearful Ben who pressed against his mum. Lachlan sat quietly on her lap, his eyes closed. The family had driven eighty kilometres that morning in search of a doctor and, within an hour of seeing the RFDS, they were on an emergency flight to Adelaide, their holiday cut short as Lachlan was rushed to theatre for an operation to save his sight.

An elderly Aboriginal man came in, took a seat in a corner of the waiting room, and smiled and nodded. I pulled out my notebook; I was here to work after all.

'How are you?' I asked, which was a stupid question to ask someone sitting in a doctor's surgery, I know.

'I'm good,' he said. 'Yep, I'm good.'

'And what do you think of the Flying Doctor?' Great, another lame question that didn't deserve an answer. What happened to 'Hello, my name's Deb, what's yours?' This was the first Aboriginal person I'd ever met and I was unaccountably nervous. I'd spent too much time in the privileged enclave of Sydney's inner west, where Aboriginal people and white people don't generally meet.

'They're good,' he said. 'They treat me right. Can't complain. Yep, I'm good.'

Before I could ask any more dimwitted questions the man was called in to see the doctor. He stood up, and his slim body was so twisted and bent out of shape that he almost fell over with the effort of putting one foot in front of the other.

'Nice talking to you,' he said, giving me a gap-toothed grin as he shuffled away.

I loosened my grip on the pen I'd been clutching, not a word written in my notebook, and looked up to see a nurse standing beside me.

'I called in to see him last week,' she said. 'All he had at home was a bed, a wooden chair and a fridge, which was largely empty. I wanted to know if there was anything I could do, anything I could get him. He said he was fine, said he didn't need anything.'

I've been so attached to possessions that I've dragged them halfway across the world and back. I've had furniture and boxes stored in Sydney, and in numerous attics and sheds in England,

and I couldn't truthfully tell you what was in any of them. I had a healthy body, money in the bank and food in the fridge . . . and I could still feel sorry for myself at the drop of a hat.

Even if you never meet the man of your dreams (or in your case, meet him and then mess up) you've got nothing to worry about. Get over yourself.

Thanks, PK. Sound advice.

*

Back in Broken Hill, with an hour of daylight left after the flight to the clinic in Ivanhoe, I jumped in the car and drove out to Silverton, foot hard down as the sun slipped lower in the sky. 'They reckon you can see the curvature of the earth from Mundi Mundi,' the cheery young man in Broken Hill Tourist Office had told me earlier in the week. 'Worth watching the sunset from there,' he added.

Three campervans were already parked on top of the escarpment, a clutch of couples in deckchairs snuggled under blankets, thermos flasks of something hot and steaming on the ground beside them. I parked a polite distance away and we smiled but didn't speak, honouring the silence of that surprisingly lonely place.

I stood outside the car, listening to couples shuffle closer together as the sun sank lower in the sky and the temperature dropped sharply. The frenetic activity of the last few weeks fell away and suddenly there was no escaping my own loneliness. I was fortunate in so many ways and blessed with good health, yet still I felt as empty as the landscape, sad for all the silly mistakes I'd made. Sunset was disappointing and I left the campers to it.

Driving back, the sky soot black, I stopped the car and got out to stare at the stars, so densely packed and close-fitting I felt I could almost bump my head on them. The thought of what might be out there with me, lurking in the darkness on either side of the road, soon had me scuttling back to the safety of the car.

Monday morning, tarmac shimmering with heat haze, I resolved to concentrate on work. I was waiting at the airport to meet Adam, a freelance photographer and documentary film-maker who lived in Sydney. Adam was a creative type, just the sort I'd be likely to fall for, and he sounded lovely on the phone, which wasn't good news.

I once asked a man out on the strength of talking to him on the phone. Listening to Craig talk was like sipping a mug of Belgian hot chocolate, a rich, sweet experience you never wanted to end, only better, heaps better, because there were no calories. Needless to say it didn't work out.

As I waited for Adam's plane to land I sent up a silent wish. Please don't let this be A4. Please let me just get on with the job I'm being paid to do and stop chasing men.

I needn't have worried about Adam; he had long hair. Maybe it's my age but long hair on a man makes me queasy. I may be a crystal-gazing, Tarot-reading, left-wing vegetarian but when it comes to men I prefer old-fashioned types, with short back and sides.

Adam strolled over and shook my hand politely, and I looked at his obviously clean hair, held back in a neat ponytail, and I was convinced it smelt like an extractor fan in a Glaswegian chippy. See? I can't help it.

We spent the morning taking photographs at the base, Adam operating with methodical care while I flapped around taking notes and, I suspect, generally getting in the way.

'Hey Mike, that incubator's got a patient.'

'Yeah?'

'Picked up last night on the road to Mutawintji.'

I spun around in disbelief. 'Are you saying someone found a *baby* on the side of the road?'

The flight nurse laughed. 'No, we were clearing out equipment from the medical campus last week. They found an old incubator that still worked and donated it to the local wildlife rescue group. It's got a baby kangaroo in it now.'

I dragged Adam to a house in South Broken Hill, where the incubator had ended up, thinking we might get some shots for a cute news story. The house was filthy and I had to press my cardigan to my nose to block the smell of pee and wet dogs. Nestled in an incubator near the closely drawn curtains of the front room was a baby kangaroo, so small as to be completely hairless, with the gangly limbs of a young colt and scared black eyes.

'His mum was run over,' said a man with bushy eyebrows and grubby shorts, frown lines etched on his forehead. 'Road kill. They found this joey in the pouch.'

We soon gave up on the idea of taking photos; the tiny kangaroo was too distressed, knocking its head on the side of the incubator.

'Do you want to hold it?'

'Yes, please,' I said, despite my fears of being peed on or getting fleas.

'Have a seat.'

He gestured to a nearby sofa, sagging under the weight of two large dogs. The dogs made room for me and I settled into a still-warm spot on the baggy lounge, ignoring the cushions beside me that were covered in dog hair, and I opened my arms to a furry, three-month-old joey. He nestled in my arms, tucked inside an old cardigan, and sucked with force from a full bottle, no different to a child.

I cradled that little joey and forgot all about the smell of pee and wet dogs. This was a warm inviting home, and it was full of love.

*

On my last night in Broken Hill the CEO invited me to join him for dinner, a solo invite excluding Adam, which seemed odd. For a second I wondered if it was a date, then I thought maybe he didn't like long hair on men either.

It was work, of course – why would it be anything else? – and we were joined by Anne Wakatama, an experienced RFDS doctor who was leaving Broken Hill for a nine-month stint in Canada, to explore spiritual direction. She was slated to be the next Chief Medical Officer on her return.

We ate in the restaurant on top of the slagheap, choosing from a menu that offered chargrilled crocodile, smoked wallaby, emu sausage and grilled kangaroo.

'Stuffed mushroom, thank you.'

The town was laid out beneath us in a carpet of light, nothing but black space beyond, and I did my best to keep pace with the flow of medical conversation that frequently left me baffled. I tried to give the impression I was a competent, eager communications professional, instead of the lost-in-space heartbroken spinster who didn't know what she was doing half the time.

The CEO dropped me off in his comfortable old Ford and I was home by nine o'clock. I fell into bed exhausted.

chapter eight

'We're getting into some tricky driving conditions now. This is going to test the skill of our driver. Woah, this car is sliding all over the place! Hold tight . . .'

I was on a satellite phone, midway through a live radio interview, in the front passenger seat of a Nissan Patrol that was struggling through a dense, glistening soup of mud somewhere north of Byrock. Imagine driving across parallel bars soaked in treacle, or an ice rink smeared in grease. Add rain. Add darkness. Add a windscreen covered in mud.

'I don't know if you can hear it, pounding the roof of the vehicle, but the rain is pouring down here, visibility is terrible! There's mud everywhere and we're caught in a torrent of it, it's like we're surfing a tidal wave of mud!'

Until that morning, rural New South Wales hadn't seen a single drop of rain for seven months. Now it was thundering down. The innocuous dirt road we'd been following from Byrock to Cunnamulla had turned into a treacherous swamp. Every dip in the road threw a shock of orange mud across an already opaque windscreen and the wheels refused to grip the squelching, slippery ooze. A steep camber on either side of the slim dirt track encouraged water to run off and left no room for error; the slightest mistake and we'd have been spun off the road and dumped in a ditch.

I was blithely ignorant of any danger. I assumed Gary, the driver, was saying nothing so I could concentrate on the thrilling radio interview I'd managed to set up. I carried on jabbering, live on air, trying to conjure up a picture of conditions on the RFDS Outback Car Trek for the listeners in Dubbo.

'My goodness the road surface is appalling out here! I can see cars stuck in the ditch up ahead and – woah! – here we go, it looks like we could be in trouble now!'

The car started to slide and I turned to Gary. His face was a frozen scowl, his eyes were fixed on the road ahead and his bloodless knuckles gripped the steering wheel. Fantastic stuff, I thought. Maybe I should ask him to comment? I pointed the microphone in his direction but before I could ask him one of my killer interview questions, he opened his mouth and spoke, loud enough for listeners in Dubbo to hear. 'SHUT UP,' he said, never once taking his eyes off the road.

In the silence that followed, all I could hear was rain drumming on the roof of the car and the furious swish of windscreen wipers at maximum speed.

'I think I'm losing the signal, I might have to –' I cut the connection and shrivelled in my seat.

'Sorry.'

Gary battled to keep us upright, the Nissan squirming and splashing its way through a darkening storm, and I thought back to the start of this peculiar adventure.

Three days after I got back from Broken Hill I had dragged myself out of bed at 5 am to catch a Saturday morning flight to Dubbo, eyeballs gritty with lack of sleep. My face looked like it had been moulded from a piece of play dough that had been stored too long in the back of a cupboard where it had picked up traces of breakfast cereal, flour, salt and the odd weevil.

The day before, I'd finally moved into the skinny house on Rowntree Street (gratefully inheriting second-hand white goods from the previous owners, furniture from Anny and a desk from Kate), then it was off to Dubbo for the start of the RFDS Outback Car Trek.

I was revved up and running at a million miles an hour, dragging press lists and press releases with me, wondering what kind of lists A3 was drawing up for his impending wedding. There would be guest lists and a gift registry, hymns, flowers, wine lists, menus, hotel rooms . . . I slammed the lid on my wayward thoughts and concentrated on work. How was I going to make it through the next six days? I'd forgotten anything I ever knew about PR long ago (and let's face it, that wasn't much in the first place) and this event was the Flying Doctor's biggest annual fundraiser. I was expected to generate publicity for it and the only way to do that was to join it.

There was no mistaking the Trek support vehicle parked outside Dubbo airport: a Nissan Patrol bristling with orange lights, satellite dishes and roof-mounted aerials, with a sturdy roo bar at the front and a roof rack groaning with gear. The back was full of telecommunications equipment and serious emergency medical gear – stretchers, evacuation mats and defibrillators. IT manager Gary Oldman was a man on a mission. A stocky bundle of cropped hair with a bristling grey moustache, he was the self-appointed driver of the car and keeper of the kit. Gary grudgingly found space for my bag, one of the few that disappointingly for him contained nothing to plug in or switch on, and over a breakfast of bacon and eggs in a local café I met the rest of the Flying Doctor support team: Canadian doctor Bill from

Broken Hill, and Aussie flight nurse Di from Dubbo. I smiled politely and picked up the menu.

Who's that big hairy biker?

Miss PK had her sights trained on the final person at the table. He looked like Dennis the Menace's grandfather, with straggly grey hair spilling down his back and a beard as long as it was wide, sprawling over his ample chest and crawling across his shoulders. He had so much hair I couldn't make out what he was saying. It might have been the weight of his beard trapping the sound in but I could have sworn he said he was one of the crew. Miss Prissy Knickers came over all English and polite.

'I'll have a pot of tea, thank you.'

*

The sleepy township of Mudgee was the starting point for the Trek and it was overrun by hairy bikers, all of them sprouting fertile beards and lacking evidence that any of them were riding bikes. A fleet of pre-1971 Dodges, Mercs, Mustangs, Chevrolets, Fords, Porsches and Holdens lined the historic streets: cars plastered with official logos and bizarre personal touches. There was a Chevrolet Impala with a full-size model Brahman bull on top, another that could play sixteen different versions of 'Greensleeves', a Mustang with horns on its roof and a Dodge panel van covered in shag-pile carpet – a replica of the fur-covered truck used in the film *Dumb and Dumber*.

Some of the hairy bikers were in fancy dress and they were clearly bonkers. There was a Justice of the Peace and his co-driver who were planning to spend the six-day trip dressed as Bananas in Pyjamas; RFDS Board member Terry Clark and his crew were dressed as extras from Dad's Army; there were Mexican banditos, surfing dudes, Men in Black, suited kangaroos and a woman with rabbit ears.

You said you wanted to have fun.
I did, PK. I did.

*

'Hey Mick, how you doin'? How's that old heapa rust o' yours?'
'More likely to make the distance 'n yours, mate!'

Six hairdressers from Sydney had set up a makeshift salon at the back of a crowded pub on the first night and the roar of men shouting competed with the electric buzz of hair clippers. It was like a giant sheep-shearing contest, spruiked by the effervescent TV personality Grant Denyer.

'Fifty dollars to shave his eyebrows off.'
'One hundred to shave one off and keep the other!'
'Two hundred dollars if you'll shave his legs!'
'Wax his chest, go on, $100 says you won't!'

By the end of the night most of the hairy bikers were bald, laughingly stripped of the hair they'd been growing for the past six months in readiness for the first-night fundraiser. Those who weren't completely bald had bizarre crop-circle haircuts, or the mark of Zorro etched on their heads. Gary had lost his treasured moustache – the first time in twenty years he'd been seen without it – and I went to bed before someone spotted that I still had all my own hair. I fell asleep smiling.

Next morning the shaved heads made their way to a chilly Mudgee racecourse for a 6 am feast of eggs, bacon, sausages and minced meat on toast.

Outside, excitable drivers revved their engines and blasted their horns, competing with each other to see who could make the most noise, like a herd of wildebeest calling across the plains. One man had the advantage of horns from an express train mounted on the roof of his car. He was a clear winner in the Battle of the Big Horn.

Clouds of smoke billowed from shiny fat exhausts as spirits rose to intoxicating levels, not that anyone was drinking. The rum being sold by a man dressed as a polar bear was for consumption later that night, when the day's drive was over. Bananas in Pyjamas slapped smiley-face stickers on people and the platoon from Dad's Army marched along the line of cars, barking incomprehensible orders.

The only people unmoved by the wall of sound and the heady mix of adrenalin and petrol fumes were the occupants of a bright red Dodge Kingsway Coronet. They were waiting patiently at the front of the line, like characters from an F. Scott Fitzgerald novel: she a beautiful woman of indeterminate age in full make-up with red lipstick and neat headscarf, he an elderly well-groomed man with dark-rimmed glasses, resting a neat gloved hand on the steering wheel. They could have been Sunday drivers, out for a spin in 1950s Cornwall.

'It's the only time they'll be at the front of the pack,' whispered a man standing beside me. 'They paid $10,000 to be the first car to leave.' There was more than a hint of jealousy in his voice.

Lying on the woman's lap was a bound document, open at the first page, with precise instructions on the day's route – turn left across a stock grid at 16.5 kilometres, fork right at a large tree at 27.3 kilometres.

And then they were off, waved away by RFDS Chairman Tim Fischer at a sedate pace, each car despatched at precise two-minute intervals. I clambered into the back of the Nissan and joined a stream of cars heading slowly out of town for the start of a marathon drive, snaking across 3383 kilometres of largely dirt roads through remote parts of New South Wales and Queensland, ending up six days later on Fraser Island.

The first night was spent at Byrock, a town of sixteen inhabitants with a single pub and a village hall. Acres of flat, empty landscape surrounded it, broken by an occasional tree and a clutch of scrubby bush. It was such a remote spot Trek organiser Stephen Knox arranged for a fuel tanker to stop by, so cars could fill up for the next day's long haul to Cunnamulla.

As darkness fell drivers pitched their tents or threw swags onto the floor of the village hall then piled into the Mulga Creek Hotel, where I was relieved to find I had a room. Publicans Gloria and Peter Pimlott somehow managed to feed more than 300 people on a fleet of barbecues set up outside. 'If it's for the Flying Doctor, we're happy to help,' said Gloria, pulling another schooner of beer.

Wood fires crackled and spat in upturned oil drums as hungry Trekkers roamed the garden, clutching beer cans and burgers dripping onion and tomato sauce. I lost sight of Gary in the scrum and felt like a nervous outsider among the high-spirited groups of people. They formed circles of friendship around the fires and I felt reluctant to join them.

A lone Aboriginal man sat quietly to one side, hunched on a small stool, his body stooped forward. Sipping a can of coke, watching the circus of activity swirl around, he looked like a rock with ants swarming around the base of it. The Trekkers didn't seem to notice him – in their high-spirited exuberance his silent presence was invisible – but I felt drawn towards his stillness and the sense of peace that emanated from him. Remembering my failure in Ivanhoe, I sat down on the empty seat beside him and introduced myself.

'Hello. My name's Deb.'

He turned to look at me. In the darkness I could just make out a long beard, bushier and longer than those the hairy bikers had sported, and limpid brown eyes rimmed with white.

'G'day Deb. My name's Ernest.'

He spoke quietly and slowly, as if words were something he

wasn't familiar with. It sounded like each one held a weight and significance far beyond its actual meaning. It occurred to me that he might have been quite happy sitting on his own, watching what was going on, and maybe I was intruding, but having sat down I couldn't get up and walk away.

'Do you live here?' I asked.

He nodded. 'Out bush. Got a little camp. Trying to do the right thing. Live right.'

His words struck a chord. If only I could live right and make up for my bad behaviour of the past, the senseless obsessions about men and the stupid decisions, I might feel better about life.

'Do you live on your own?' I asked.

He nodded again, slowly and thoughtfully. 'Trying to live like spirit says to live. Been doing it five years now. Do you believe in God?' he asked.

The question took me by surprise. People around us were laughing and drinking, the air smelt of fried onions and char-grilled burgers, and the pub garden resembled a busy fairground on a Saturday night. It was the kind of atmosphere that called for a flippant response but sitting beside Ernest I knew with absolute certainty that I couldn't possibly fudge it. This was no time for jokes or maybes; I'd been asked a serious question and he was expecting a serious response.

'Yes,' I said quietly, feeling tears prickle behind my eyes. 'I do believe in God. I don't know what or who God is, but I do believe God exists.'

'Where do you think God is?' Ernest said.

'I think God is in the land,' I said. Until the words came out of my mouth I had no idea that was the reply I was going to give. When I heard myself speak I knew it was what I had always believed and only now did I realise it.

'That's why I like gardening,' I said. 'It brings me closer to God.' I was glad it was dark because yet again there were tears running down my cheeks and there was nothing I could do to stop them.

The quiet interlude with Ernest stripped away the frenzy of activity I'd been hiding behind, the bustle of a new job and a new place to live, checklists and tasks, forced laughter, people to interview, places to go. Set all that aside and what was there? Sadness. Nothing but deep, overwhelming sadness. I was sad I'd wasted so much of my life, sad love was something I couldn't handle; sad I'd hurt so many people along the way.

The circus around us faded, leaving just me, Ernest and a conversation that meandered from one topic to another, flowing through a river of ideas. We spoke about Jesus, the notion of God, the philosophy of Socrates and the kindness of the Dalai Lama.

'I met him. At the Aboriginal Tent Embassy in Canberra. He asked to have his photograph taken with me.'

Ernest's words were slow and gentle, the pauses full of reflection, and it was tempting to let all my pent-up sorrow overflow. I listened with a lump in my throat as Ernest described meditating under a tree.

'I was tiny, like an ant, and I could see all the blades of grass. Next thing I was up in the tree, looking down. Been living in the bush a long time now, trying to follow the teachings of spirit.'

He watched me to gauge my reaction, nervous that I might laugh or mock, but there was a quiet sincerity to his words that silenced any doubt. Ernest was convinced he had flown above the trees, and why was that so difficult to believe? Was his story any different from so many others that are impossible to prove?

I have a friend, I'll call her Sarah, who is a mature-aged woman with traditional views and a conservative outlook on life. She votes Liberal and is a life-long Christian. Sarah is convinced an angel appeared in her bedroom one night, an angel as real to her as any person. He was a clearly defined presence standing at the end of her bed, wearing a blue robe and a beautiful smile. The angel spoke no words but conveyed a sense of reassurance that the child Sarah was worried about would be looked after. So why wouldn't I believe Ernest?

The air grew chilly and I drew my jumper around me. Ernest was wearing shorts and a t-shirt. In the darkness outside the pub it was hard to tell his age; I guessed early to late sixties.

'I'm following the teachings of my uncles, my Aboriginal elders, learning traditional Aboriginal culture. My ancestors, they're with me, all the time,' he said. 'They leave me behind when I walk into town and they join me again when I walk out.'

I thought back to the time I took my mother to a spiritualist church in London. A stranger told her the baby boy she'd lost was alive and well in the world of spirit and I turned to Mum, expecting her to shake her head and indicate they had the wrong person: Mum had four girls. To my surprise there were tears streaming down her face. Later I found out that Mum had given birth to a son who died before any of the rest of us were born. Neither I, nor my three sisters, had known that. How could a stranger know? There was so much I didn't understand and couldn't explain.

It was getting late, people were drifting off to bed and we had an early start the next day.

'It was nice talking to you,' I said. 'I'd better go.'

'Would you like to visit me in the bush one day?' Ernest asked, taking me by surprise.

My answer was even more surprising.

'Sure,' I said. 'And let me know if ever you visit Sydney.'

I gave Ernest my phone number.

chapter nine

The quiet interlude with Ernest had dug so deep it unnerved me, and I felt a sudden urge to get back to work, to keep busy.

'I must work, I must work. The reason we are depressed and take such a gloomy view of life is that we know nothing of work . . .' Throw me the whip, Chekhov.

When I'd first said I wanted to go on the RFDS Outback Car Trek the CEO had told me that only those who were part of a support team, or working, deserved a place. I had no intention of being a freeloader. I wanted to throw myself into work and send some pictures to a newspaper or a magazine. I wasn't sure which but I had a list; I'd find someone (like I said, it had been a long time since I'd worked in PR).

I walked into the bar and collared one of the official photographers who sat nursing a beer. 'How did it go today? Get any good shots?'

'A few.'

'Excellent.'

'Yeah, we put them on a DVD at the end of the trek. Everyone gets a copy.'

He drained his glass and tried to catch the barman's eye so he could order another beer.

'Any chance I could get some sooner?'

He turned back, wary now.

'How soon?'

I fished about in the bottom of my bag and pulled out a data stick.

I followed the photographer into the community hall, where dark lumps had spread across the floor like a pile of shuffling seals. Enormous bellies swelled inside the shifting swags and the wooden floor thrummed to the sound of snoring. I must have been talking to Ernest for longer than I'd realised. I was about to apologise and beat a hasty retreat, when a voice hissed out of the darkness.

'Where the hell have you been, mate? We need to go through these shots!'

A second photographer, more eager than the first, appeared from a side room, so we fired up the laptop and the photographers downloaded a set of pictures, only to find that Gary, the keeper of the keys and guardian of the satellite, had gone to bed. I scurried off to my motel room and slept soundly.

*

'Why are those guys still wearing shorts?' I asked, staring at the shivering extras from *Hawaii Five-O*. Early risers had huddled in the garden to get as close as they could to the barbecues that had been fired up again and were now offering a breakfast feast of bacon, egg, tomato and sausage; all four crammed into a bread roll and smothered in tomato sauce seemed the go. With the temperature barely six degrees, the surfing dudes were wearing cut-off jeans, short-sleeved Hawaiian shirts and thongs. Their breath billowed in puffs of white and their legs had turned a funny colour.

Gary looked up from his dripping sandwich.

'Unwritten rules of the Trek,' he mumbled, licking his sticky fingers. 'Start in costume, stay in costume.'

I looked around the garden. The Mexicans were all right, snuggled under ponchos, and the Men in Black wore thick suits (although the sideburns they'd drawn with marker pen had started to run). The platoon from Dad's Army lolled about in camouflage, and the Bananas in Pyjamas looked warm, snug and happy – something to do with wearing pyjamas all day, no doubt. Pity the poor surfing dudes.

I did my best to make appropriate and intelligent car conversation.

'So, you're driving a Chevrolet, is that right?'

'Yep, 1966 Chev.'

'I understand some of these cars have powerful engines.'

'Yep, 390.'

'What does that equate to – 1.8 litres? Two litres?'

'Nope, that's 6.4.'

The disastrous live radio interview I attempted while driving through the mud with Gary took place later that afternoon. For a while after that I thought silence might be my best option. We listened to drivers up ahead radioing for help.

'Car 234, calling X234, got your ears on?'

'This is X234 support, what's the problem?'

'Stuck in the mud, mate. Can you give us a tow?'

The silence in our vehicle stretched on as we aquaplaned our way in darkness through kilometres of thick red mud. Eventually I offered Gary a jelly baby and it helped to break the tension.

We arrived in Cunnamulla two hours late for dinner, to find most other drivers swapping 'how I nearly lost control' stories in the bar of the local community centre. Gary plunged in with glee, recounting his own desperate struggle to survive.

'Sorry about earlier,' I said, during a break in the chatter.

'No worries,' said Gary the Great. 'You never know what to expect on the Trek. We've had PR people arrested before; one of them streaked naked around a field late at night as a bit of a lark one year. Never had a PR person try to do a radio interview before, though. That's a first.'

*

The race official tipped his head back, drained the can of soft drink he'd been clutching and then stood beside me, leaning his bulk against the wall. We were in a gymnasium crammed with Trekkers bidding at auction. Raucous laughter and loud banter bounced off the walls and reverberated off the floor, encouraged by a frenetic auctioneer; it was like a giant party. I was uneasy in such exuberant company – I was meant to be working after all – so I stood to one side, helping to spot potential bidders. I'd managed to set up two more interviews on breakfast radio (with Trekkers this time; I'd learnt my lesson), followed by a newspaper interview at lunchtime. My mind was on work and I was only half listening to the official standing beside me.

'I had a breakdown not so long ago,' he was saying. I assumed he was talking cars so I settled my expression into one of polite interest.

'Oh yes?'

'Overwork. Couldn't stop. Couldn't cope. Doc said I should slow down, take things easy.' He scanned the crowd, then turned to me with kind eyes. 'Hope you don't mind me saying this, but I can see the sadness in you. Don't be too hard on yourself,' he said.

Was my struggle so blatant? I thought I was doing OK, burying my head in work, running at a fast pace so I wouldn't have to think about A3's impending wedding or picture the late-night planning sessions, the dress fittings and, most of all, the vows that would be taken in less than three weeks. *Haven't you ever wanted to get married?* Tears welled up and I shook them away. 'Thank you,' I managed to say. He nodded, crunched his empty can in a massive fist and disappeared into the crowd.

The following day, in a bid to find out more about the Trek, I caught a ride with the organiser, an erudite, expansive gentleman with a neatly clipped white moustache and closely cropped hair – no other word but gentleman would do for Stephen Knox.

I'd barely fastened my seatbelt when he caught me by surprise.

'My wife suffered from depression a while back,' he said.

Please, not here, not now, I thought. I can't bear to make a fool of myself and burst into tears.

'It took a while but she got over it. It's not something to be ashamed of.'

'That's good. I'm glad. Could I try driving for a while?'

Kindness has always made me want to cry.

*

I kept a tight lid on my emotions over the days that followed and watched with interest as the hardened petrol heads enjoyed a feast of mud-soaked fun. The more fun they had, the more the decades dropped away. They'd started out resembling elderly Hell's Angels and ended up looking more like excitable school-children. Never judge a book by its cover, isn't that what they say? Judgement's my middle name. Tatts, piercings and a long beard? Lock the door.

The Trekkers grew visibly younger as we drove through a rollcall of Australian outback towns – Charleville, Augathella, Tambo, Blackall and Isisford, where a Jack Russell launched itself at a panel mounted on the back of a ute and somehow managed to clear seven metres. A Holden panel van broke down and had to drive 170 kilometres in first gear, but did the drivers complain? No, they laughed.

The sun finally shone for the surfing dudes as we left Barcaldine, birthplace of the Australian Labor Party, and we followed a dusty gravel track that snaked its way through steep wooded hillsides to penetrate deep into Queensland's remote gemfields of Sapphire and Rubyvale, where electricity only arrived in 1977. The drought was a long way from breaking here. From Rubyvale we crossed cattle grids and dry riverbeds to reach the small town of Cracow, famous for a two-storey Queenslander run by circus folk Fred and Sandi Brophy.

It was like walking onto a Harry Potter set. The bar was full of magical circus memorabilia and the garden teemed with fire-eaters, singers and musicians. Towering over the proceedings was Fred himself, an enormous lion tamer of a man with a handlebar moustache and bright red braces. He was missing only a whip, which was surely under the counter somewhere.

I checked into my room and went in search of a shower to wash off several layers of sweat, grease, dirt and sand accumulated over the two days since my last shower. The bathroom was at the end of a long veranda. As I drew closer I noticed a scrap of white paper pinned to the door. 'No Showers,' it said. Underneath someone had scribbled, 'Sorry, water tanker didn't arrive'.

I turned round, headed down to the bar and ordered a beer. Who cared about cleanliness? After a solid week of company I was craving solitude so I sat alone in the darkened garden, watching the performers until a line of ants clambering over a tree root caught my attention. I thought back to the conversation with Ernest on the first night of the Trek outside the pub in Byrock, and everything that had happened since. I'd spent six days in the company of 300 men, nearly all of them away from their wives and girlfriends, and I hadn't chased any of them. I'd done my job – seven live radio interviews, twelve press interviews and dozens of photos placed in local papers – and there were times, yes I think I could safely say, there were times I'd actually had fun. What an extraordinary week it had been.

*

Kate linked her arm through mine as we walked along the shore. Cool sand squeaked beneath our feet, shifting, settling and trickling between our toes. A salty breeze blew off the ocean and the sun felt warm on our backs. It was hard to believe it was midwinter.

If you believe the *Guinness Book of Records*, Hyams Beach has the whitest sand in the world. It's a sweeping unspoilt bay two and a half hours south of Sydney, part marine sanctuary, part national park. In places it's nothing short of a windswept, pristine wilderness, the shoreline thickly forested with scribbly gums, casuarinas and paperbark trees that reach down and touch the sand.

Two weeks earlier Kate had rung me. 'We're planning a long weekend at the beach,' she'd said. 'Would you like to join us?' The date coincided with A3's wedding (why did he have to tell me the date?) and all I'd been able to think about was Central Park, New York, where the ceremony would be taking place: horse-drawn carriages, champagne cocktails and lovers smiling for the camera. I didn't need asking twice.

Kate's recovery from the breast cancer had been slow and steady, her body gradually healing and gaining strength.

'How are you doing? Really doing?' I asked, as we strolled along the sand.

'I can't feel anything in these new breasts; they're like heavy lumps, fastened to the front of me, and I won't be happy until they add nipples.' Then she smiled. 'But I've got a flat stomach.

And I'm alive.' She stretched her arm around my waist and pressed against me. 'And how are you doing?'

I felt strangely calm. Now that it was here, the day I'd been dreading, it was almost a relief. 'I'll get there,' I said.

'I'm glad you're back,' she said.

'Me too.'

The weather changed as quickly as a cloud passing across the sky. Without warning, the kookaburras, crimson rosellas and rainbow lorikeets that normally sat in the trees took flight as the wind picked up, turning the ocean from innocent aquamarine to slate grey. In minutes the sea was a mass of churning water, flashing teal blue and foaming white as sharp sand whipped off the beach to scour our faces.

We retreated to the old fibro and timber house that Kate and James had rented for the weekend, overlooking the ocean, to find Ben and Hanne hunkered down in front of the fire and their Danish granny Inga ensconced in a squashy sofa, reading a book.

'Who's for a glass of red wine?' said James as we hurried out of the wind.

That night an electrical storm flashed around the bay and we listened to rain drum on the roof as we rugged up, threw another log on the fire and watched *As it is in Heaven*, by Swedish director Kay Pollak.

Everyone shed a quiet tear at the end. Long after everyone else had dried their eyes I was still crying. It was something about the beauty of the film and the joy of being in the company of such a close and loving family. Why was that so hard to bear? Maybe because I wanted it so much. I suddenly felt desolate, old and single, with no one to blame but myself. It was too late for children and probably too late for love. And why would anyone love me anyway?

Get over yourself.

PK was right; that was the last glass of red talking. I pulled myself back from the brink, sobered up, stopped crying and reminded myself how lucky I was. Sure, I'd never married, but I'd never had a major illness either and I had loving friends, a close family and a good job. Besides, A3 was married now. What was it Buddhists said? This too shall pass.

Friendship should be a two-way street and the last few years had been one-way traffic. I'd been as needy as a child, crying over things (largely men) I couldn't have. Kate had never once turned me away or told me to sort myself out. That's friendship for you.

*

The next day was breezy and overcast, the air full of sound: waves pounding the beach, young ferns rustling and gum trees creaking overhead. We walked through an eerie graveyard of charred blackbutt trees in Booderee National Park, the smell of scorched earth from the last bushfire lingering in the air. In the midst of all that devastation were signs of life: green shoots unfurling at the base of blackened tree trunks.

At Stony Creek we clambered across a bed of shells that crunched underfoot and then took a swim in the still-warm ocean, bobbing contentedly in the water until we felt wrinkled. Only when we got out did we realise that dolphins had been swimming a few metres behind us.

chapter ten

'Hello. Can I help you?'

It was late Monday afternoon back in Sydney and the phone hadn't stopped ringing all day. I was racing to catch up on work and there was silence on the other end of the line. I tried again, brisk and efficient.

'This is the marketing department. How can I help?'

'Hello?'

The voice on the other end was deep and tentative; it sounded familiar. Then I heard the old-fashioned sound of a coin dropping into the bottom of a phone box. I hadn't heard that sound for years.

'It's Ernest . . . the Aboriginal man you met in Byrock. Do you remember?' I recognised the warmth in Ernest's hesitant voice, and his slow, measured way of speaking.

'Of course! How are you?'

'I'm good,' he said. 'I'm good.' Another coin clanked to the bottom of the box and I struggled to catch what he said next.

'Sorry?'

'Sydney. I'm in Sydney.'

Now I was the one hesitating. What was he doing in Sydney? Why was he here? I thought I could guess the answer and I wasn't sure how I felt about an unexpected visitor.

'Uh . . . Ernest, can I call you back?'

'I don't think so,' he said, slowly. 'I can't see a number on this phone.' I heard another chunk of money being pushed into the it.

'Where exactly in Sydney are you?'

'I'm on a big main street. I got off the train and I started walking.'

The obvious question had to be asked.

'Ernest, what are you doing in Sydney?'

'I've come to visit you.'

More money grumbled past. The synapses in my brain weren't working fast enough. What should I say? What should I do? I know I said he should look me up if ever he came to Sydney, but that was a scant three weeks ago. I wasn't expecting him to . . . well, I don't know what I was expecting. I probably wasn't expecting him to turn up at all. We'd had an hour-long conversation outside a pub in Byrock and all I knew about Ernest was that he lived alone in the bush and he was trying to 'live right'.

I played for time. 'Ernest . . . the thing is, I'm at work.'

'That's OK, I can wait.'

'But where can you . . . I mean . . .'

A heavy coin clattered into the box.

'Nope, I don't mind waiting. Only I'm running out of money. That was my last dollar.'

There was no time to think or plan. 'Ernest, go back to the station and wait for me outside the main entrance. I'll be there in an hour.'

'OK.'

Miss PK wasn't impressed.

*

I finished work and caught a taxi to the station, nibbling on the inside of my lip as I wondered how to deal with the situation. Could I really invite a complete stranger to stay with me?

Tell him to get a room.

What if he doesn't have any money?

Not your problem.

He invited me to stay with him.

So?

So I should return the favour.

He turned up out of the blue, he didn't check if it was OK.

PK's uncompromising stance didn't help.

Apart from the patient in Ivanhoe, Ernest was the only Aboriginal man I'd ever met. Our conversation in Byrock meant something; it opened a door to a culture I knew nothing about. I was working in a country that for 40,000 years had been inhabited solely by Aboriginal people. This was a chance to find out more, to extend a welcome to an Aboriginal man I had enjoyed talking to. He'd invited me to visit him, so why shouldn't I return the favour?

Because you don't know him.

It was true. Ernest hadn't been introduced by a mutual acquaintance who'd said 'I'd like you to meet Ernest' or 'I'm sure you two will get along' or even 'I've known Ernest most of my life, he's a good man'. I'd blundered into an encounter with him and now all I had were my instincts.

I thought back to our conversation. He'd come across as a man with a strong faith and a desire to talk about things that mattered, and he'd left me with an impression of calm serenity. But what else did I know about him? Nothing.

I decided to trust my instincts. If it felt like the right thing to do when I met him at the station, I would offer him a bed for the night. If I had any doubt, I would take him to the nearest hostel.

I sat in the back of the taxi, trying to remember what Ernest looked like: black face, big beard, brown eyes. It wasn't much to go on. I fidgeted in my handbag for my glasses and felt inclined to agree with PK. I wasn't sure I liked the idea of a stranger descending so unexpectedly. How long must it have taken him to get to Sydney from that remote little town? It had to be at least 700 kilometres and there was no train station in Byrock. Not even a bus stop, come to that.

The taxi dropped me at the front of Central Station on Cleveland Street and I stood opposite the main entrance, watching the rush-hour stream of people – suits, students, back-packers bent under the weight of bulging rucksacks, mums with strollers, old people with walking frames, the odd person in uniform and no one who even remotely resembled Ernest.

We'd met in the dark outside a pub, with only the light from open fires to see by. Although we'd talked for over an hour all I could remember were his long beard and his brown eyes. Ernest spent the entire conversation sitting down so I didn't even know how tall he was.

After ten minutes outside Central Station I was starting to draw attention to myself, staring at Aboriginal people, offering them a tentative 'do I know you?' look. Maybe Ernest wouldn't recognise me either.

I wandered away from the main entrance, wondering if I'd missed him. Then in the distance I spotted a large black man standing by a fence, picked out by a pool of light that fell from a nearby streetlight. He was wearing jeans and a dark grey t-shirt and there was a rucksack lying on the ground at his feet. The clincher was the long grey beard that stretched almost to his waist.

I walked towards him and he smiled, nodding encouragement. The closer I got the bigger he got and by the time I reached him I realised Ernest was at least six foot six, maybe six seven.

'Hello.'

He towered above my five foot four, an unexpected giant of a man. We shook hands and Ernest smiled with a shy tilt of his head.

Now I know this will seem like an odd thing to say, but he made me think of the pictures of Jesus I had seen at school. Make Jesus a blackfella and add a long grey beard and he could have been standing there in person. Ernest was the most striking person I'd ever seen. He looked at me from under lowered eyelids with a hesitant glance, almost as if he was trying to disappear, and this will sound even more bizarre but an image of Princess Diana popped into my head. I reckon if she'd been born Aboriginal she'd have come out looking like Ernest, if you see what I mean.

That's ridiculous.

But true.

'How was your journey?' I asked.

'It was long,' he said softly, with another shy smile.

'And here you are!'

He smiled and nodded again. 'Haven't been to Sydney since I was fifteen.'

'How old are you now, Ernest?'

'I'm forty-four.'

I'd been way off the mark with my guess of mid-sixties, but standing under the glare of an urban streetlight, with a long grey beard stretching to his waist, Ernest looked a lot older than forty-four. I'm not sure what surprised me most – that Ernest was only forty-four or that he'd made his way to Sydney. A man who lived alone in the bush, on the outskirts of a remote town with a population of sixteen people, had travelled 700 kilometres to a city of over four million – a city he hadn't visited in almost thirty years – to pay me a visit. I couldn't turn him away.

'Let's jump on a bus and get out of the city,' I said briskly. Ernest reached down for his rucksack, and it looked no bigger than a daypack in his enormous hands.

'Sydney must have changed a lot since you were last here. How amazing that you're back. Gosh, well, here you are.'

I marched Ernest down the slope from the train station, chattering nonsense to cover my nerves, and when we hit the intersection with George Street we were assaulted by sound and fury – a busker playing electric guitar, students shouting, taxi horns blaring and traffic thundering past. Ernest shrank from the noise and edged closer.

'If I get nervous, is it OK if I hold onto you?'

I changed my mind about the bus and splashed out on a cab.

*

The house on Rowntree Street had never felt overly large but filled with Ernest it seemed far smaller. I bustled around, showing Ernest the bathroom and the spare bedroom, pointing out how you could just glimpse the Harbour Bridge if you craned your neck and, all the time I chattered, Ernest just smiled and nodded.

'Are you hungry?'

His smile widened. 'I could eat something,' he said.

He sat in the subterranean dining room that adjoined the kitchen, as motionless as a sleeping cat, while I cracked eggs into a bowl, fussing over bits of shell that fell into the mix.

'Would you like cheese in your omelette? Or mushrooms, I could do you a mushroom omelette. I don't have any ham because I'm vegetarian. Did I tell you I was a vegetarian? Maybe cheese. Are you happy with cheese?'

Ernest nodded. He seemed perfectly comfortable with a level of silence that unnerved me.

'Put some music on if you like,' I said.

He flicked through my CD collection and picked an album by Beautiful South, *Blue is the Colour*. When the album was first released they had to edit the opening track for radio so the lyrics would be less offensive. In the song 'Don't Marry Her' lead singer Jacqui Abbott tried to persuade a man not to marry his girlfriend. Have me instead, she suggested on radio. The lyrics on the original album had one small but critical difference. I whipped six eggs into a frenzied lather while Jacqui begged the man to leave his fiancée. Don't go through with the wedding, she pleaded. Why not fuck me instead?

Ernest quietly listened to the music, head tilted to one side, as the words rang out clearly through the silence. He seemed as still and calm as a deep waterhole in an ancient forest, covered by slow-growing moss and ferns. I was a shallow puddle, wind scuttling across the rain-splashed surface. I kept whipping while Ernest kept listening and the song seemed to last an eternity.

We ate an exceptionally frothy omelette in near silence, then Ernest put down his knife and fork.

'That was good,' he said. 'Thank you.' Then he looked at me with calm brown eyes and said, 'Tell me about yourself.'

The wind whipped across the surface of my shallow pond. I wanted to run away and hide. I was used to interviewing other people; that was my job. I was on safe ground searching for stories, getting other people to talk. Ernest waited, in silence. In the face of his quiet sincerity there was no option but to tell the truth.

'It's been a tough year . . .'

And suddenly I was crying, great gulping sobs that couldn't be contained. The truth was utterly miserable. I'd lost what felt like my last chance at love, and it hadn't even been a real chance. I felt old, used up and unloved. Ernest pushed back his chair and stood up.

'Can I hug you?'

Unshed tears choked my voice so I just nodded. Ernest walked around the table, put his arms around me and held me tight, in a kind, loving, generous hug that asked for nothing in return. Then the doorbell rang.

'Hi, Aunty Deborah.'

It was Hanne, Kate's 22-year-old daughter, holding an armful of spare bedding. I'd rung Kate earlier from the office and told her about Ernest.

Hanne introduced herself to Ernest.

'Nice to meet you,' he said, ducking his head.

'Where are you from, Ernest?'

'From Byrock, out west.'

'And how long are you planning to stay in Sydney?'

I couldn't help smiling. Hanne was sussing him out, sweetly trying to make sure I was OK.

Ernest nodded his head again and lowered his eyes.

'That's up to Deb,' he said.

I walked Hanne to the front door. 'He seems nice,' she said. 'Are you sure you're OK?'

'Yes,' I said. 'Everything's fine.'

And it was.

*

We spent the rest of the evening talking about the world of Spirit. Ernest had an avowed connection with the Holy Spirit, the spirit of the land, the spirit of animals and the spirits of his many ancestors who walked beside him, in constant communication.

'I was staying with an uncle, an elder, and he kept chooks.'

'Chooks?'

'Chickens. We were sleeping in this caravan and one morning, early, there was a big fuss outside. The door was open and a chicken appeared. It just stood in the doorway.'

Ernest paused in his slow, measured telling of the story to make sure I was listening.

'My uncle, he sat up in bed. He looked at that chicken and he said, "Well come on then, tell me what the fuss is all about." So that chicken came into the caravan. It hopped on the bed and it sat on my uncle's chest. There was a lot of squawking and I reckon that chicken told him what was going on because my uncle, he said, "OK, I'll be out in a minute, you go and tell them to calm down." So the chicken went back outside and it all calmed down.'

Maybe I'm gullible. Maybe a scientist would have asked questions like, do the chooks normally get fed at that time in the morning? All I know is, after listening to Ernest, I was convinced communication between humans and animals was possible.

Ernest saw messages everywhere, in the trail left by an ant, in the touch of a dog's nose. 'The call of a currawong first thing in the morning? That's my uncle,' he said.

I was starting to think he was almost Shakespearean in his adherence to dreams and portents, then he blew it by admitting he read his horoscope every day and believed every word of it. His touching naivety about horoscopes aside, I was impressed by the stories he told of elders who communicated with animals in a way we'd forgotten how to, or perhaps we never knew.

It was fascinating to spend time with someone who spoke so openly about talking to animals. I relaxed to the point of offering Ernest a beer or a glass of wine but he shook his head.

'Given up the grog,' he said. 'Can't talk to Spirit when you're on the grog. Have you got another can of coke?'

I handed him a cold can from the fridge and he popped the top.

'Have you ever been married?' he suddenly asked, tipping his head back to drink.

'No,' I said, lips tightly pressed together.

'Why not?'

Some of my closest friends wouldn't dare approach me on that touchy subject but Ernest strode right into the mouth of the volcano, and instead of erupting I burst into tears, again.

'I don't know!' I wailed. That led to another hug.

'If I get scared tonight can I come and sleep with you?'

I was suddenly wary and Miss PK was on full alert.

What did I tell you? If he sets one foot on those stairs he's in big trouble.

I had to agree with PK: that wasn't what I wanted.

'Ernest, you have to stay in your own bedroom.'

He nodded. 'OK.'

What's to stop him slipping upstairs in the middle of the night?

The attic room where I slept didn't have a door – the stairs simply led to an open space under the eaves – but some instinct told me Ernest wouldn't do that. I sensed a streak of decency in him.

You don't know anything about the man!

Calm down, PK. I believe I can trust him.

Ernest could have easily overpowered me but as I lay in bed waiting for sleep to come, I didn't feel remotely nervous.

'Good night,' he called up the stairs.

'Good night, Ernest. Sleep well.'

chapter eleven

'I don't wear clothes in the bush. I don't want to scare you while I'm here so I'm keeping my clothes on.'

Ernest was standing in the kitchen, sipping a mug of sweet tea, and he was naked from the waist up. On the bottom half he wore a pair of loose-fitting pyjama bottoms that sat low on his hips, revealing jutting hipbones and a lean torso. I pressed a spoon against the teabag in my cup and watched leaves float to the surface.

'That's good, Ernest. I'm glad you'll be keeping your clothes on while you're here. You'll notice I'm keeping mine on too.'

'Will it be a problem when you visit me? I'll be naked then.'

I ran through a few options in my head. When did I last spend any time alone in a forest with a naked man? Would it bother me? Too right it would. I was unnerved by the proximity of a half-naked man, especially one as attractive as Ernest. I'd had so many disasters in the past I didn't trust my reactions towards men anymore. Whatever I did or said would be wrong. I settled for something flippant and non-committal.

'Just as long as you don't expect me to be naked too.'

Ernest looked disappointed. 'Maybe once you get to know me better, and you relax, you'll feel OK about it.'

I concentrated on fishing tea leaves out of my cup. Oh, yeah right, I thought, like *that's* going to happen. You haven't met Miss Prissy Knickers. And then I wondered if it might happen in the bush. Ernest was a good-looking man and I allowed myself to wonder what his skin would feel like if I were to reach out and touch him. I banished the thought as quickly as it appeared.

I had come to Australia to do a short-term job that would get me out of England and away from A3. I wanted to enjoy myself but I wasn't looking to start a new relationship, have casual sex or get involved on any level other than friendship. The conversation in Byrock had been fascinating but I'd crossed the Rubicon. Besides, I still felt uneasy about the way Ernest had turned up out of the blue the day before. I wasn't even sure I would be making a trip out to his camp any time soon. I glanced at the clock, swallowed the last mouthful of tea and rinsed my cup in the sink.

'I hope the little hairies won't put you off,' Ernest said from behind me.

I switched off the tap, unsure if I'd heard correctly.

'Little horrors? Are there children at your camp?' I asked, wiping my hands on a tea towel and turning back to face him.

Ernest frowned at the floor, clutching his empty mug. 'There are no children, it's just me and the little hairies.'

I was discombobulated by the talk of nakedness and kept expecting a joke to unfold.

'A little hairy? What's that when it's at home?'

I should have known better. Ernest didn't have a flippant side.

'It's a creature about two or three foot tall.' His voice was careful and deliberate, as always. 'You don't see them very often because they move too fast, but they're out there.' He frowned again. 'Don't let them worry you, though; you'll be all right.'

The air was thicker than it had been a moment ago. Was he serious? There was an Aboriginal man in my kitchen and he was talking like a character from Lewis Carroll. It felt like I was staring down the rabbit hole, wondering if I should follow. Ernest was telling me, in all seriousness, that if I were to visit him in the bush, not only would I have to contend with a fully naked, six-foot-six-inch Ernest, I'd also have to watch out for small hairy creatures that moved incredibly quickly. I didn't bother to ask if they would be naked. I think I knew what the answer would be.

I looked at the clock again. There was no time to pursue the conversation; I had to get to work.

My hand hovered over the fruit bowl where I kept a spare set of keys. Could I trust him? I didn't know much about Ernest but he was a guest in my house, I had allowed him to stay, and I couldn't now treat him like a prisoner and lock him in. Or out. Besides, he'd done nothing to make me think I couldn't trust him. He'd made no attempt to climb the stairs during the night and he seemed as open and honest as his name suggested.

'You'll need these to get back in if you go for a walk,' I said, handing over the keys. 'I'll be back by six thirty – help yourself to any food you can find in the fridge or in the cupboards.'

I left him standing in the kitchen, a young man with an old-man beard nestled incongruously against his bare torso.

*

The day passed quickly and I barely had time to think about Ernest. Everyone in the marketing office was working like crazy, including the lovely Janis Joplin who kept us all supplied with freshly brewed tea. Lovely as she was, there came a time when I had to stand up to her. I was copied in on an exchange of emails, in which Janis offered to write an in-depth feature on medical training for a professional magazine. I was impressed; that was a complex job that would require hours of research and interviews to do it justice.

Twenty seconds later an email pinged into my inbox. 'Looks like I put your hand up for some more work,' she wrote, adding a smiley face at the bottom of the email.

I could feel my heart thudding. I was the person who always said yes, no matter what was asked of me, in work and in life. But I'd never been under such intense pressure before. I was working weekends and evenings just to get through the workload. I thought about the photo shoots I had to arrange, the four-page advertorial for *The Sydney Morning Herald* I had to organise and the next issue of the newsletter I was meant to write, never mind the website that hadn't been updated and the weekly news that hadn't even been started.

I was forty-nine years old and I had never stood up for myself in a workplace before. It was one of those 'now or never' moments.

'Looks like you put your own hand up,' I replied, adding a smiley face of my own. That may sound insignificant but it was a major step forward (and it was also the end of the smiley faces).

I called in to Woolies on the way home and picked up a cauliflower for dinner. A few weeks of walking up Darling Street had left my clothes looser and my thunderous thighs noticeably less flabby. The long slog uphill, inhaling scent from flowers and listening to birds singing overhead, beat going to a gym any day.

As I turned the key in the lock I wondered if Ernest would still be there. My clichéd view of Aboriginal people, gleaned from tourist images and an English primary school education in the 1960s, was that they went walkabout, roaming the land for months on end.

I found Ernest sitting perfectly still in an armchair in a corner of the living room. He got up when I came in, moving with a slowness that wouldn't be stopped until he'd reached his full height, like a whale slowly breaking the surface of the ocean. After an unexpected hug hello, I asked what he'd been doing all day.

'I had a sleep,' he said in that tentative, even way that wouldn't be rushed. 'And a bit of a cry.'

His answer took me by surprise. 'Why were you crying?'

'I lost all my money.'

Ernest crumpled back into the chair and empty space pushed at my stomach.

'What happened, Ernest?'

'I lost it on the pokies.'

'How much did you lose?'

'Everything I had.'

My heart beat faster. I sat down opposite and fought the instinct to respond with dramatic intensity. Instead I took a breath and slowed the conversation down to match his pace.

'Ernest . . . how much did you have?'

'Three hundred dollars.'

Relief that he hadn't lost more vied with shock at discovering all Ernest had in the world was $300. Now he didn't even have that.

'Why did you do it?' I asked, as gently as possible. I could see he was upset. He stared at the floor, slowly moving his head from side to side.

'It was the bad spirits. They made me do it.'

I tried to get on the same wavelength as Ernest when I answered. 'Why didn't you listen to the good spirits?'

'The bad spirits don't want me to be on the path of goodness.'

'But why did you listen to them?'

'I didn't have a choice.'

His answer shocked me. Surely we all had a choice when it came to good and evil; I'd always believed that. I don't know if it was Ernest's quivering lip and lowered shoulders, or the strangeness of what he was saying, but suddenly I knew I'd had a choice when it came to A3. I wasn't a victim of fate; I could have chosen to believe him when he said he wasn't interested and I had chosen not to. And now, here in Australia, I could choose to nurture my sadness about the fact that he was married. Or I could choose to let it go and get on with life. Choices. We all had them. It seemed an important point, one I wasn't willing to let go of.

'Ernest, what if the bad spirit told you to do something terrible, something really bad. Would you do it?'

'They don't want me to stay on the right path.'

'Ernest, you can choose to listen to the good spirits.'

'The bad spirits want me to fail.'

'What about personal responsibility? What if the bad spirits told you to bash someone? Would you do it?' I could hear my voice rising. I was selfishly worried for my own safety. What if the bad spirits told him to take a pop at me? Would he be forced to do it? Would the good spirits intervene in time? Ernest shook his head and tears fell on his cheek.

'Where do you figure in all this talk about good spirits and bad spirits, Ernest? What about your own will?'

'They want me to fail,' he repeated miserably.

It was pointless to continue the conversation so I let the subject drop and made cauliflower cheese for supper.

*

'My uncle Dave told me a riddle I don't understand. He said I'd understand it one day.'

After dinner it had seemed like a good idea to get out of the house, so I took Ernest on a short stroll along the quiet back streets of Balmain; now we were sitting on a park bench over-looking Birchgrove Oval. Ernest was reluctant at first, eventually admitting he'd been moved on by police earlier in the day when a concerned resident 'reported' him for sitting on a bench in that very park. Try moving him on now, I thought, suppressing the fury that made me want to ring every doorbell and find out who had been so bigoted.

It was a clear night, cool near the water with a faint sprink-ling of stars above. Here those stars were competing with light pollution from a city of four million people and all that went with it: cars, houses, buses, ferries, museums, supermarkets, office blocks, high-rise apartments, skyscrapers. Out in the desert or at sea they would be diamond sharp. I had an inkling of what Ernest meant when he said his ancestors left him behind when he walked into a town. How could any spirit reach him in the middle of all this distraction?

'What was the riddle?' I asked.

'Whether you're a butterfly or whether you're a snail, when the magpie comes pecking you'll remember who you are.' He turned his head. 'Do you know what he meant?'

Maybe I did. In spite of his size, Ernest seemed as gentle as a butterfly. He was as slow as a snail too, every movement considered and purposeful, his speech never hurried. His uncle had chosen the metaphors well. I tried to link my answer to the bad spirits, hoping to find a way to help Ernest get over what had happened.

'Maybe what your uncle is telling you is that the bad spirits are like magpies. When they peck at you, even if you're gentle and slow, you have to learn to defend yourself. You have to remember that you're a man and find the strength you need to do the right thing. When bad things happen, when the magpie comes pecking, that's when life is teaching you a lesson.'

Ernest nodded but he didn't look convinced. It's hard to interpret the guidance others give. How often has the universe tried to teach me a lesson? I'm pretty sure well-meaning friends must have tried many times to let me know I was chasing the wrong men, and wasting my life in the process. But did I listen?

*

Next morning I left Ernest some emergency money, first extracting a promise he wouldn't spend it on the pokies, and I caught the bus to work. The passenger sitting next to me was reading *The Sydney Morning Herald*, and as I glanced across I couldn't help noticing an article on the Dalai Lama. He was in Australia, running a series of workshops on meditation for aspiring monks, nuns and students. On Saturday night there was a public talk, 'Finding Purpose in Life'.

The coincidence that Ernest should be in Sydney at the same time as the Tibetan spiritual leader seemed serendipitous; Ernest had met the Dalai Lama in Canberra and I'd always wanted to hear him speak. When I got to work I booked two tickets. As an afterthought I booked a combined train and bus ticket to get Ernest back to Byrock the following Monday. The path Ernest had chosen – living alone in the bush in search of redemption and cultural knowledge – was not an easy one but it was time he went back to it. A week with an unexpected house guest was long enough.

In the days that followed I took Ernest to dinner at a friend's house and he endured our fellow guests' curiosity with good-natured head nodding and quiet conversation. I was finding out that there was no such thing as small talk for Ernest. It was all deep and meaningful: spiritual discussions, visions, Jesus versus the devil, the battle between good and evil. I was relieved to let others spend time in the spotlight of such intensity.

Well, aren't you liberal, taking an Aboriginal person to a dinner party in Balmain.

Bad spirit, I thought, banishing PK's puffed-up pride. Go away.

*

Good spirits were there in abundance on the Saturday, led by a portly man sitting cross-legged on a cushion. Ernest sat mesmerised in the audience, head and shoulders above the rest of the six thousand followers gathered in the exhibition centre at Sydney Olympic Park. His long grey beard and dark skin made Ernest look like a budding guru himself, and there were plenty of sidelong glances.

I was glad we'd made the effort to come. After almost a week of full-strength Ernest conversations about the Holy Spirit I'd endured about as much as I could take. I was getting impatient with Ernest's lack of motivation too, and the kindly message of the Dalai Lama was just what I needed to hear.

The Dalai Lama had none of the ego-driven pride that often comes when an important man addresses an adoring crowd of several thousand people. His Holiness laughed a lot, giggled even, and talked through an interpreter about compassion, kindness, generosity, and finding purpose by helping others. The resident of Balmain who rang the police to 'report' Ernest for sitting on a park bench would have done well to take note.

I hoped I wasn't being unkind by banishing Ernest back to Byrock, but he needed to get on with his life and I wanted to get on with mine.

'Question what I tell you,' the Dalai Lama said. 'Analyse my teachings and see if they work for you.'

'What's in the bag you always carry?' asked a member of the audience. The Dalai Lama chuckled and reached into his shoulder bag. He held up a bread roll.

'For when I get peckish,' he said, his face full of mirth.

I reminded myself that Ernest would need food for his journey back to Byrock; money too.

*

I was dozing in and out of sleep early on Monday morning when I heard the creak of a stair tread. I opened my eyes and saw Ernest, one hand on the banister at the top of the stairs, looking at me lying in bed.

'Can I come up?' he asked tentatively.

'NO, Ernest, you cannot!' I said, banishing him with a Miss Prissy Knickers glare that left no room for doubt.

Later, over breakfast, I reinforced the message.

'Ernest, I'm not looking for a boyfriend.'

He slowly shook his head. 'No. I'm not looking for a girlfriend either.'

'Good, that's settled then; just as long as you understand.'

*

I got home to find the spare set of keys back in the fruit bowl and the house spotlessly clean. Ernest may not have contributed financially but he'd helped in other ways: chopping vegetables, doing the dishes and now it looked like he'd vacuumed the house (the first time the vacuum cleaner had been used since I'd moved in).

I sent him a silent thank you, kicked off my shoes, opened a bag of chips and curled up on the sofa to watch whatever mindless drivel I could find on television.

When I went to bed I found a note resting on my pillow. It was a heartfelt thankyou note – nothing untoward or suggestive in it, but even so I felt uneasy. If Ernest had left it on the dining room table it would have been sweet and lovely. Putting it on my pillow, in my bedroom, was wrong.

*

Ernest rang a few days later to let me know he'd arrived home safely.

'You shouldn't have left that note in my bedroom,' I said.

'I just wanted to say thank you,' he said, sounding hurt. 'Did I do the wrong thing?'

'No, it's just . . . oh never mind.'

'When are you coming to visit my camp?'

'Work's very busy. I'm not sure I'll be able to get out to Byrock.'

'Maybe I could visit Sydney again, in October or November.'

That was still another four months away; I might even have gone back to England by then. I took refuge in polite English manners. 'Of course,' I said. 'Anyway, I'm glad you got home safely. I'd better go now, goodbye, Ernest.'

Two days later Ernest turned up on the doorstep, with no money in his pockets at all. Did he even go back to Byrock? I bought him another train ticket, the earliest I could get, and sent him packing after a fractious twenty-four hours. It's fair to say we parted on bad terms.

A week later there was an apologetic letter, a heartfelt missive with references to the Holy Spirit and Jesus, only this time there was a twist in the tail.

I just needed to let you know I'm sorry for the way things have turned out between us . . . I'm 99.9% sure that you wanted to have sex with me . . . and I'm letting you know

114

that if you want, the next time we meet we can make love all day and all night, no strings attached.

Crikey. Somehow Ernest had picked up on the sliver of momentary curiosity I'd experienced in the kitchen and turned it into a ninety-nine per cent slab of certainty that I wanted to sleep with him. I will never know how he did that but I did know we wouldn't be seeing each other again.

He rang to see if I'd received the letter and Miss Prissy Knickers answered the call. 'Ernest, there will be *no* next time. I don't want to sleep with you, I told you that. I told you I wasn't looking for a boyfriend!'

'I know. That's OK. I'm not looking for a girlfriend either.'

*

Over the next few weeks I fielded several calls from Ernest. His behaviour hardly amounted to stalking – it was more like wilful persistence in choosing to interpret the friendship I offered as an indication of something else – but it was a sobering reminder of my own behaviour. How often had I done that, and in ways far more devious and sneaky than Ernest's?

When A3 said all he could offer was friendship, I agreed. Then I schemed and plotted and desperately hoped for something else. Why not simply accept the situation? Was my self-esteem so low that I needed to prove I could 'make' someone fall for me? Was I happier to live with fantasy than deal with reality? If I needed fantasy I should have looked no further than Alice in Wonderland – *say what you mean and mean what you say*. I said nothing, not out loud. Internally I could argue, split up and then get back together with A3 (with any of the As – in fact with most boyfriends I've ever had) without ever speaking a single word to any of them. I'd locked my feelings away for so long that I could no longer voice them and relied instead on interior monologues so vivid and intense it was easy to forget that no one else was taking part in the conversation. And it was easy to ignore the fact that I was stalking A3.

Looking back, I've witnessed several stalking episodes. Early one Friday evening I was sitting on a bench in a crowded shopping centre in West London, reading a book and waiting to meet my close friend, Helen, when a well-dressed woman in her early twenties sat down beside me.

'I want to apologise,' I heard someone say. 'I want to apologise.'

I looked up and an older man was standing in front of the young woman sitting beside me. He was dressed in jeans and a navy polo-neck jumper, with greasy black hair dragged into a ponytail, and he was staring at the girl in a way that spooked me.

'I want to apologise,' he kept repeating. 'I want to apologise.'

'Go away,' she whispered.

There was something so menacing about the situation I felt compelled to step in. 'I think she wants you to leave her alone,' I said. The man ignored me.

'Do you want me to call the police?' I asked the girl, loudly enough for him to hear.

'Yes please,' she whispered.

I called the local police station, making sure the man could hear what I was saying. He didn't move. While we waited for the police to arrive the young girl told me the stranger had broken into the residential college where she was studying, and he'd been spotted several times lurking behind the stacks in the library. Each time he was ordered to leave. The last time it happened he doubled back, broke into her student accommodation through a bathroom window and hid in the wardrobe. When she found him, several hours later, he ran away.

She had sensibly taken out a court order warning him not to go within fifty metres of her, yet here he was, standing less than a metre away. He clearly had no idea he was a stalker because when the police arrived he made no attempt to leave. 'I just want to apologise,' he said, as they led him away.

Then there was the time I had a small role in a Bertolt Brecht play, *Fear and Misery of the Third Reich*. I was cast as a woman who cried a lot. (Easy.) The cast included Samuel, a confident guy in his mid-thirties with a broad cockney accent and a live-in girlfriend, and Astrid, a nervous kitten in her early twenties. Astrid would always stand with one leg in front of the other, toes pointed at a forty-five degree angle, front leg slightly bent, like a catwalk model waiting to be photographed. She once confessed she thought it made her look slimmer. (It did.) She was a beautiful princess, as silent as a statue, and it was obvious that something went on between Samuel and Astrid during the play's run.

After the final performance, when most people had gone home, I was sitting outside the theatre, finishing my drink, when Samuel appeared, trudging along the footpath with his head down and his hands in his pockets. Astrid was following a few paces behind. Every time Samuel stopped, she stopped; he turned, she turned.

'Leave me alone,' he said. 'I'm going home and you can't come with me.'

He turned. Astrid followed.

'Astrid, go away!'

Astrid said nothing, she just stood there. Samuel pleaded with her, first politely then with growing desperation, but nothing he said drew any reaction. The moment he walked away, Astrid followed. He shooed her away like a dog and she stopped, but as soon as he walked on she followed.

Samuel gave up trying to go home and walked over to me.

'Astrid won't stop following me!' he declared.

'Why?' I asked, already knowing the answer.

He sighed. 'Because I slept with her. But it was only once and now she won't leave me alone!'

The thought of his long-term, live-in girlfriend's reaction was clearly troubling Samuel (a shame it hadn't troubled him earlier, but there was no point arguing with him now).

'You have to let him go, Astrid,' I said. 'It's over.'

Astrid gave no sign she could hear me. She just planted herself next to Samuel with a sad look on her face.

'Astrid, can't you see? He's not interested. Leave him alone. Go home.'

Samuel walked away and Astrid followed. He turned; she turned. Without warning, I flipped.

'Stop it, Astrid! You're an idiot! He's not interested and we're all bored with your bloody stupid behaviour and we all want to go home so just stop it! Leave him alone, for God's sake!'

It broke the spell. Astrid slumped down beside me and burst into tears; Samuel legged it. I don't blame him but I was left trying to comfort the distraught Astrid, who couldn't get over the fact that Samuel was only after a good time and had no intention of dumping his long-term girlfriend in favour of her, no matter how elegant she might have looked standing with one leg slightly bent or how alluring she might have looked lying naked in his bed.

And what about that case in Holland of a Dutch woman who called a man 65,000 times in one year? That's an average of 178 calls a day, never mind the emails and text messages she must have sent. She had several mobile phones at home and saw nothing wrong in it.

My own behaviour seemed timid by comparison but it was stalking all the same and I should have spotted what I was doing and stopped it. Know thyself, said the great Socrates. Easier said than done.

If I'd been more honest about what I wanted from A3, if I'd communicated more openly, would I have stood a better chance of success? Who knows? I certainly wouldn't have wasted years stalking someone who wasn't interested.

chapter twelve

Here's where I have to admit that I haven't been telling you the whole story.

You see, while Miss Prissy Knickers was 'earnestly' shoring up her defences against a possible breach of security, someone else was making his way across the outlying wasteland that surrounds Fortress Frosty. Like some crazy escapee from a World War II film, unwittingly tunnelling in the wrong direction, he seemed oblivious to the threat that lay ahead.

Maybe he didn't realise he was heading for danger? Maybe he didn't spot that he was placing himself directly in the line of fire? Either way, Captain Considerate, Fearless Adventurer, Slayer of Dragons and Saviour of Middle-aged Spinsters, mounted an assault when the troops were busy elsewhere.

He snuck under the wire, crossed the frozen wastes and breached the walls of Fortress Frosty before any defence could be mounted. When he tried to claim his prize he found Miss Prissy Knickers snarling at him. Lesser men would have given up and gone home, but Captain Considerate calmed and soothed the She Devil until *she* gave in.

How the hell did that happen?
Persistence, PK, sheer bloody-minded persistence.

*

Captain Considerate asked me to have dinner with him, in that old-fashioned, polite way people used to before Facebook and text messaging took over. The note arrived on my desk at work. 'Would you like to have dinner with me?' his note said – his *handwritten* note.

I wondered what a normal person would do. I know that sounds crazy but with a relationship history like mine I had no idea what normal looked like when it came to men. I phoned Kate.

'I've been invited out to dinner.'

'Great.'

'Yes, but what should I do? I mean, what does the note mean? Is it a date? Should I accept? What would you do? I don't even know if I want to go on a date with this man. And what if it's not a date? Why is he asking me out to dinner?'

Kate stepped in before the twisted rubber band of my anxiety could snap. 'Go and have dinner with him,' she said. 'That way you'll find out.'

Part of my anxiety stemmed from the fact that the note came from the CEO, the cycling fanatic I'd met in Broken Hill. Extensive cellulite crammed into too-tight cycling shorts and lack of any demonstrable skill on a bicycle hadn't deterred him. Let me say now that Captain Considerate was not my type, not remotely. There wasn't one thing about him that made me think, ah yes, he's the type of person I fancy. He was tall, for one thing, and skinny, whereas I prefer bulk; give me a warm pillow of flesh I can snuggle into any day. He also had all his own hair and I have a thing for bald men – always have, ever since Yul Brynner in *The King and I*. (I hate to admit this, but even Kojak did it for me.)

Captain Considerate also had nothing to do with theatre or the arts, both of which I love.

So even if I hadn't been pining for lost love, nursing a broken heart and grieving over a man I couldn't have, there was no danger I would fall for Captain Considerate. I accepted the invitation.

*

'I thought you'd enjoy the view,' he said, drawing a patio heater closer to our table. It was an unusually cold night and we were the only people sitting outside the café on the strip leading from Circular Quay to the Opera House.

'Thank you,' I said. 'It's lovely.' In fact, I was shivering. My choice of what to wear had been limited by the colourful summer clothes I'd brought from England (the thought of winter in Sydney hadn't crossed my mind). I'd opted for wide hippie pants, with a pink and blue flower embroidered at the ankle, a sky blue singlet top and a thick green Marks & Spencer cardigan. I must have looked like an ageing leftover from an anti-war demonstration.

Captain Considerate wore a white shirt and striped tie, navy slacks (no other word for them: they were slacks) and a navy double-breasted blazer with gold buttons. With his grey hair parted on the side he looked to be somewhere in his mid-sixties. What anyone would have made of us, God only knows, although CC did remind me of my uncle Jim, which in retrospect was no bad thing since I really liked my uncle Jim.

The magnificent view was lost on me because I wasn't seeing too straight, having downed a couple of glasses of wine before I'd left home to calm my nerves, then ordering a gin and tonic as soon as we'd met. Captain Considerate was sipping a lemon, lime and bitters.

'Would you like white or red?' he asked, squinting at the wine list in a way that made me think he normally wore glasses.

'White, please.' I told myself I could have one more glass, two at most. Any more and I'd be sloshed. The waiter brought a bottle of chilled sauvignon blanc.

'Would you like to taste the wine, Sir?'

'The lady will taste the wine.'

I made a passable imitation of a lady who knows how to taste wine and sipped demurely. CC held his hand over his glass.

'Sparkling mineral water for me, thank you.'

The waiter nodded and left.

'You're not having any?'

He shook his head. 'I don't drink.'

'Not at all?'

'Not anymore.'

'Why not?'

'I drove home from a function one night and realised I was over the limit. I could have killed someone in that state. So I stopped drinking.'

'Why did you order wine if you don't drink?' I asked, helping myself to another glass.

'I thought you'd enjoy it,' he said.

I did. By the time the food came I was sloshed; well and truly pickled, off my trolley and floating away with the fairies, which could explain why I happily told Captain Considerate all the lurid details of my early life – sexual misadventures included. I didn't hold back. I wasn't trying to impress this man so what did I have to lose? I told the truth about the mistakes in my life while he recounted all the amazing achievements of his.

We shivered our way through a mediocre meal as I heard about his successful career as a geological surveyor in oil and gas fields (I think), followed by an equally successful career as a pilot. He seemed fit, happy and emotionally intelligent. (And since when did that ever describe anyone I normally fell for?) He got out of the stock market before it crashed and he won the George Medal for bravery in his early twenties. By the end of the meal I'd worked out that Captain Considerate had enjoyed a stable marriage that lasted twenty years before it ended in divorce (I'm guessing; there wasn't much of the bottle left by that stage), and he had a cordial relationship with his ex-wife and a grown-up son he loved.

'I'd run a mile if any of my ex-lovers crossed my path,' I said.

'What's the longest relationship you've ever had?'

'It was only t . . . uh . . . oh, let me think . . . five years.' (Maybe I did care what he thought after all.)

'And now you're single?' he asked.

'Yes. And you?'

He nodded.

Having watched me slip inexorably into a drunken stupor, Captain Considerate asked if I'd like to have coffee at his hotel, in that terribly polite way that only someone wearing a blazer can get away with.

'How far is it?' I asked. By that stage my legs felt numb with cold. Or alcohol. Either way I'd have trouble walking.

'Five minutes.'

I figured it had to be worth it to get out of the cold.

We passed through a quiet wood-panelled lobby (thankfully deserted) and stepped into a lift. Moments later I was propped in the doorway of a dimly lit lounge room with an adjoining bedroom.

Being so far gone there seemed no point stopping, I reached for a glass of red wine from the minibar, then slumped onto the sofa. Before I could get the screw-top off Captain Considerate had slapped a ladder against the fortress wall and was clambering up the side, poised to leap over the top. I slapped him back down.

'Don' *doo* that!'

'I'm sorry,' he said. 'I thought you wanted me to.'

'Whaddever gave you thad idea?' I said, forgetting the rollcall of sexual misdeeds that I'd cheerfully recounted over dinner, some in graphic detail. I wrapped myself in what I could muster of my tattered virtue and stood up, grabbing hold of the door jamb to stop from falling over.

'I am gonna gedda takshi,' I declared.

I tottered down the corridor to the lift and Captain Considerate followed, presumably to make sure I didn't fall over. He appeared at my side while I stood swaying on the pavement outside.

'I've had a lovely evening, thank you,' he said politely.

I squinted at his fuzzy tie and succeeded in raising my eyes high enough to meet his. He seemed genuine.

'Me doo,' I mumbled.

'Are you sure you're OK to get home? Would you like me to come with you? I'll come straight back.'

'I'm abshloodly fine. Thangk yoo.'

He flagged down a taxi and helped me in. As I sprawled across the back seat he reached across to pay the driver. 'Please make sure the young lady gets home safely,' he said, making me feel like a Victorian.

I dimly remembered my manners and scrabbled into an upright position. 'Thangk yoo for dinner,' I managed.

'My pleasure,' he replied. 'Almost.'

Miss Prissy Knickers glared at him with drunken displeasure and his grin widened as he waved goodbye.

*

The next morning I dragged my sore head in to work by bus, feeling every jolt on the journey. My queasy stomach protested at the parade of aftershave and perfume that wafted past and as soon as I got to the office I shut the door. I slumped at my desk with my head in my hands and stared at the proofs of the next newsletter. Lines of text swam across the page like startled ants.

Five minutes later, there was a knock at the door and I peered through splayed fingers to see a pair of navy slacks standing in front of the desk.

'Looks like you had a big night,' said Captain Considerate. 'Did it go well?'

Judging by the barely concealed laughter in his voice, Captain Considerate wasn't remotely embarrassed by the previous night's encounter. I was at a loss for words. Having dinner with the boss was bad enough, but I hadn't just had dinner with the man, I'd had dinner, got drunk, spilled the beans on my disastrous love-life, and then gone back to his hotel and told him to piss off when he made a pass at me. Did it get any worse? The only thing saving me from personal and professional ruin was the fact that I would be leaving the RFDS, and Australia, in less than four months' time. Plus he lived in Broken Hill.

Sometimes I'm the kind of person who can think on her feet and come up with a witty rejoinder; sometimes I'm not.

'Uh . . .'

Another note appeared on my desk while I was at lunch.

'I enjoyed your company tremendously last night. Perhaps you would allow me to invite you to the cinema, or the theatre; I will be in Sydney for the next few days. I promise not to tease or embarrass you if you prefer to decline.'

Once the fug of alcohol had cleared from my system (the sense of embarrassment took longer to fade), I realised that if you took away the awkward fumble at the end of the night, I had enjoyed his company too. And it was such a sweet note.

That fact that he was the CEO didn't bother me unduly; I wasn't about to start a relationship with the man and he wasn't married. I didn't report directly to him, or even indirectly, and I worked in the marketing department, twelve hundred kilometres away from his office in Broken Hill. I wasn't even a permanent member of staff and, anyway, going out to the theatre didn't commit me to anything else.

So I upped the ante and took him to a left-wing theatre group in Newtown, run by a bunch of humanists and socialists, with the odd communist thrown in, some of whom were my friends. He passed with flying colours, chatting happily to strangers in the foyer on King Street and saying nothing about the packing tape holding the New Theatre seat covers together. He even said he enjoyed the show (which was going a bit far – we both knew he hadn't, but you get the idea).

'I'd like to see you again,' he said at the end of the night, this time making no attempt to persuade me to go back to his hotel. 'Perhaps we could have dinner again the next time I'm in Sydney?'

I liked the fact that he'd braved an onslaught from Miss Prissy Knickers and hadn't given up; he'd smiled in the face of the icy winds that blew across the tundra and laughed at the stony silence that greeted him when Miss Prissy Knickers found him standing on the wrong side of her defensive wall.

Captain Considerate was hardly Captain Fantastic, and he was a long way from being Mr Right, but I liked his laid-back approach to life and his mischievous sense of humour.

'I'd like that,' I said. 'It could be a lot of fun.'

chapter thirteen

In the interest of fairness we went to a Sydney Swans game at the SCG, where I met and liked Captain Considerate's grown-up son. I can't say AFL floated my boat but each to his own, I thought. And, as simple as it sounds, that was a major step forward.

I'd never been out with anyone whose interests diverged so widely from my own. In the rare case that the object of my desire might not have enjoyed theatre or the arts, I quickly dropped my interests to fit in with theirs (which, by the way, is the fastest way I know of becoming a boring, needy appendage). So I feel I should declare, here and now, that no matter how gorgeous that Hallberg-Rassy yacht was, I never really enjoyed sailing (A2); the whole idea of crawling down a dark, wet cave in a boiler suit and hard hat actually filled me with dread (A3); and I'm not nearly as adventurous in bed as you thought I was (A1, and just about anyone I've ever slept with).

Maybe it was easy to accept that Captain Considerate had totally different interests because, for once, I wasn't looking for a long-term mate. I wasn't weighing up his every move to see if he was 'the one'. I was having some fun, and hard as it is to admit this, I was also marking time. I had flown to Australia, pledging to have fun while I got over a broken heart, and here was a single, attractive man with a good sense of humour who wanted to take me out. There was no reason not to enjoy his company.

Mind you, as much as I tried to minimise it, the fact that we both worked for the same organisation was tricky. He was the boss, and the people that I reported to reported to him. What's more, after five or six dates – all of them charming, proper, good fun and light-hearted – I saw no reason not to sleep with him (hardly a ringing endorsement, I know).

CC was keen to do the right thing and advise the Board about our fledgling relationship but I resisted. What if it didn't last? What if this was just a fling? The only way to find out was to take drastic action.

'I think we should go on holiday,' I said sternly when I saw CC next. 'We need to find out if this is a fling or a proper relationship and if this *is* a proper relationship, then we have to decide what to do about it and the only way we're going to find out is if we spend some time together so I think we should go on holiday.' I paused to draw breath. 'If you agree,' I added, rather lamely.

'Sounds like you've got it all worked out,' CC said. 'Where are we going?'

In the weeks leading up to the holiday I thought about phoning and saying, this is a bad idea, let's not do this. How did I end up agreeing to spend a week in Bali with a man I barely knew?

I hate hurting people. I once got engaged to a man I didn't like kissing (he was as desperate as I was to avoid being single; not exactly a match made in heaven) and rather than admit I hated the way he shot his tongue between my lips at unexpected moments, rather like a lizard trying to catch a fly, I got engaged to him. Brilliant plan. That way he never suspected a thing. In the end, when I thought I'd gag if he kissed me once more, I broke off the engagement and the poor man was left wondering what went wrong.

I was worried I might be doing the same with CC. Nice guy, not sure I wanted to have a relationship with him, so hey, why not go on holiday and spend a week together. Another brilliant plan!

You have a rubbish track record with holidays.

It's true. I've had some monumental foreign fuck-ups in my time.

When I decided the time had come to move back to England in hot pursuit of A3, I booked a stopover in the Far East, hoping to soak up some rays so I could arrive tanned, relaxed and irresistibly attractive. If nothing else, it would stave off the reality of an English winter with no job.

I splashed out on a beachfront resort on the island of Koh Samet off the east coast of Thailand and pre-paid for a five-night all-inclusive stay. The resort emailed me confirmation that a bus would pick me up from a Bangkok hotel.

The driver greeted me with a smile, then looked around the lobby.

'No Mister.' he said. 'Where Mister?'

I smiled good humouredly and said, 'No Mister.'

He raised his eyebrows. 'You go Ao Prao Resort?'

I nodded. He shrugged, picked up my case and led the way to a waiting tour bus, where two young couples were already onboard. I took a seat on the single side. Three hours later we got off in the town of Ban Phe, where the resort had its own ferry that shuttled between the mainland and the island of Koh Samet. I joined a queue of people at the ferry check-in desk.

'Hello Madam, you on your own?' The demure girl with a pink frangipani tucked behind her ear looked over my shoulder for the elusive Mister as I handed over my booking confirmation form.

'Yes, all alone,' I said with a brittle smile, dimly aware that several couples were waiting to check in behind me. As we filed along the pontoon towards the waiting ferry the throng of porters thinned out and I took stock of my fellow passengers. I was the only single person, surrounded by a sea of couples.

We landed on a small deserted beach fringed by palm trees. A line of timber cabanas and thatch-roofed bungalows nestled among the trees. Two young girls stood ankle deep in water, waiting to drape garlands of jasmine flowers around our necks, and, as far as I could tell, there were no shops, no restaurants, no bars and absolutely no sign of any other single people.

At the simple resort check-in desk the worried manager took me to one side.

'Why you come alone?' he asked. 'Why no Mister?' he whispered, not bothering to hide his shocked dismay.

'Because there is no *Mister*,' I said, panic and frustration rising by the second as I realised I'd spent the last of whatever money I had on five days in a honeymoon resort. '*I'm alone!*'

The happy honeymooners waiting to check in took a few steps back and I hurriedly signed the guest book, grabbed the keys to my room and disappeared along the beach.

At breakfast the next morning I was an oddity of pursed lips and frosty silence, the single wrong note in a symphony of loved-up couples sipping champagne and slipping each other titbits from the buffet. There was worse to come. Day three of my stay was Valentine's Day. The trees were festooned with strings of pink hearts, heart-shaped candles glistened on all the tables and a blackboard proclaimed that a crooner from the mainland would be ferried across with his keyboard to serenade the honeymooners with the world's top 100 love songs at dinner. I ate in my room.

The universe was trying to show me what love looked like and I didn't want to know. I sat grimly determined on the beach each day – a lone warning to all those happy couples that life outside the blissful state of coupledom was bleak – and at sunset I retreated to my room, unable to bear the sight of honeymooners kissing on the still-warm sand as the sun slipped below the horizon.

The only saving grace was a small library of paperback books in a cabana overlooking the beach. I ignored a couple smooching on the sofa behind me and knelt down for a closer look. The authors were typically undemanding honeymoon fare but I didn't care; I would have read anything to get me through those five days. I peered at the titles and my heart sank as I realised the books had all been published in foreign languages. I could have read John Grisham's *Det målade huset*, Danielle Steel's *Herzsturme*, Barbara Cartland's *Hjerter dame er trumf* or Maeve Binchy's *I år blir det nog bättre*.

Just as I was beginning to think I'd have to tackle the Binchy (something about being blathered after drinking too much egg nog), I spotted a lone novel in English, tucked away at the back of the shelf. It was a dog-eared, water-logged copy of Raymond Chandler's *Farewell, My Lovely*. I grabbed it, hoping I could make it last, and opened the battered front cover to discover the first twenty-seven pages were missing.

I never did find out who Moose Malloy was.

*

In order to make the cost of the holiday fair and equitable, CC and I agreed we would each pay a proportionate amount of the total cost. I had no idea how much CC earned (and no wish to) but it had to be at least four times my salary, so he paid three-quarters and I paid a quarter. A sensible, grown-up solution.

I sank a couple of glasses of wine to calm my nerves in the Qantas lounge (courtesy of CC's Qantas Club membership) while

he had a coffee and a sparkling mineral water, and pretty soon
it was status quo: me well on the way to being sloshed, Captain
Considerate stone cold-sober. Mid-afternoon, we boarded the
plane and I made polite conversation as we took off.

'Have you been to Bali before?' I asked.

'Yes, several times.'

'When was the first time?'

'On my honeymoon.'

'Oh.'

'What part of Bali did you stay in?'

'Ubud.'

We were on our way to Ubud and I was the one who'd chosen
it. I pressed the call button for another glass of wine.

The six-hour flight from Sydney to Denpasar was followed
by a ninety-minute drive. It was after eleven by the time we left
the airport and the city lights quickly thinned as we drove inland
until nothing remained but dense vegetation and the flash of
passing motorbikes. A lone guard on the boom gate at the resort,
set high in the hills outside Ubud, swept a mirror under the car
when we arrived. He wasn't taking any chances, even in this
remote spot; the Bali bombings in 2002 had rocked the tourist
industry on this small island.

We stood in the centre of a deserted lobby, like guests who'd
arrived after the party had finished, until a smiling night porter
appeared and presented us each with a garland of fresh marigolds
and frangipani flowers. This time, it made me feel special instead
of lonely and out of place.

The gentle porter led us past a swimming pool, stars reflected
in its flat, still surface, through landscaped gardens dense
with dark shapes and the sound of crickets calling from deep
within the foliage. He stopped in front of a carved wooden door,
unlocked it with a key that could have unlocked a dungeon, and

pushed open the heavy door to reveal a garden of swaying palms and fragrant jasmine.

The stone villa had floors of polished marble and dark wooden furniture set against pale white walls. Fine mosquito netting hung from a wooden frame around a massive bed set on a plinth in the middle of the bedroom, and in a delicate touch of welcome, there was a banana leaf on each pillow. It held a chocolate cupped in the middle, with a handwritten note etched on the leaf: 'Have a nice sleep.'

We climbed into that huge, welcoming bed and fell asleep immediately.

chapter fourteen

CC stirred in his sleep. I lay awake in our bigger-than-king-size bed, listening to the gentle sound of someone sweeping leaves outside the window. The cotton sheet felt cool against my skin and fine white mosquito netting softened the early morning light that filtered through the wooden shutters. A low murmur of words spoken in a language I didn't understand rose and then faded. I turned over, quietly so as not to wake CC.

This was a new sensation. I hadn't lost myself in a tortured angst of passion, I wasn't standing on the edge of a cliff, poised to swoop and soar or plummet to my death – sometimes both. I had a lover I liked and we had a week to get to know each other. It was a relief to know I wouldn't get swept along by feelings I couldn't control and that lack of angst had unexpected benefits, freedom even.

CC's body beneath the sheet was lean and long. He had the legs of a ballet dancer and the muscled torso of a long-distance runner . . . or a cyclist. I thought back to that scorching-hot day, my bulky thighs squeezed into cycling shorts two sizes too small, my face a sweaty beetroot, and I marvelled that he'd found something attractive in that.

Did he marvel that I found him attractive? In sleep his face looked ageless; the skin graft that stretched from his cheekbone down to his chin was smooth and hairless, suggesting the skin of a far younger man. I wondered if he'd been wearing glasses when he'd been burnt. The skin around his eyes looked to have been spared but his nose had suffered badly; his lips too. An arm above the sheet showed the extent of the damage: deep scar tissue running from his shoulder to his elbow, a twisted mass that distorted the skin. The scars faded as they reached his wrist; there was a clear patch where the leather strap of a watch must have offered some protection and then the spider web of distorted lines started again, extending to the tips of his fingers.

He blinked and I looked away, embarrassed to be caught staring.

*

'It was a helicopter crash.'

The cloud above us was milky white as we lingered over a second cup of coffee on the terrace after breakfast. Rice paddies of deepest green stepped down from the high side of the hotel, dropping to an unseen river below. It was so humid you could have reached out a glass, scooped it full of sky and gulped it down. I sipped my coffee, waiting for CC to expand on his answer to my question: what had happened?

'I was working for Geosurveys. I was part of an airborne team conducting gravity surveys on the Cape York Peninsula. There were two of us working this particular section. I was the surveyor and Jim was the pilot. He would land in a small bush clearing, I'd jump out to take a reading, and then we'd take off again. We plotted our course with a control centre so they would always know where we were in case of accidents, but on that partic- ular day one of the landing spots was too wet, so we changed

I was raised in the picturesque English village of Framley Coddrington. As a child I spent many a wet afternoon devouring fairytales at our local library. The dream of a handsome prince riding to the rescue burnt into my psyche.

I'm Mum's second daughter, born after Wendy and before Elizabeth and Rachel. My sisters all married boyfriends they met at school. They enjoyed the sweet innocence of young love while I pursued unsuitable older men. We're pictured here at a cousin's wedding in 1970, when I was twelve.

At fourteen I insisted on taking part in the Bristol Bordeaux Student Exchange then spent a month in France crippled by shyness. I barely spoke a word of French to my fellow student, pictured here at the start of her month in England. Her English improved massively.

After a series of short-term flings in my twenties and thirties, I gave up chasing men and threw myself into work as a writer and part-time actor. On stage I could cry at the drop of a hat; off stage I battened down the hatches and let no one in.

Mum and Dad were engaged within three weeks of meeting and they remained happily married for forty-eight years. They had a great sense of humour and a playful approach to life, something I failed to emulate for a long time.

The prospect of leaving England in mid-winter and heading back to the sunshine of Sydney was very appealing.

Me with the Royal Flying Doctor Service (RFDS) marketing team in Sydney. I couldn't have been more nervous applying for the job with the RFDS. I pledged to myself that if I got the job I would stop stalking and start living.

With my long-time friend Kate at Hyams Beach. Kate spent many hours mopping up my tears and listening to tales of woe about men. As a trained family therapist she always dispensed wise advice, which I frequently chose to ignore. Kate and her family welcomed me into their home when I first arrived in Sydney.

It took me a long while to stop obsessing over men and appreciate the true value of girlfriends like Kate. We're pictured here on Wendy Moore's 'Colourful Journey' in Nepal.

Friendly blokes with beer and big hats were a feature of most pubs
we visited on the Flying Doctor Outback Car Trek, the biggest annual
fundraiser for the RFDS. I spent ten days in the company of three hundred
men, working hard and having fun. This was taken at the Crakow Pub.

The only things that kept the surfing dudes warm were their wigs, especially
on early mornings when it was a chilly six degrees. They were laughing by
the time we got to Queensland and the sun finally came out.

The unwritten rule of the Trek was that if you started in costume, you stayed in costume. For these two that meant wearing pyjamas all day, every day. Some of the participants had a lot of fun. And some were clearly bonkers.

When the super-fit CC said 'would you like to come cycling?', the answer should have been no. I wasn't expecting an off-road expedition into the desert at seven a.m. on a Sunday morning. CC is pictured fourth from right, next to his equally fit bestie, David. I'm the sweaty lump second from left.

Jenny and Keith Treloar host a regular RFDS clinic on their Wiawera property near Broken Hill. They're pictured here at celebrations in the hangar to mark the 85th anniversary of RFDS. Left to right: Trish Treloar, RFDS SE President John Milhinch, Jenny Treloar, me, Keith Treloar and John Treloar.

Captain Considerate wasn't my type, not remotely. There wasn't one thing about him that made me think, ah yes, he's the type of man I normally go for, and for that I will be forever grateful.

I didn't know him then but Captain Considerate clearly cut a dash in his 1970s RFDS pilot's uniform. Left to right: the Hon Tom Lewis Premier of NSW and President of RFDS SE Section, Chief Pilot Captain Kevin Wiggins, CC and Captain Arthur Day.

Me in Bali while on holiday with CC. Because he wasn't my type I could relax and enjoy myself without wondering if CC was Mr Right. We didn't fight, split up or run out of conversation while we were away. We just had a lot of fun. On our return to Australia I convinced myself the relationship could never work.

When I moved to Broken Hill I thought free-range chooks in the back garden would help me feel at home, in an elegant *House & Garden* sort of way. How wrong I was. This is a rare moment when the chooks appear to be pecking contentedly at the lawn, when in reality they were planning their next assault on the vegetable patch.

How could anyone resist? Part-beagle with pick-me-please eyes, long legs and the softest coat, I fell in love with the adorable Benson before we'd even left the RSPCA car park. I was alone in thinking Benson was the ideal dog.

Maggie arrived looking scruffy and in need of a bath. The first time she got in the car, I sat in the back seat with her and I was terrified she might try to rip my arm off. Winding the window down transformed her from a potential killer into a family pet.

Members of the RFDS Women's Auxiliary taught me the value of community, commitment and dedication to a cause. I have the greatest admiration for these women, some of whom have been producing these fundraising puddings annually for almost fifty years. Left to right: Cynthia Langford, Julie Horsburgh, Jo Hayes, me and June Files.

Towards the end of the second week every available space was taken up with racks of calico-wrapped puddings hung up to dry. The drying room was already full – this is the overspill.

Me and my gorgeous sisters at my nephew's wedding. Wendy, Elizabeth and Rachel all live within a few miles of the village where we grew up. They are all in long-term committed relationships, hold down regular jobs and have raised happy, well-adjusted children. Spot the difference.

Thank God for girlfriends. On my fiftieth birthday, Kate and Andrea arrived with a bottle of champagne and they whisked me off in a water taxi for lunch at Ripples in Chowder Bay. I floated through the day in a sunny haze of friendship and laughter. It was a perfect day but for one missing ingredient.

HRH Crown Princess Mary of Denmark met her prince in a pub opposite the Sydney marketing office of the RFDS. She's pictured here with mine, arriving in Broken Hill to launch a new breast care service for the RFDS.

It wasn't all dust and flies, far from it. The annual RFDS Women's Auxiliary Dinner Dance in Broken Hill was a chance for everyone to frock up.

I was just as happy in a swag; I gave up the nightlife of the Sydney Theatre scene and the buzz of Balmain restaurants to spend evenings in a creek bed, barbecuing steak and eggs over a fire built from the fallen branches of a Coolabah tree.

You can stand at the edge of Broken Hill and see nothing but desert. I was scared of such solitude until I learnt to embrace the natural beauty of the Australian outback.

My entirely unexpected mate was completely the wrong man for me, or so I thought. The isolation of our desert home meant quitting wasn't an option, and after a shaky start I realised just how beautiful Broken Hill was, and how right CC was for me.

direction and flew to a new site. Jim radioed through the change but for some reason the message didn't get through.'

'How old were you?'

'Twenty-one.'

At twenty-one I was cruising my way through a part-time job teaching English as a foreign language in Madrid, sleeping in, staying up late and partying hard. It was my first job out of university and my only concern was where to find a decent tapas bar.

'About four in the afternoon we landed in a small clearing. I took the reading we needed, got back in the helicopter and Jim took off. Unfortunately the main blade clipped the top of a tree and the helicopter crash-landed. A fuel tank behind my seat exploded and I was thrown clear but Jim was trapped in the burning helicopter. I went back in to try to release him.

'That's when the second fuel tank exploded. I remember seeing my hands on fire and feeling no pain. I knew my head was on fire too but Jim was in a really bad way, he was on fire all over. I dragged him clear and tried to put the flames out.'

The waitress hovered to see if we wanted more coffee, then sensed our discussion was serious and left us alone.

'We crashed not far from a creek. An old tin of peaches we'd been carrying in the back of the helicopter burst open so I used the empty tin to carry water back and forth from the creek. I kept dousing Jim's body and gave him sips of water to drink. I thought we'd be rescued quickly but they didn't know our position. I kept going back to the creek for water and when it got dark Jim would call out so I could find my way back to him. One time, part way through the night, he didn't call. That's when I knew he'd died.'

CC's voice was quiet and measured. He lifted his coffee cup, drained what was left and held it for a moment in his hands before placing it back on the white saucer.

'When did they rescue you?'

'About twenty-four hours after the crash. They flew me to the burns unit in Cairns Hospital and I remember lying in hospital listening to a radio report about the crash. "One dead and one survivor, who isn't expected to live," they said. That was me.'

CC smiled. 'I was lucky,' he said. 'I died twice on the operating table but I pulled through. And I was doubly lucky because a top burns specialist treated me. Every day since 4 June 1966 has been a bonus.'

Lucky? To be involved in a fatal helicopter crash that left him with first, second and third degree burns to eighty per cent of his body? That didn't sound like luck to me but I was beginning to realise that CC was a glass half full kind of man.

He shot a challenging glance at me. 'My girlfriend at the time came to visit me in hospital. She took one look and walked out. I never heard from her again.'

'What a despicable thing to do,' I said.

'I don't blame her. There's no point being with someone if you don't want to be.'

I heard what he was saying loud and clear. Whatever happened, I had to be honest: there was no point leading this man on with any kind of false expectation. I knew I liked him but I wasn't going to fake a passion I didn't feel.

*

Bali was beautiful and Ubud a quiet backwater of easy grace (this was just before the explosion of growth that followed the publication of *Eat, Pray, Love*). The hotel was a haven of frangipani trees, thatched roofs, brick walls, stone paths, moist green ferns, fruit trees, ivy, jasmine, gardenia, heliconia, hibiscus and a profusion of flowering plants I couldn't even begin to recognise.

The men and women who worked at Kamandalu were gracious and always ready to smile, going about their business with purpose. There was no loud music and no radio blaring; just the sound of a besom broom sweeping leaves, a motorbike putt-putting sharply in the distance, a tree being felled in a forest far away, wood pigeons cooing softly to each other and the call of a cricket, swallowed by the silence like a star falling into a black hole.

CC insisted on learning a few phrases of Balinese from our waitress, whose name was Ketut. *Rahajeng semeng*, good morning; *sukseme*, thank you; *sukseme mewalt*, you're welcome. He mispronounced the phrases and used them frequently, often at inappropriate moments. As a linguist, I should have thought it cringe-worthy but I found myself admiring his willingness to have a go.

We hired bicycles and followed tracks that cut through the rice fields, waving at children who were immaculately dressed in pristine white uniforms, the girls' hair braided into long plaits, on their way home from school.

'Hello,' they called, giggling to each other. 'How are you?'

We smiled and called back. 'Very well, thank you, how are you?'

I'd shed another couple of kilos over the weeks before we left, thanks to a new routine of cycling to work. It took seven attempts before I made it across Anzac Bridge without getting off and pushing, but once I made it there was no stopping me: I joined a peleton of regulars, clinging to the back of the pack as we swooped and soared through traffic, spiralling down to the fish market and then climbing up again over Darling Harbour. I didn't feel as useless on a bicycle now as when I'd ridden in Broken Hill with CC.

According to the guidebook, no trip to Ubud would be complete without a visit to the Monkey Forest, a sacred area of temples and forest that was home to a collection of long-tailed macaque monkeys, so we bought two small clumps of bananas at the entrance and wandered past groups of well-fed monkeys basking in the sun, grooming each other.

I had worked out by now that Captain Considerate liked a joke. We once took a cab from Balmain to North Sydney, stopping first at Circular Quay for CC to get out. We kissed goodbye and he stood on the pavement, holding the car door open.

'Say hello to your husband,' he said, then shut the door before I could think of a rejoinder and waved as the taxi pulled away from the kerb. No amount of righteous protest would convince the grinning driver that we weren't having an affair.

Given CC's fondness for humour, it came as no surprise when he hid his bananas in his pocket. We sat on a wall to feed the inquisitive monkeys and a small male tugged at CC's pocket, knowing what was in it. CC stood firm. The monkey clambered onto his lap and CC wouldn't relent. Finally it leapt onto his shoulder. Still the bananas stayed hidden. In the end the monkey climbed onto CC's head, sank its long filthy teeth into his scalp and bit hard enough to draw blood. After I'd stopped laughing I told him not to worry.

'I've got some tea-tree oil back at the hotel,' I said.

Nurse Nightingale dabbed at the angry-looking bite and kissed it better. It was only later, when we got back to Australia, that we discovered rabies was a serious risk. He was luckier than I gave him credit for.

The days slipped by in an easy rhythm of late breakfasts, long massages, frequent lovemaking and hours spent lazing by the pool with a good book. We were content to drift with no real plan and I could tell by the way people looked at us that we must have seemed like one of those loved-up couples I'd found so confronting on Koh Samet, which was odd because I knew I didn't love him. But I liked him. I liked him a lot.

Captain Considerate was patient, emotionally mature and level-headed. He reckoned there was a guardian angel looking out for him and I had to agree because, in the course of seven days in Bali, quite apart from being bitten on the head by a potentially rabid monkey, he fell over playing tennis and drove the motorbike we hired the wrong way around a busy intersection, narrowly avoiding killing us both. I know I can be impulsive, headstrong, accident-prone and likely to get into some tricky situations, but I was a non-starter compared to him.

The seven days we spent in Bali were a joyful reminder of how to have fun. And I quickly forgot CC's burns – they were nothing compared to his atrocious dress sense. It amazed me that someone with such an incredible physique had no idea how to wear casual clothes. He'd always looked stunning in a suit but in Bali I discovered that CC's idea of casual wear was track-suit pants with a rugby shirt. Not so terrible, you might think, but wait, what if you were to tuck the aforementioned rugby shirt into the elasticised waist of those tracksuit pants? And how about very short shorts with trainers and long white socks, pulled up to the knees? Was it just another of his cunning ploys, so I'd prefer to see him naked? I wouldn't have put it past him.

One afternoon we climbed up to the private Balinese day bed that perched above the roof of our villa like an observatory, offering 360-degree views of the whole resort. The day bed was sheltered under a gazebo-type roof with mosquito netting shielding the open sides. It seemed totally private and secluded, an ideal place to shed those tracksuit pants and relax. So that's what we did.

Something happened up there that I struggle to explain. I remember reading Hemingway's *For Whom the Bell Tolls* in my early twenties and in the novel the elderly Pilar talks to the young Maria about how the earth can move when you make love, how a person is fortunate if it happens once in a lifetime, and how it can never happen more than three times. I had no idea what she was talking about.

What nonsense, I scoffed, absolute bunkum. Rubbish. As you can probably gather, I'd never had an orgasm. I eventually worked out what orgasms were but I still didn't get the whole earth-moving business; it seemed such a massive exaggeration. Now I know what Pilar was talking about.

The earth shifted up there on our Balinese day bed – I was there, and not there. I was connected and disconnected; unhinged and easily moved, like the way sunrise can slip unnoticed across the sky and tinge the clouds pink.

I glimpsed a parallel place; a tranquil, kind, loving place I'd never visited before. I have no idea if I was happy or not, all I know is I felt more alive than I'd ever felt before. It was more ephemeral than physical, a sense of belonging to each other and to the world around us, of being human and in place, a place of me but not me, a blurring of the edges, a different reality. Is that what it means to become 'one' with someone? It felt larger than that. I was 'one' with CC and everything else in the universe. I was nothing and nowhere and everywhere simultaneously. There were no edges, no inside or outside, no skin, no bed and no body.

CC saw it happen. 'You shimmered,' he said afterwards.

At breakfast the next day we realised the Balinese day bed wasn't as private as we thought. We would have been visible, relaxing and shimmering, to the entire restaurant. Over the following three days we worked out we would have been visible, relaxing and shimmering, to anyone who might have been sunbathing by the pool, playing tennis or walking by the river. In fact, there wasn't a single place in the hotel where you wouldn't have been able to spot us, relaxing and shimmering. It's a wonder we didn't get arrested. It might explain why on the last night they upgraded us to a private villa with a pool and left a cake in our room. The icing on it said, 'Happy Honeymoon.'

By the end of that week in Bali I felt ten years younger. I forgot all about the 'we need to work out if there is any prospect of this being a long-term relationship' nonsense, and I had fun. Fun was what I'd wanted and fun was what we had. Miss Prissy Knickers, frosty ice maiden and suspicious single stalker, melted on holiday with CC. We got naked. We laughed and joked and I would even go so far as to say I frolicked. When did I last do that?

CC was funny, kind and sexy, and seemed to think I was too. He was thoughtful, dependable, strong and supremely confident, a Machiavellian chancer who believed in the world of spirit; a happy, jealous, sensual man, prejudiced against anyone with tattoos or body piercing, crap at speaking a foreign language, accident-prone and a terrible dresser. In short, he was human.

We didn't argue or split up. I didn't sulk, throw a tantrum or threaten to walk out. The force was with us. Captain Considerate, Master and Commander, conquered the ice maiden. Hallelujah, ring out the bells!

Now that *was the best holiday you've ever had.*

chapter fifteen

But that was a holiday, not real life. Within days of getting back to Sydney I'd convinced myself it could never work; the holiday had been a fluke. All that sex had been great in a five-star resort with massages every second day and nothing else to do in between but lie by the pool with a beer and a book (really great, actually) but by the end of it, to be perfectly honest, I felt a bit overwhelmed. There's only so much sex a woman can take (only so much this woman can, anyway) and while CC came back keener than ever, all I wanted was a rest and a lie down – on my own.

Back in the real world I had a stressful job and I was working long hours, struggling to make ends meet on a small salary, and trudging back and forth to Woolies without a car. I didn't want more sex. I wanted companionship. I wanted someone I could talk to. And, let's face it, CC and I simply weren't compatible.

I've been a vegetarian since the age of fifteen and I hate killing anything. I apologise automatically whenever I kill spiders, ants, even flies. A photograph of a starving child never fails to have me reaching for my (normally maxed-out) credit card. I studied languages and I've worked as a teacher, a librarian, a workshop co-ordinator and, for several years, as a struggling actress. I treasured the hard-won Equity card that had finally allowed me to work professionally, even if I did get it by pulling on a kangaroo suit and playing the lead in a primary school production of *The Bunyip and the Black Billabong* (seems prophetic in hindsight).

I write poetry (mediocre, but who cares) and I've been known to transcribe Shakespeare onto my living-room walls, even onto the curtains. I like camping, reading, gardening and fringe theatre festivals. I'm a workshop addict. You name it, I've done it – mime, movement, clog dancing, flamenco, mask making, Reiki healing, yoga, jewellery making, pottery, cake decorating, creative writing, wood carving, painting, photography, wine tasting, sacred singing, abseiling and windsurfing.

I believe in Tarot cards, spiritual healing and messages from the dead.

Dig deep and you'll find a flaky old hippie.

From what I could gather, CC worked and worked and then he worked some more. When he wasn't working he swam, cycled or played tennis, then he went straight home (not via the pub) to consume a large steak and check his stocks and shares. He was driven, competitive and conservative.

Captain Considerate was a good-looking man with a great physique hidden behind heavy gold cufflinks and thick-striped shirts in navy and white that made him look like Del Boy in an episode of *Only Fools and Horses*. All he needed was a silk hankie poking out of his top pocket to match his tie and he'd be all set to sell you a Ford Cortina or a case of Player's No. 6 cigarettes.

Did I mention that he ate a lot of meat? Lunch never wavered – a regular beef and shredded lettuce sandwich, with no butter, salt, pepper or mayonnaise – and dinner was steak, peas and beans or lamb, peas and beans. He would happily have eaten the same thing, day after day, until the end of time. The only variation was fish and chips on a Friday.

'What about slow-roasted beetroot, served with braised asparagus tips and sprinkled with shaved parmesan?' I asked him one night.

'What about it?'

'Would you like some?'

'No, thanks.'

*

In spite of my reservations there was something so fundamentally decent about CC that I couldn't help but like him. I agreed to see him whenever he was in Sydney, and each time I found out more about him.

'I was born in Persia . . . Iran.'

I wasn't expecting anything quite so exotic.

'Dad was working for the Anglo–Iranian Oil Company.'

'Was he Iranian?'

'No, Scottish.'

'How did you end up in Australia?'

CC snapped off a piece of popadum and dipped it in his creamy beef korma. The All India at the top of Rowntree Street had become a local. It never had more than a handful of customers mid-week and the staff were friendly, the music unobtrusive and curry was a meal we both enjoyed. I dabbed a corner of naan bread into a plateful of lentil dhal.

'My father was running the Abadan Oil Refinery in Iran when it was nationalised by the Iranians; this was in the early 1950s.'

I had dim memories of reading about some kind of coup at school. I wasn't born until several years later.

'My father was detained in Iran in order to keep the refinery operating. When the Shah was installed following the revolution, my father was released and allowed to leave. He went from a life of luxury, with a polo pony, a Daimler and a yacht, to a life of unemployment in the UK.'

'What happened to you?'

'My mother, my sister and I stayed with relatives until my father was released. We lived on a converted lifeboat for a while, sailing round the Scottish islands, then Dad decided we should emigrate, start over again. He used what money he had left to buy a pub in William Creek.'

'Where's that?'

'A small town in South Australia.'

Small is an understatement. You'd be hard-pressed to find anywhere smaller, or more remote, than William Creek. It's way out on the Oodnadatta Track, not far from Lake Eyre, with a population that fluctuates between three and six people (which presumably depends on how many are living at the one and only pub).

'Why did he pick William Creek?'

'I don't think my father really knew where it was. He saw the pub advertised for sale, decided to buy it and we emigrated. Mum was shocked when we arrived. 'Where are the servants?' she said. Dad had to tell her there weren't any. 'You're looking at them,' he said.

'What did you think?'

'I loved it. It was like living in a Boy's Own Adventure story. I was ten years old, riding bareback across the outback, setting traps for dingoes and selling the pelts for pocket money. I used to gallop alongside the train that came through every week and the guard would throw me a bundle of newspapers. I never dropped a single paper,' CC said with pride, mopping up the last of his korma sauce with another piece of naan bread.

'My father gave me a poddy calf one day –'

147

'What's that?'

'An orphan calf.'

I got a warm fuzzy feeling picturing CC as a ten-year-old hand-rearing a doe-eyed calf until I remembered he was a committed carnivore.

'Dad said I could raise it, sell it and keep the profit, so I lavished attention on that calf. I fed it and fattened it and eventually I sold it for fifty dollars. I thought I was rich. Then Dad presented me with a bill for the feed, the vet's bills and the slaughterhouse and it wiped out all the profit. He was teaching me a lesson about profit and loss.'

'What did you do?'

CC looked up from his plate and smiled. 'A group of stockmen were working nearby and they came into the pub one night. I heard them talking about how they were planning to head off and muster brumbies, so I decided to join them. I packed a bag, took my horse and left a note for Dad on the kitchen table.'

'What did it say?'

'I've gone mustering. I reckon it will be easier to make money that way.'

CC laughed at the look on my face. He was an accomplished storyteller and he enjoyed seeing the effect the story had on me. It was incongruous, listening to him talk about brumby mustering when he was sitting in a restaurant in Balmain wearing a suit and tie. I tried to imagine him as a ten-year-old boy, hooking up with an outfit of men, sleeping in swags, eating damper and dried meat, sitting around the campfire at night and galloping across the open country by day. It conjured up an image of the Man from Snowy River.

'The stockmen knew my father and, with hindsight, they probably had his blessing. Anyway, they tolerated me and let me tag along. They probably thought I'd give up and go home after a few days. One afternoon, not long after, a group of brumbies they'd been herding broke free. The ranchers shrugged; they thought it wasn't worth trying to catch them.

'I leapt onto my horse, bareback, and I chased them. Looking back, it was idiotic. I was galloping at full stretch and my horse could have stumbled and thrown me at any point. No one would have known where I was but I was determined to get those brumbies. I rode hard for half an hour or so, caught up with them, rounded them up and brought them back. When I went home I had money in my pocket.'

It wasn't the conservative upbringing I'd been expecting.

We walked back from the restaurant after dinner, me clutching the remains of a bottle of red (I'd restrained myself – there was still half left), then later in bed, just as I was drifting off to sleep with my head resting on his shoulder, he said something that woke me up.

'I shot a man once.'

I sat bolt upright. Miss Prissy Knickers stared at him.

'You did what?'

'Don't get excited, I only shot the top of his boot off.'

The thought of CC pointing a gun at someone, then firing it, had Miss Prissy Knickers reaching for the reins. She leapt onto her high horse and galloped towards him.

'How could you? How could you do such a thing? What if you'd missed? What if you'd shot him? What if he'd had a gun as well? What if you'd got into a shooting match?' A passing thought made PK pause. 'Was it live ammunition?'

'Yes.'

'It was!' Miss Prissy Knickers got out of bed and grabbed her dressing gown. 'So instead of lying here telling me this story you could be in prison right now, serving a life sentence for killing a man! How would you feel then? Hmm?'

CC waited for Miss Prissy Knickers to blow herself out, she and her high horse snorting with righteous indignation.

'It was a long time ago and I was a very good shot.'

'Oh, and that makes it OK, I suppose?'

'Do you want to know what happened, Frosty?'

'Frosty?'

'Well, I don't detect much warmth coming off you right now.'

True, I was ready to call the police and hand him over, but curiosity finally got the better of me. 'Go ahead then, tell me what happened.'

'I was working for an oil and gas exploration company on a camp in South Australia and most of the guys were out surveying. I was only nineteen and pretty junior so they left me behind at the camp with a couple of girls who did the cooking. I heard some guys from a nearby town were driving around in a ute; they were drunk and looking for trouble. They wanted girl action and they knew where they could get it.'

It sounded like he was reading from a script in a Clint Eastwood movie.

'So this beaten-up ute arrived with five drunken blokes in it and I loaded my .22 revolver and walked across to meet them. I said, "If you set one foot out of that ute, I'll blow it off. There's nothing for you guys here, so why don't you just get back in your vehicle and drive off." The guys were so drunk they didn't believe me. They laughed. The driver climbed out and he stood there facing me, daring me to do something.'

'What did you do?'

'I shot him.'

Miss PK's high horse reared out of control. 'What if you'd killed him? What if the others had had guns too?'

'Calm down, Frosty, I was an expert shot. I just nicked his boot, that's all. Besides, those guys were drunk, I had to do something. If I hadn't, they might have grabbed the girls and raped them.'

'What happened next?'

'They got back in the ute and drove off.'

Miss Prissy Knickers was forced to admit that maybe Captain Considerate had a point.

She slid off her horse and CC opened his arms. Much to her surprise, she found herself admiring his courage, his ability to take decisive action and protect the defenceless young girls (who in all probability could have whacked the drunks around the head with a frying pan and decked them, but never mind). She even – God forbid – admired his skill at using a firearm. Miss Prissy Knickers was confused. Captain Considerate, he of the pressed slacks, striped tie and double-breasted blazer, was not as conservative as he looked.

I drifted off to sleep and dreamt of Clint Eastwood.

But what about romance? What about chocolates and flowers and whispered words of tender sweetness? Romance mattered to me; in fact it mattered so much that once, while I was pining for A2 and mourning the fact that he'd fallen in love with someone else, I ran a service called 'Say it with a Sonnet'. I set it up in time for Valentine's Day and, for a small fee and a stupendously large dose of self-flagellation, I offered to read love sonnets over the phone.

'Hello,' I would say, in low, dulcet tones. 'I have a message for you; it comes with love from Mike.' (Or Betty, or James or Julie.)

'Shall I compare thee to a summer's day? Thou art more lovely . . .'

'How do I love thee? Let me count the ways . . .'

By the end of the day I was weeping with self-pity that no one had sent *me* flowers or offered to read *me* a poem, neatly overlooking the fact that some of the romantic souls I'd spoken to had a rather shrewd approach to love.

A woman called Sally rang and asked me to read Sonnet 57 to her husband.

Being your slave what should I do but tend
Upon the hours and times of your desire . . .

'No problem,' I said. 'Do you have a message you'd like to add?'

'Tell him I love him more than life itself.'

'What a lovely message.'

'And then I want you to ring Michael, on this number.' I noted down the number she gave me. 'And I want you to read the same sonnet,' she said.

'Um, any message at the end?'

'Same message, thanks.'

Then there was Brenda, who wanted me to jump out from behind a tree in the Domain near Parliament House while she and her loved one were having a surprise picnic. It sounded like an ideal publicity stunt so I contacted a local news station and suggested they might like to get some footage of it. I then thought (belatedly, I did tell you I was rubbish at PR) that maybe I should let Brenda know what I was planning.

'That won't work,' she said, flatly.

'Oh but it will!' I gushed. 'They love the idea!'

'I don't think so.'

'You won't have to do anything, you can just carry on having your picnic.'

'We don't want to be filmed.'

'But the TV crew is really keen.'

'I don't think you understand. We *can't* be filmed.'

'Oh.'

In the end I had to find a fictitious couple, arrange a fictitious picnic and jump out from behind a (thankfully real) tree for the TV cameras, while Brenda and her secret lover were discreetly picnicking elsewhere in the park. When the TV crew left I had to do it all over again for the blushing Brenda and her publicity-shy lover.

The experience didn't put me off; if anything it heightened my desire to find the romantic lover of my dreams. Having spent most of my adult life longing for romance I could swoon at the mere hint of anything approaching a romantic gesture.

A1 had arranged a surprise picnic on a summer afternoon in England. He drove us to a deserted field of poppies and we lay on a blanket drinking elderflower champagne, watching the poppies sway above us, bobbing red against a cloudless blue sky. Gorgeous.

A2 had taken me sailing at dusk. He produced a chilled bottle of vintage Bollinger as we drifted through Sydney Harbour, electric green phosphorescence glowing in the wake of the boat. Beautiful.

A3 had wooed me with a selection of chocolate bars, spread out on a clean white handkerchief like something out of an Enid Blyton storybook. Exquisite.

None of those relationships worked.

So what? There were flowers, chocolates and whispered words of poetry. There was romance! Isn't that what love is all about?

When it came to romance, CC was baffled. He couldn't see what all the fuss was about.

'Quite frankly, I think it's a load of nonsense,' he said. 'Don't expect me to send you flowers, roses, chocolates or any of it. Valentine's Day is a commercial rip-off.'

So while he may have been an expert shot and a courageous hero (when I asked him if he would go back into a burning plane to rescue someone again, he said yes without hesitation), CC was no romantic.

'What's the point, Frosty?' he said, searching in his briefcase for a pair of glasses so he could read the paper in bed. The nickname 'Frosty' had stuck, indicating he knew me better than I thought, especially when he put the paper down and peered at me in a way that suggested I was about to get a dose of reality.

'I've met several versions of you now,' he said. 'First there was the ice maiden – cold, intellectual, unapproachable and unassailable.'

'Which didn't stop you,' I said, pressing my lips together. I wasn't at all sure I was going to like this.

'On holiday I met a different version, the up-for-it, wanting-to-please Frosty who suspected it might all be over by the end of the week so there was no harm in being nice. Along the way she found she could enjoy herself too.'

I didn't respond. There was more coming.

'Then there's the post-Bali Frosty, who is analytical, don't you dare tell me you love me, what's love got to do with anything, we like each other and that's all there is to it, so don't get carried away. Just because I slept with you in Bali doesn't mean I'll want to do it again and I could run away any time, so don't look for some kind of commitment from me.'

There was a pause.

'So what's the point in sending you flowers? Am I right?' he added, with a triumphant look on his face.

'You tell me, since you seem to know me so well,' I snapped, annoyed at being so quickly (and accurately) summed up.

There was a lot to like about CC but I hadn't fallen for him. I was nursing a broken heart, secretly pining for someone I could never be with. The hurt of knowing that the man I loved had married someone else was still raw. I still loved him.

PK did her best.

The man you thought *you loved is married! He was never interested in you!*

Stupid, isn't it?

You're not giving Captain Considerate a chance.
I know.
He's a lovely man.
I know.
And life's too short to stuff a mushroom.
What's that got to do with anything?
Don't be such a bloody vegetarian all the time!

chapter sixteen

'What were you two laughing about?'

Bonnie walked into my office just as CC walked out. Until she spoke I didn't even realise we *were* laughing. For the life of me I couldn't have explained why, so I shrugged and tried to concentrate on the email I should have been composing. Bonnie was a shrewd, perceptive New Yorker with a big heart. She was around my age and there wasn't much she missed.

'It's good you get on so well,' she said, glancing at CC's retreating back as she passed me a set of proofs she'd corrected. 'Some people find him intimidating.'

'Really?' I backspaced to delete the rubbish I'd just typed.

'I think he's lovely,' she added. 'Really decent.' She gave me a look that suggested she knew there might be something going on and I gave her a look back that said you might be right but please can we be discreet about this? Bonnie had met her husband at work many years earlier and I knew I could trust her not to blab.

But how long could this relationship continue? In spite of the occasional laugh, my frosty insistence that there would be no snatched moments in the office had introduced a level of tension between us that was hard to counteract. I insisted on stern professionalism at work (or so I thought) and found it hard to switch it off outside the office.

CC was keener than ever to advise the Board but I dreaded going public with the relationship because, with my track record, there was every likelihood the relationship wouldn't last. Even when I'd been madly in love with someone I'd never been able to make a relationship work so what were the chances with CC? Slim. This was no great romance and the messy fallout of a failed affair would, at the very least, be highly embarrassing for CC. It could have been catastrophic for me.

I'd grown to love my job, and there was a slight chance they might ask me to stay in some capacity when Rachel came back from maternity leave. A failed relationship with the CEO wouldn't help my chances.

I got no pleasure from hiding the relationship and no illicit thrill in sleeping with CC because I didn't consider him superior. He wasn't my boss; he was my equal (and if I'm being really honest, I thought I was a teensy bit superior to him). But no matter how well we might have been getting on, and no matter how 'equal' I considered us to be, I was under no illusions about the power gradient between a CEO and a lowly communications co-ordinator. I would never have contemplated embarking on such a radically inappropriate relationship under normal circumstances, but . . . but what? These weren't normal circumstances? That sounded like a pretty lame excuse and I doubted if anyone would welcome me into the workplace if things went wrong.

With CC living in Broken Hill we hadn't seen much of each other since Bali. His dedication to work was fearsome, and on the odd occasion he was in Sydney he started early, finished late and often had dinners to attend, which relegated me to the role of warm body at the end of the night. The bitter disappointment of A3 had been a wake-up call and I knew, finally (yes, I know, it took a while but I got there in the end), that secret love affairs and lonely nights spent waiting for someone to climb into bed with me only to slink off the next morning held zero appeal. I wanted a straightforward, simple relationship. But could I have that with CC?

*

'You OK in there?'

'Yep.'

'You sure?'

'No problem.'

CC was standing on the other side of the locked bathroom door. He'd noticed I had been in there a long time, which can't have been difficult since the log cabin we were renting only had one bedroom, a combined living/kitchen area and a small bathroom. I wasn't in the bedroom and I wasn't in the kitchen so I had to be in the bathroom.

We'd hired a car and driven towards Windsor, an hour north of Sydney, heading for a simple log cabin for a long weekend, another attempt on my part to find out how compatible we might be, away from a five-star luxury hotel. The cabin was tucked out of sight on thirty acres of native bush, midway between Windsor and Dural. Other cabins dotted about the property were far enough away to be out of sight, so it was just us and the kookaburras, the alpacas and the kangaroos. Beyond our cabin was a cleared paddock, where hammocks were strung between the trees, and a small creek with a couple of old kayaks pulled up on the bank. 'Help yourselves,' the owner had said when he showed us around. It was a far cry from Bali.

I wasn't helping myself to anything. I'd woken up with a raging headache and sore throat the morning we left Sydney, and by the time we arrived I felt so miserable I went straight to bed, which may have been precisely where CC wanted me, but not like that. He mixed me hot drinks, fed me aspirin and placed cold flannels on my sweaty forehead. He prepared inhalations and put up with my sneezing, coughing and moaning. When the fever went down I was left with a stinking cold and a hacking cough. CC took it all in his stride.

'Thank you,' I mumbled, lying back on the sweat-soaked pillows, my nose red and streaming. 'You're a very kind, considerate man.'

'It's in my interest to get you better,' he said bluntly.

By day three of our long weekend I felt much better, but I had a problem that wasn't going away, no matter how hard I tried. Let me take this opportunity, if I may, to point out one of the essential differences between vegetarians and meat eaters. Meat can take up to five days to pass through your body. Vegetables are speedier, decomposing as fast as you can eat them; the more you eat, the faster they decompose and the sooner they leave your body. There's no hanging around with fruit and fibre; vegetarians are in and out of the bathroom up to three times a day, as regular as clockwork, quick as a flash, no messing. Maybe it was the cough lollies or the vast doses of vitamin C or maybe it was the aspirin, I don't know, but something interfered with my normal rhythm.

CC knocked on the bathroom door.

'Let me know if I can do anything.'

'Sure.'

Like what, I thought? I was so fed up wasting time I made a monumental effort and experienced a pain so intense it terrified me. I had no option but to retreat from the brink and I emerged from the bathroom feeling weak and shivery.

'How did you go?'

'Fine.'

'Liar. Frosty, if you've got a problem, we've got to sort it out,' he said, opening drawers in the small kitchen.

'What are you looking for?'

'A pipe.'

'What do you want a pipe for?' I had a horrible feeling I knew the answer.

'You might need to flush your system out with soapy water.'

'No, I won't,' I said decisively. 'I don't want any William Creek outback remedies, thank you all the same.' I retreated to the bathroom.

Half an hour later CC knocked on the door again.

'Frosty, what about olive oil?'

That sounded better than a pipe. 'Won't it make me sick?' I shouted.

'Why would it do that?'

'If I drink too much of it.' I swear I could hear him smile on the other side of the door.

'Frosty, you don't drink it,' he said.

I stayed in there another twenty minutes. When I eventually emerged, feeling weaker than ever, CC was peering at a bottle of brown sauce, one of those squeezable types, with a nozzle on top.

'We could empty it and –'

'NO!'

'Calm down, Frosty, I'm only trying to help.'

What surprises me most is that neither of us thought of the obvious solution, which was to get in the car and drive to the nearest chemist, buy an over-the-counter cure and wait for it to take effect. It must have been something to do with the isolation of our remote log cabin that persuaded us to attempt a Bear Grylls-type remedy with olive oil, but at least it worked.

The few hours we had left were spent sitting on the balcony, reading books and hand-feeding kookaburras perched on the railings waiting for scraps. All too soon it was time to pack up and leave so we emptied the cabin (sorry about all the olive oil), filled the car and paused on the balcony before the drive back to Sydney.

Bright sunlight was filtering through the trees and then, without warning, it started to rain. There were no clouds that we could see and it only lasted a few seconds, but that was long enough for a rainbow to appear. The appearance of that small but perfectly formed arc, clearly visible from one end to the other shimmering in between the eucalyptus trees, seemed a good omen. I silently thanked the universe for showing me that a practical man can sometimes be far more desirable than a romantic one.

*

'I like you, Frosty, in fact I more than like you,' CC said, crushing me in an embrace that made it hard to breathe. We were standing in the skinny corridor of the house in Birchgrove at six o'clock the following morning, waiting for a taxi to arrive to take him to the airport for the journey back to Broken Hill.

'I like you too,' I mumbled, keeping my face pressed against his jacket.

The blast of a horn signalled the arrival of the taxi.

He picked up his briefcase. 'Look after yourself, Frosty.'

'You too.'

*

I made a cup of tea after he'd gone and sat in the sunroom looking out over the water. Captain Considerate had fallen for me, that much seemed clear, and I should have thanked my lucky, sparkling, vigilant stars and my guardian angel, that someone so sexy, attractive, good, decent, kind, intelligent, thoughtful, fit, healthy, happy and solvent had fallen for me. So what was the problem? Why did it matter that he wasn't my soul mate?

I have a friend, Nicole, whose first husband was her soul mate; anyone who saw them together thought the same, two people meant for each other. They used to go out to the airport and watch planes together, take a picnic and make a day of it. One day he rang and said, 'I'm at the airport.' She said, 'Great, I'll pack a picnic, meet you there.' He said, 'No, you don't understand, I'm at the airport because I'm leaving you.' And that was it. Eight-year marriage. Gone.

CC and I may not have been soul mates but we were good together. Sure, we didn't agree on politics or on matters to do with finance – or food, sport, theatre, books or films, come to that – but I liked him. I trusted him. He was the most stable, reliable, dependable man I had ever met and he made me laugh. We made each other laugh.

Which was all well and good, but CC had jumped into the raging river and he was being swept along. I was standing on the bank, watching him.

What was it about falling in love that I always resisted? Was it that sense of letting go and having nothing stable to hold onto? I fought it all the way, like a salmon struggling upriver, swimming against the tide. Love had led me to some dark places and I no longer trusted it.

Instinct told me that if I let go and trusted the rushing tide, I wouldn't drown. In quiet moments I pictured a sheltered bay with deep water and a calm, stilled peace but when had I ever trusted the current to carry me that far? And what if there was no shallow, secluded inlet at the end of the river? What if there were rocks instead? What if the ocean flung me against those rocks and smashed me to pieces?

On the odd occasion that I had ever been persuaded to plunge in, I've grabbed the nearest rock, clamped my eyes shut and waited for the swirling to calm down, spluttering against the force of rushing water and struggling to breathe. That's what love has always felt like to me.

The feelings I had for CC were calmer, quieter and altogether different. But were they strong enough?

Of course, part of my reluctance to jump in the river with CC was the dwindling hope that A3 might resurface, which was a ridiculous notion. In spite of all the affection and encouragement I'd showered on him he'd chosen someone else. I was never even a contender.

Why wouldn't that fact sink in? Why couldn't I get it through my stupid, thick head that A3 was in no way suddenly going to announce he'd made a monumental mistake? He wasn't about to call and say, 'What was I thinking of, getting married, I'm aching to be with you, could you ever forgive me because you and I were meant for each other, let's run away to a cottage in the country and live happily ever after on fresh air and cheap red wine, you're all I need.' It wasn't going to happen, end of story. So why couldn't I stop hoping that it would?

Because I still loved him, and it takes a long time to get over lost love.

chapter seventeen

Dream catchers spun from the ceiling, rainbow-coloured scarves covered the counter and the shelves were full of crystals and self-help books. It had to be the right place.

Metro Mike operated from a converted semi-detached house sandwiched between a butcher's and an op shop on a busy main road near the Metro Shopping Centre in Marrickville, hence the name. I hadn't entirely weaned myself off Tarot cards (in my defence, Metro Mike came highly recommended) and I was curious to know if the universe had any advice about CC.

I followed Metro Mike down the narrow side passage that once would have been an empty space between two houses. The hazy corridor was covered with corrugated plastic to keep out the rain and the walls were draped in multi-coloured fabric. It was barely wide enough to drag a bin down yet Metro Mike had somehow managed to squeeze a table and two chairs into the narrow space. This was his consulting room.

The box of tissues on the table was a bad sign – I'm like Pavlov's dog when I spot a box of Kleenex – and sure enough Metro Mike had barely started speaking before a pile of soggy tissues started accumulating in front of us. He said some pretty hard-hitting stuff.

'You're good at failure, but you're afraid of success,' he declared. 'Why aren't you writing more?'

I blew my nose. Had I told him I was a part-time writer? I couldn't remember.

I'd written stories, poems and scripts that I'd shown no one because I was convinced they weren't good enough. It was that search for perfection again. Writing was the one thing I loved doing more than anything else, but it was easier to give up and call myself a failure at it than try to succeed and have someone else tell me I was no good. The truth of what he'd said had me reaching for another tissue. 'You're doing a job that helps people but you shouldn't be doing it. You've been putting off what you really want to do and now it's time to get on with it. Do you sometimes write things that seem really intelligent and profound?'

I nodded, sobbing into my tissue, feeling a little glow of self-satisfaction as I wondered how he could possibly know about the hidden talent I sometimes thought might be worth sharing with the world.

'Fifty per cent of what you write isn't yours,' he said bluntly. 'It comes from your guides.'

Oh that's all very well, I thought sourly, thanks for the vote of confidence, but what about what I really came here for? What about relationships? What about the future? What can you tell me about those, Mr Smarty Pants?

'Stop worrying about the future,' he said, when I hadn't said a word about the future. 'And you've got a good relationship,' he added, before I could say a word about relationships. 'Enjoy it. It was working but then something got in the way.'

He peered at me rather accusingly, as if it was somehow my fault. And of course, it probably was. Secretly longing for an old flame to reignite is hardly the best way to encourage a new relationship.

'Accept love,' he said firmly. 'You're good at giving love to other people but you're bad at accepting it for yourself.'

Where was he getting this stuff from? How did he know that the sum total of all my experiences had led me to believe I wasn't worth loving? I blew my nose again and asked the question that had to be asked. 'There was someone else once,' I mumbled, 'a long time ago, an old relationship, more of a friendship really, and I was just wondering, could it ever . . .?'

I knew the answer before I'd even finished speaking. I've known the answer for years, yet still there was a moment when I wondered what Metro Mike might say. It was like a small, ever-reducing spark of fire sucking at oxygen, a speck of glowing embers that shines brighter the moment before they are extinguished forever.

'No,' said Metro Mike, decisively. 'It won't. That's over. Let it go. Write him a letter if you have to, tell him everything you need to, then burn it.'

I knew that wouldn't happen. I'd written countless letters, all of them declaring undying love and none of them sent (I'm really quite an unobtrusive stalker; you'd hardly notice me at all unless you were looking). There was no need for another one.

And suddenly, to my surprise, no need for the Kleenex either. The sense of disappointment as Metro Mike spoke was so small as to be hardly noticeable, quickly and easily overcome, a final acceptance that life had moved on, a realisation that all those times that I'd laid in bed alone, longing to be with A3, were over. All those years (although it wasn't that long, only four) that he kept insisting all he wanted was friendship, he meant it. There was me, thinking he was battling with a desire as strong as mine and he wasn't; he wanted friendship.

He wanted precisely what he said he wanted and silly me for thinking otherwise.

I paid Metro Mike, thanked him for the tissues and caught the bus home.

As I sat on the half empty bus back to Balmain I knew I'd been clinging to a falsehood, nurturing a fantasy that should have died long ago.

Had I ever really understood what love was? I used to think it was romance and passion; I thought it was all about being with the one you loved at any cost, moving heaven and earth to be with that person, and if you met someone you loved then what you did once you'd fallen in love wasn't important. That bit (which I never got to) would take care of itself! Relationships were all about falling in love or being in love, a sensation I resisted yet found overwhelmingly attractive at the same time. That was all that mattered and I couldn't see beyond it. In other words, I hadn't grown up.

I'd reached middle age without ever getting beyond that breathless stage, when you feel like you'll die if you can't be with the person you love. The passion that made me feel like a giddy teenager was precisely that – teenage, starry-eyed desire with nothing grown-up about it.

I set out wanting something from all of the As – marriage, stability, family – with little understanding of what I had to offer and even less regard for what any of them wanted. Getting what *I* wanted was what mattered. When I didn't get it, and more importantly when I couldn't face the disappointment of not getting it, I refused to give up. The love I'd felt mutated into something far more sinister.

What's the big deal about passionate love anyway? Sorry if that sounds like heresy, but really, is it so important? Sure, it's exciting, but it's not reliable or trustworthy. Passionate love won't be there when the bins need to be taken out, or when the dish-washer needs to be emptied, or when you just want to sit in silence, content to have the kind of companion who is happy to do his thing while you do yours, a companion who will try hard not to hurt you or let you down. A companion like CC.

CC and I were very different people but we shared similar core values of kindness, integrity, respect and honesty (apart from the odd spot of obsessive behaviour but that was behind me now). I was beginning to understand that a loving relationship with a partner might not be that different from a loving relation-ship with a friend. Other people probably worked that out years ago. I didn't. It was like when I was sick in junior school, missing several weeks of maths, and never caught up. I don't understand long division to this day.

For a wily old goat like CC, our relationship was about compromise, which roughly translated into negotiating, manoeu-vring and positioning to get his own way. I was doing the same of course, so maybe we weren't so incompatible after all.

By the time the bus reached Newtown I knew I didn't want the anguish of a passionate relationship (I've never been able to handle them anyway). I wanted, and it seemed I might have found, companionship, laughter, pleasure and joy. I had met someone who was good company, someone who could laugh at himself and at me. CC, my unexpected mate.

I hesitated to say I loved him because what I felt was so comfortable, like a favourite cardigan I was glad to reach for and slip on again. In the past, sexual arousal had come from an element of danger; it was forbidden fruit that was troubling, passionate and ultimately destructive. I was having to re-learn what I thought I knew about sex and find passion within the security I felt with CC.

Perhaps it was that sense of security that confounded me?

Of course, I probably wasn't all that CC wanted either. At my age I wasn't that bothered about sex, so it was ironic that after all those early years of communicating largely through sex, a lot of the time without any real pleasure, I had finally found someone I felt comfortable with, someone I could talk to, quietly and calmly, and he was the one who wanted all the sex.

It served me right for asking the universe to send me someone sexy. I clearly remember putting that at the top of the list I wrote out late one night when I was living under the flight path in Leichhardt. *Please*, I wrote, (it always pays to be polite) *bring me someone sexy, kind, funny, intelligent, solvent and compassionate. And make it someone who wants to be with me and me alone,* I added.

It looked like I got my wish.

*

'What did he say about us?'

'That we were good together.'

'There you go, Frosty, approval from a higher source.'

I told CC about the reading when we spoke on the phone that night and he gently mocked my reliance on spiritual guidance and psychic advice. His next sentence took me by surprise.

'Maybe I should go and see him.'

'You?'

'Why not? No harm in giving it a go.'

This was a man who existed on work, meat, sex and sport, and he was agreeing to see a psychic. I had seriously underestimated CC.

The appointment was for the following Saturday morning, when CC was in Sydney, so I hung around the crystal shop in Marrickville while Metro Mike did his stuff. I went for a coffee, went shopping, had another coffee and by the time CC emerged almost two hours later I was burning with curiosity.

'Well? What did he say? Were you impressed? Did he make any sense?'

'It was largely work related; he picked the fact that I was in management, but that wouldn't have been difficult.'

'True.'

'And he said I don't suffer fools gladly.'

'It wouldn't have been hard to work that out either.'

CC laughed. 'I apologised for being late, then I said, "But you would have known I was going to be late anyway, wouldn't you?"'

'Good start.'

'He said I might travel to India one day.'

'India?'

'It's feasible. Caroline spends half the year there.'

'Who's Caroline?'

'My foster sister. I should call her Nagasuri really. She's a Buddhist monk.'

He said it in a way that suggested having a sister who was a Buddhist monk was nothing unusual. 'You never said. And I didn't know you had a foster sister.'

He shrugged. 'I've got two.' We drifted away from the topic of Metro Mike and chatted about family.

Later that night I discovered there was a nugget he'd kept to himself. He'd been holding it in his pocket, polishing it, smoothing it and examining it when I wasn't looking. He held onto it through Saturday evening while we watched *The Lives of Others* on DVD, through Sunday brunch, an easy breezy affair with friends, through cleaning the patio and sweeping up the leaves, through a trip to the cinema to see *Samson and Delilah* – a heart-breaking film of brutal beauty – and through snuggling on the sofa on Sunday night until, finally, we went to bed.

'Metro Mike said there were other men around you.' His voice was hard and flat and I was shocked at the sudden revelation.

'I'm not seeing anyone else if that's what you're worried about.'

I may not have had a great track record when it came to men, and I admit I've been guilty of trying to pinch someone else's boyfriend on more than one occasion – a betrayal of sisterhood that now shames me – but I'd never been unfaithful, not since I was a teenager. At seventeen two boys got wind of the fact that I was seeing them both and they turned up on my parents' doorstep simultaneously. The shock was enough to put paid to any more of that nonsense for the rest of my life.

'Metro Mike said you wouldn't be unfaithful.'

'There! See?'

'But you've never really had a successful relationship, have you?'

Not for the first time I wished I hadn't had so much to drink on our first date. CC had the memory of an elephant. It was selective memory too, recalling the fact that I'd never had a successful long-term relationship and ignoring the equally relevant fact that the only time I'd ever been unfaithful was when I was seventeen.

'Hang on. Metro Mike said there were three women around you and he said they would all make suitable partners. I didn't get my knickers in a twist about that, did I?'

'No, you didn't.' The look of disappointment on his face told me he rather wished I had. The implication of his words settled like dust in an empty room.

I attempted a bungled explanation about how jumping in wasn't my thing but the more I spoke, the more defensive and elusive I sounded. 'I'm taking my time, that's all, standing on the bank, you know, waiting, I don't want to dive into deep water . . . until . . .'

'I didn't realise,' he said quietly. After a pause he added, 'I jumped in, as soon as we met. I thought you had too.'

CC was hurt to discover that he'd jumped in alone. More worryingly, he was concerned I might be standing on the bank waiting to see if someone better came along.

'Are you seeing someone else?'

'No.'

'What about that Aboriginal guy. Did you sleep with him?'

'No!'

'Have you seen him again?'

'No, I haven't heard from him in ages.'

'What about that photographer?'

'Don't be ridiculous, I'm not seeing anyone else.'

'He fancies you.'

'That's hardly my fault.'

'He's into all that creativity you think is so important, he's more your type.'

'Stop it! I'm not seeing anyone else! I'm taking my time, that's all, because I want to be sure I'm with the right person.'

'And are you?'

I took a deep breath. And avoided answering the question.

'The right person is someone who won't let me drown . . . who will always wait for me to catch up if I fall behind.'

CC wasn't in the mood for creative answers.

'Do you think I'm stupid?'

'No, I don't.'

'Do you think I don't know what's going on?'

His eyes darkened and he quizzed me on every man I knew, trying to find out if there was anything going on. I'd never seen this side of CC before. His lack of trust infuriated me.

'Stop asking questions! I haven't cheated on you, I'm not cheating on you and I won't cheat on you! We agreed at the start we wouldn't do that.'

'How do I know I can trust you?'

'You don't know, that's the whole point of trust!'

'I need confirmation.'

'Oh that's ridiculous. You can't *confirm* trust. It's like faith; you either have it or you don't. And if I was the kind of person who was willing to cheat on you, I'd also be the kind of person who would be willing to lie about it, so your endless questions are *pointless.*'

The argument petered out with nothing resolved and CC looked as drained as I felt. I mentally vowed to stand my ground. I may not have come clean about A3 but I'd done nothing to be ashamed of. I certainly hadn't cheated on CC. Before I fell asleep I briefly wondered if he was the one doing the cheating.

*

There was a time when I would have cowered in the face of rage like CC's. In the late 1980s I was working as a medical librarian at a military hospital in Saudi Arabia. Jason was an administrator with the Canadian embassy and this was the first proper, long-term relationship I'd ever had. It was just me and him (or so I thought).

As a single woman I was meant to live in a walled compound with other single women and I wasn't allowed to drive or get into a car with a man unless he was my husband, my brother or my uncle. I also had an eleven o'clock curfew every night.

I got around the travel restrictions by lying in the back of Jason's car on the floor, covered in a blanket, and I avoided the curfew by living in his flat. He would drive me to the single woman's compound early each morning and stop around the corner. I would hop out of the car, join the queue for the bus to the hospital and arrive at work like every other single woman.

We were soul mates, inseparable, inventive and compatible. We performed in plays at the American air base (another illegal activity), played darts, read books, brewed wine and threw dinner parties.

Jason went on leave for a week and I stayed behind – in the initial six-month phase of any contract you weren't allowed leave in case you never went back – and one afternoon a male friend called over for tea. It was a completely innocent visit.

When Jason got back he heard about the visit and flew into a rage. I didn't recognise him. That night he stood over me, a vein in his neck pumping blood, his face a contortion of crimson muscle as he pressed a clenched fist against his thighs. 'You are so lucky I don't hit women!' he screamed.

I cowered in a corner of the room, shocked into a stammering explanation that nothing had happened. Jason stalked into the bedroom, grabbed a blanket and threw it at me. 'You can sleep on the sofa!' he shouted, and slammed the bedroom door.

When my heart stopped hammering against my ribs I burst into tears. Jason was an affable, kind, considerate man and in front of my eyes he'd turned into a monster. I had nothing to help me understand or cope with such behaviour. My parents had never argued (or if they did it was quietly, behind closed doors) and I'd never seen anyone fly into a rage like that before. The unfair accusations hurt but the sudden withdrawal of love was far more upsetting.

So I did something that I regret to this day. In the middle of the night I crept back into our bedroom and curled up on the floor at the bottom of the bed. When Jason woke up I whispered, 'I'm sorry.'

'I forgive you,' he said.

He forgave me and I'd done nothing wrong! The force of his anger had made me feel culpable and led to my nervous apology, which no doubt confirmed my guilt.

A week or so later I found a flirtatious postcard –

After an extensive search of his drawer.

Yes, thank you, PK.

– from a woman he'd visited in England while he'd been on leave. With it was a letter he'd been composing to send to her. *'When we make love I tread the line between death and exhilaration . . .'*

The jealous rage I'd witnessed had been prompted by his infidelity, not mine.

And here's the worst part (quite apart from the fact that he had never said anything like that to me after we'd made love), I replaced the postcard, and the half-finished letter and, as on so many occasions in the past, I said nothing. I swallowed the hurt and disappointment and I carried on as normal. I dreaded the thought that any confrontation might lead to a repeat of that earlier ugly scene. I still loved Jason, and he still loved me; we were still soul mates, but the seed of our eventual break-up had been sown. That hidden letter and its contents festered like rotten fruit. I should have confronted him but I was too scared. The resulting lack of trust ultimately destroyed our relationship and we split up several months later.

The next morning, less choked by emotion, CC and I talked through what had happened.

'I'm sorry,' CC said. 'I don't know why I said those things. It was wrong of me.' Then he struggled. 'It's just that I love you. I love you so much,' he said, his voice wavering. 'I couldn't bear to think you might cheat on me.'

I pulled my chair closer, surprised at how calm I felt. I couldn't tell CC I loved him because I didn't, not then. I liked him. I liked him a lot, enough to make a solemn vow.

'Even if we don't spend the rest of our lives together, even if it turns out we're not right for each other, I will never cheat on you,' I said. 'Never. You have my word. We all have a choice when it comes to cheating.'

There was a faint melancholy in his expression; he hadn't missed the fact that I hadn't said I loved him. He reached across and patted my hand, his smile slow and tentative, and there was a mixture of sadness and hope lurking behind it. I saw what was happening. He was swimming back towards me, fighting the current that had initially swept him downstream, so he could clamber out of the river and join me on the bank.

CC was willing to wait for me to take the plunge.

chapter eighteen

'You have to pay if you want a pavement.'

'What do you mean, you have to *pay* for a pavement? What kind of nonsense is that? I've never heard anything like it.'

'Calm down, Frosty, that's normal practice out here.'

It was a Saturday morning in mid-October and we were sitting outside The Silly Goat on Argent Street. Back in April I'd thought Broken Hill was a fascinating place with an intriguing history and friendly locals. That's when I knew I was only staying for the weekend. As a place to live, a place to call home, I wasn't so sure.

I had flown up for a four-day work trip and extended it over the weekend to stay with CC, openly. Our relationship was no longer a secret. With some trepidation I had agreed we should take the step of going public, and several weeks earlier, CC had advised the RFDS Board, in writing, that he and I were conducting a personal relationship. Apart from a reminder to respect professional confidentiality there was no adverse reaction (even Queen Bee did little more than raise her eyebrows) and my colleagues in the marketing department seemed overwhelmingly positive. CC was well liked and well respected and people seemed happy for him. It was a major step to have taken but a necessary one if we were to spend more time together – in a small town like Broken Hill, if you fell off your bar stool at one end of town they'd know about it before you hit the deck at the other end. Although neither of us was saying it, not explicitly, we were both wondering if I could live in Broken Hill. My contract had been extended for another six months but I would still, in theory, be going back to England the following year.

Could an English vegetarian with vestiges of a hippie past survive in a place like Broken Hill? I grew up in a Gloucestershire village surrounded by acres of green fields, I'd lived in glamorous cities like Madrid, London, Seville and Sydney; worked on events in Paris, Rome, Brussels, Amsterdam, Vienna, Sardinia, Vancouver and Marrakesh, staying in five-star resorts and swanning around like a PR princess. Could I embrace life in a dusty Australian mining town, surrounded by scrubby desert?

From our vantage point I could see two of the town's three sets of traffic lights, although according to CC there were hundreds more underground, controlling a complex network of tunnels formed by decades of mining activity.

'The town will probably cave in one day,' he said placidly, forking bacon and eggs into his mouth.

'What kind of council runs this place?'

He took a mouthful of (excellent) coffee. 'A local would tell you the village idiot used to be mayor of Broken Hill. He was ousted by the town drunk, then the whole council was sacked and they appointed an administrator. Things have improved since.'

'How long have you lived here?'

'Thirty-six years.'

'And you're not considered local?'

CC smiled and shook his head. 'No. You're only local if you were born here. I'm from Away.'

Me too, I thought. A long way away. Mind you, it could have been worse. He could have lived in White Cliffs. I'd visited that remote opal-mining community the day before, tagging along with the RFDS on a weekly clinic run.

It had been well into the mid-thirties by nine thirty in the morning and I'd lowered my sweaty body onto a plastic chair in the clinic waiting room in White Cliffs, relieved to find the single-storey building had air conditioning. I'd taken a seat next to a middle-aged woman and struck up a conversation.

'Hello. Is your husband an opal miner?' I'd asked.

She'd lifted her weathered face and looked at me with disinterest, deep lines radiating from her narrowed eyes.

'I'm the miner,' she said. 'I've got a jackhammer and a shovel and I'm mining for opals.'

I'd hastily apologised for my naïve blunder and tried another approach. 'I understand most people in White Cliffs live underground.'

'That's right. Constant twenty-two degrees underground, summer or winter.'

'It must be a relief to escape the heat.'

'If you can afford a dugout, it would be. I can't. I live in a caravan, out on the opal fields.'

'It must be hot out there,' I'd said lamely.

'Recorded a top of fifty-three degrees last year.'

Why would anyone choose to live in such extreme conditions? I assumed she must have been hoping to strike it rich one day so she could escape the place but I was wrong.

'I love the isolation out here, wouldn't live anywhere else,' she'd said bluntly.

A litany of accidents and injuries had walked through the door, all reinforcing the harsh, unforgiving nature of that small bleak town. A man had called for a check-up following a fall down a mine shaft, a woman with ulcers on her legs needed urgent treatment and a sheep shearer presented with repetitive strain injury, nursing a dog that had clearly come off second best in a fight with a wild pig.

The nurse practitioner told me she had once attended an accident in a nearby paddock, a helicopter crash in which the pilot had died. The co-pilot was badly burnt and had multiple fractures on both legs. She'd asked him, on a scale of one to ten, how bad the pain was. 'About six,' was what he said. The nurse had smiled at my shocked expression. 'People out here are pretty resilient,' she'd said.

*

A stroll through town after brunch showed Broken Hill wasn't always so broken. The disused train station in the centre of town proudly declared that Broken Hill once had the first fully air-conditioned diesel-powered train in the British Empire. The Silver City Comet went into operation between Broken Hill and Parkes in the late 1930s, with iced water on tap in twelve air-conditioned carriages. Four powerful diesel engines pulled the carriages at a respectable 130 kilometres an hour. That's when Broken Hill was at the centre of the mining boom.

Some people came to Broken Hill in the early days to get rich and they ended up settling there. Others stayed as long as it took to make some money down the mines and then they were off. How long would I stay?

The walk back took us past 'pavements' of beaten earth and it felt oddly personal, walking on a nature strip that someone had carefully cultivated. Some owners had watered and seeded the baked red soil to encourage grass to grow and some had planted the strip with lavender bushes and eucalyptus trees, anything that might withstand the frequent droughts and fearsome summer heat. Others had left the pavement as a patch of red dirt, worn down by cars, feet, prams and bicycles that failed to quell the ever-present clutch of straggling weeds.

We passed houses where roses bloomed in profusion; fragrant petals juxtaposed against the looming backdrop of the dark slagheap in the centre of town. Streets with practical and distinctly unromantic names like Iodide, Bromide, Chloride, Uranium, Oxide and Kaolin overflowed with old-fashioned roses that flourished. I reached over a fence and pulled a full bloom towards me. If I closed my eyes I could have been in England.

Almost.

A hot wind filled with fine dust forced me to lower my head, clamp a sunhat onto my head and narrow my eyes as we struggled up a slight rise in the road. Heat swirled into my lungs and a fine sheen of moisture appeared on my skin, drying as quickly as it appeared in the thirty-five-degree heat.

We passed a small local supermarket that looked like it was struggling to survive, shelves stocked with chips, chocolate, soft drinks, lollies, and a meagre fruit and vegetable section. I picked up a shrink-wrapped packet of corn on the cob and turned it over to check the use-by date. It was long overdue. Someone had simply crossed the date out with a thick black pen.

Most roads were wide, flamboyantly so, with room for eight or ten cars to drive side by side.

'Why?' I asked, my hat jammed firmly on my head. 'Is it so you can shoot through on the way to somewhere else?' It was a feeble attempt at humour and the joke wasn't funny. CC attempted a laugh all the same.

'They were designed that way to allow a bullock team to turn around,' he patiently explained. 'Early miners would turn up with the materials they needed to build a house loaded onto the back of a dray. That's why so many houses were built of corrugated iron,' he added. 'When the ore ran out they could dismantle the house, put the sheets on the back of the dray and move on.'

It looked like some of them had left their houses behind. They reminded me of the terrapins we had at school, or the fibro shacks that sprang up in England after the war, that were only meant to last five years and were still standing forty years later. We passed one house made entirely of salvaged materials. The only thing of value appeared to be a huge satellite dish in the garden.

'Probably worth more than the house,' said CC, in his own attempt at humour.

There didn't appear to be a rich or poor neighbourhood in Broken Hill, just pockets of poverty and wealth, often side by side. Houses built from salvaged timber, iron, fibro sheeting, weather-board and old stone, thrown up quickly with the minimum of fuss, stood beside more substantial, graceful properties, brick-built by settlers in prosperous times and hidden behind tall, swaying trees.

Next door to one of the graceful mansions was a crumbling house of corrugated iron, with a fence of twisted, broken chicken wire. I looked closer and noticed that the windows were made of odd bits of stained glass. A shaft of sunlight glinting on those windows would have thrown shimmering rainbows into the house. I was reminded that making do can sometimes throw up unexpected bursts of beauty.

Towards the end of Zebina Street was a shack made of tin and corrugated iron, bound together with mud and stones that must have been collected from the desert scrub at the end of the street. The sheets of corrugated iron were laid at odd angles, the walls were crumbling, the boundary fence was broken and the garden was a wasteland. A handwritten sign hung optimistically on the front gate: 'For Sale'.

It was tempting to call the mobile number scratched under-neath to find out what the house was worth – there was a time, not so long ago, when you could buy a house in Broken Hill on a credit card – but I didn't want to get the owner's hopes up. He or she couldn't have had many calls.

CC's house was one of the last in the street, a simple brick bungalow with manicured lawns shaded by mature trees. A few more houses, a slight rise and the road petered out until there was no distinction between the end of civilisation and the start of a vast empty wilderness that pressed in close and let no one (well, me) forget that Broken Hill was surrounded by desert.

'Do you fancy a swim?'

It was late afternoon and the sun had lost some of its heat so we cycled two blocks to the municipal pool, a place of such dazzling emptiness it would have had David Hockney reaching for his paintbrush.

Sunlight sharpened the blocks of solid colour: navy and blue tiles, red flags, purple shadecloth, yellow lifebuoys. It cost two dollars to get in and we had a lane to ourselves. In fact, we had the whole Olympic-sized pool to ourselves. What's more, it was heated.

CC dived in to chase down the first of forty laps and I eased myself down the steps, luxuriating in the cool, clear water. I took long, lazy strokes, brushing aside an occasional fluffy white feather that had drifted down from the white cockatoos that were sitting on the branches of nearby gum trees.

After a while I left CC powering up and down the pool and I got out, towelling off at the side.

'Not many people here,' I said to a nearby attendant.

'No, gets busy in school holidays though.' He nodded towards CC. 'He swims most days. In winter I've seen him swim with frost on top of his head.'

That didn't surprise me.

*

'Are you sure you're not married?'

I couldn't get over how neat and tidy the house was. There were signs of a woman's touch everywhere, in the flourishing indoor pot plants, the ironed tablecloths that covered the kitchen and dining room tables, and a vase of freshly picked roses sitting on the sideboard.

'I've got a housekeeper,' CC explained. 'Heather looks after the house when I'm not here; she does all the washing and ironing as well.'

'Heather?' I said, trying to keep my voice neutral. Was that a stab of jealousy I felt? How curious. Since when did I want to look after someone else's house? And I *hated* washing and ironing.

CC looked pleased. 'Jealous, Frosty?'

'Ha. As if.'

But I *was* jealous. And that was a good sign. There was something oddly comforting about being in Broken Hill with CC. His place wasn't remotely the kind of house I would have chosen to live in, and it wasn't decorated to my taste either (I'm hard to please, I know, but pink velour curtains and matching pink velour cushions have never done it for me). Still, I felt comfortable. At the last count I'd lived in thirty-two different places, decorating each one with minimalist white or wild colour and the longest I'd lived anywhere was four years. It was hard to explain why I would feel at home with CC, in a house he'd lived in for the past thirty-six years. Was I allowed to be that relaxed, that happy? Was it really that easy?

'Are you hungry?' I asked.

'I could eat something.'

I searched the cupboards for biscuits to go with cheese and found three packets: one expired in 2005, one in 2003 and the winner by a mouldy mile expired in 1999. I fared no better with nuts and an old jar of marmalade, not that it mattered much; the block of cheese in the fridge was seven months out of date.

CC seemed to exist on a diet of yoghurt, protein powder, steak and peas. Why would such a conservative carnivore be attracted to someone like me? I supposed for the same reason I was attracted to him.

Yin and yang.

North and South.

Jack Sprat . . . and his wife.

*

'Let's go out, we can watch the sunset at Mundi Mundi and get takeaway on the way back.'

I didn't admit I'd been to Mundi Mundi already; CC was eager to show me the sights and I didn't want to disappoint him. We folded two deckchairs into the back of the car and took a packet of peanuts, a bottle of wine and a rare bottle of beer for CC.

The Silverton Road took us across the Barrier Highway – Adelaide 500 kilometres one way, Cobar 450 kilometres the other – and into a landscape of desolate plains and low hills.

'You'll recognise this next bit of road. It's where they filmed the big chase scene in *Mad Max*.'

CC had told me, with some pride I might add, that the first *Mad Max* film was shot on location on the outskirts of Broken Hill in the late 1970s. Location scouts must have been thrilled to find somewhere that so clearly said 'end of the world' with such finality, but I can't say there was anything familiar about the seemingly empty scrub that passed in a blur on either side of the road.

'Here it is,' said CC.

Apart from a slight rise and bend the next bit of road looked exactly like the last bit. I was oddly touched that he thought I might recognise it, even more so when he revealed he had flown an aircraft in the film and had had to land on a stretch of road further on (which looked a lot like the stretch of road further back).

We parked at the lookout (a rocky outcrop I did remember) that afforded a view of distant plains stretching across a big fat slab of landscape and I tried in vain to see the curvature of the earth's surface.

The air was gritty with dust, the landscape strewn with rocks, and we unloaded the deckchairs in a determined wind that slapped against the car.

'At least the wind will keep the flies off,' said CC, optimistically, settling the deckchairs onto the rocky ground next to the car.

It didn't. We had to part our lips like bombproof letterboxes at Heathrow Airport to cautiously sip our drinks, slipping peanuts between the thin slits, mindful of flies that were trying to slip in as well.

I once read that the average person will swallow three flies in a lifetime. I dismissed the report. I'd never heard of anyone swallowing a fly, except maybe the odd motorbike rider. Now I understood how statisticians must have arrived at that figure – the residents of Broken Hill had skewed the average. There were flies so desperate to find a drop of moisture they were willing to crawl up our nostrils. I wondered how many flies CC had swallowed in his lifetime and decided now was not the time to ask.

Dusty plains stretched into the distance and I felt a pang of longing for Sydney Harbour; views of sparkling beauty I'd taken for granted on a daily basis. Images of green fields and dry stone walls in the English villages of Castle Combe, Chipping Norton and Moreton-in-Marsh superimposed themselves across the parched desert. I thought about English country houses and well-stocked kitchen gardens. I remembered the rugged beauty of Cornish fishing villages with tall cliffs, blue seas and cobblestone streets, the majestic beauty of elegant chateaux in the Loire Valley surrounded by formal gardens, the swaying fields of sunflowers, serried ranks of vineyards . . .

Stop it.

I would never see the beauty in this desolate flat landscape if I kept comparing it to somewhere else.

We sat in our deckchairs, sipping wine, slipping in peanuts and watching the sun dip lower in the sky. As we relaxed together in companionable silence, like the couples I remembered from my first trip to Broken Hill, I began to understand how such isolation and peace might be attractive.

Five minutes before the sun finally sank below the horizon another car pulled up and four chattering teenage girls clambered out. They threw down blankets and pressed together on the ground a few metres in front of us, arms linked as they lined up to watch the sunset, giggling softly to each other. After a brief pause one of them filled the silence with a question.

'So, Brad Pitt or George Clooney? Who would you shag?'

CC and I sat quietly in our deckchairs, sipping wine and slipping in peanuts. We were invisible to the giggling girls, a middle-aged couple well past our use-by dates.

The sunset when it happened was fleeting and ordinary so we packed up our deckchairs and left what remained of the evening to the carload of giggling girls (Brad Pitt fans, by the way).

We got back to Broken Hill and, on a whim, put our deckchairs on the grass in the garden to watch the stars of the Milky Way appear above our heads. Forked lightning flashed across the sky and the distant rumble of thunder held the promise of rain.

I decided I might enjoy a return trip to Broken Hill.

chapter nineteen

'Sasha couldn't get enough time off work for Sydney so we're meeting in Cairns. I'll have a few days on my own while the conference is on. Could I cadge a bed? If it's a problem, don't worry, I can book into a hotel.'

I scanned the email, text flickering as I scrolled up and down the screen. My heart was racing as I hit reply. 'No, of course it's not a problem, come and stay, there's a spare room,' I wrote. I hit send before I could change my mind.

The occasional email had pinged back and forth since A3's wedding – how are things, what's the weather like in Australia? Great thanks, how are you? It was all very grown-up and polite, only now he was planning a trip to Sydney. He would be speaking at a conference in Darling Harbour and his wife would be flying over when the conference ended, joining him for a diving holiday on the Great Barrier Reef.

A3 was coming to Sydney, and he was coming without his wife.

The request set my emotions spinning. Why was he coming? Why did he want to stay with me? And why on earth did I say yes? I'd done such a good job of persuading him – and to a lesser extent me – that I was over that ridiculous infatuation nonsense that he thought there was nothing wrong in asking to stay. And I stupidly said yes. Oh crap, crap, crap, crap, CRAP.

CC was back in Broken Hill and he wouldn't be in Sydney for another few weeks. In the meantime, the man I had pursued for so long, so desperately and doggedly, without any hope of success or sign of interest on his part, had suddenly asked if he could come and stay. I should have said no. I should have lied and told him I'd be away. I could have made up any number of excuses, I could even have ignored the email altogether.

But you didn't.

No. I didn't. I invited him to stay.

A3 had left an imprint on my life like a stain that couldn't be rubbed off. I'd tried to stop loving him and I wasn't sure how successful I'd been. Not very, judging by my reaction to his email.

What chance did CC have when I was still longing for A3? No. Longing was too strong a word; it was more of a vague, niggling, annoying hope that A3 would want to be with me. But why? Why would I want to be with someone who'd rejected me? Was it because I refused to accept reality? Was it easier to live in a fantasy world than face the truth? Or did I still nurture a faint hope that things weren't working out, that his newly minted marriage might be on the rocks already? And even if he did arrive and suddenly declare that his bright shiny new marriage wasn't working –

Stop right there.

– why would he want to be with me instead? And did I really want to be with him?

No, you don't.

So why was I so churned up about his visit?

He's coming for work and he wants a free bed.

Yes I know, but what if –

What if nothing. He's a cheapskate academic and he wants a free bed.

I know but –

No buts. He's married. Get over it.

Miss Prissy Knickers was right. Of course he wasn't coming for any reason other than work. I tried to remember how it felt when I was living in England and A3 avoided my calls, ignored my emails and made excuses not to see me. None of it calmed my jittery nerves. Hope rose like a helium balloon above a busy fairground.

What was behind his email? Was it, at long last, his chance to reveal that he'd spent the past four years fighting a burning desire to be with me? Had he been struggling with a passion so intense it threatened to overwhelm him and prevented him (pretty much ever) picking up the phone and calling me?

I should have grabbed that gaudy balloon and jabbed it with a sharp pin. I should have squashed that burgeoning sense of hope and told him not to come.

But I didn't.

People who play with matches start fires.

*

'Who is he?' CC asked with suspicion when I explained on the phone there would be someone staying for a few days, while he was in Broken Hill. The gentle, considerate man I thought I knew sounded like a Rottweiler with his hackles up.

'An old friend, someone I knew . . . we've kept in touch.'

'Just a friend?'

'Relax, you don't need to worry.'

Say that to someone like CC and he worries. I'm glad he couldn't see me because I felt a flush of blood creep up my neck.

'Frosty, are you and he –?'

'No! Of course we're not! A long time ago I sort of . . . anyway he wasn't interested. He's married now and he's just a friend. Just a friend,' I finished lamely.

I hesitated to tell Kate, knowing she would disapprove, so I waited until one Friday evening, when we were sitting in her back garden, sharing a gin and tonic. By then A3's visit was less than two days away.

'Kate, is there any chance I could borrow your car on Sunday?'

'Sure, going anywhere nice?'

'I have to pick someone up from the airport.'

'Ooh, tell me more – sounds interesting!'

'It's no one special, just that guy I met in Canada.'

Kate drained her gin and tonic, rattled the ice and placed the glass on the table. She wasn't fooled for a minute. 'You mean that guy you fell for who got married?'

'That's him.'

'Is his wife with him?'

'No, he's meeting her later, up in Cairns.'

'Is that a good idea?'

'He asked if he could stay. I didn't feel I could refuse.' What a lame, feeble excuse. I didn't refuse because I didn't *want* to refuse. 'There's nothing between us,' I added. 'There hasn't been for years.'

'You were pretty upset about him, though, weren't you? Be careful, Deb. You've met someone here who sounds lovely.'

'Seriously, you don't need to worry. Nothing's going to happen!'

Come the Sunday of A3's arrival, I was a mess. The only way to calm my jitters was to keep busy. I washed and dried the sheets, made up the spare bed, found clean towels and vacuumed the carpets. I cycled to the fish market and picked out two plump tuna steaks from De Costi's, which they packed in ice and wrapped in plastic for the cycle home. I put them in the fridge and then cycled to Darling Street, shopped for groceries at Woolies and came home to put a bottle of sauvignon blanc in the fridge – followed by another, just in case.

A3 was on a Singapore Airlines flight, arriving at four thirty. From lunchtime onwards I clawed my way through a wardrobe of clothes that made me look too fat, too old and too frumpy. I flung a low-cut top onto the growing pile of discards. What was wrong with me? I never worried about what I wore with CC and here I was fretting like a high-school student at her first school dance. It was embarrassing nonsense and Miss PK had stern words.

Get over him.

Despondency struck like a blow from an unseen assailant lurking down a dark alley. What did it matter what I wore? He wouldn't care. He wouldn't even notice.

The international arrivals hall at Sydney Airport teemed with people in constant ebb and flow. A tidal surge of emotion washed over the hall as family members who hadn't seen each other for years were reunited, then drawn through the double doors into the steamy atmosphere outside.

What a lot of luggage everyone had. There was a time when suitcases were small and compact, made of leather or pressed cardboard, and easily carried. Now they're the size of a trunk for a three-month sea voyage: cases with wheels so we can cram in more clothes and drag more belongings behind us; hand-bags, shopping bags, briefcases, plastic bags full of duty free, hand luggage stuffed with treats and lollies, toys, games, books, BlackBerrys, iPods, iPads, iPhones. Stuff. Baggage everywhere, mine included.

I wandered over to the newsagent's to kill time and dawdled in front of racks of glossy magazines – *Beautiful Homes, Gorgeous Gardens, Inside Out* or *Upside Down* – the title was less important than the attention-grabbing headline. 'Free Goody Bag!' one cover shouted. A bag the size of a small knapsack was stuck to the outside, full of more stuff no one really needed.

I once took a train from Bomaderry, on the South Coast of New South Wales, to Sydney and a young Aboriginal couple got on with me. It was clear from their conversation they were going to Sydney but they wore no shoes and carried no bags. When the ticket inspector arrived it turned out they had no money either, which was a bit of an issue, but I was struck by how much I was carrying and how little they felt they needed.

There was a recession on and instead of learning to consume less we were being encouraged to consume more. *Buy one, get one free, two for the price of one, fifty per cent extra in the bag!* My handbag weighed heavily on my arm, crammed with a purse containing too much small change, a cardigan in case it got cold, a notebook, newspaper, reading glasses, tissues, lipstick, nail clippers, old receipts, used bus tickets, mints, toffees, a hair-brush that could do with a good clean, and detritus caught in the torn lining. Stuff.

'Hey!'

The unremarkable figure of A3 swam into view, a slight figure in chinos and t-shirt, fair hair darkened by sweat and the beginnings of a beard after twenty-four hours on a plane. His appearance inflated my balloon to the point where my feet barely touched the ground.

He smiled and I gave him a quick hug, then grabbed his trolley for ballast. 'I've borrowed a car; it's parked just outside. How was your flight? Did you get much sleep? God, it's hot, isn't it? How's married life? What's the weather like in England?'

I pushed the trolley towards the exit. It was too soon, too raw, I shouldn't have invited him to stay and I was so glad to see him.

*

'Do you mind if I Skype Sasha?'

'Sure, go ahead. Use my computer if you like.'

Twenty minutes later they were still chatting and I sat in the subterranean dining room, my balloon well and truly deflated. What a dope, what a sad, deluded empty-headed fool I was to have ever harboured the slightest hope he might have been coming to Sydney for anything other than business. The sooner I got my mutton-brained head around the incontrovertible fact that he had never been remotely interested in me, the better. Why had I invited him to stay? It felt like I had nothing stable to hold onto, as if I was suffering from vertigo.

CC called and we had a strained conversation that I cut short. I couldn't explain how I felt. How could I admit that I'd been a prize fool? The tuna steaks could stay in the fridge: I had to get this man out of my house.

'Let's eat out; there's a good pub around the corner,' I said as soon as he was off Skype.

A3 looked miffed that I was bundling him out of the house as soon as he'd arrived but I couldn't face the thought of the two of us eating alone in my house.

'A brisk walk will do you good,' I said. 'Help you get over jet lag.'

*

The Royal Oak thrummed with activity. Voices in the packed dining room bounced off the vaulted ceiling and rebounded from the wooden floor. Chefs in the open-plan kitchen shouted to make themselves heard above the clatter of pans and the loud music, and waiters did their best to dodge young children running between the tables.

'I'm thinking of grilled red snapper . . . or crumbed calamari. Oh, but the steamed Tasmanian mussels sound good.' A3 looked up from the menu and gave the waitress a helpless smile. 'I can't decide,' he said. I'd seen that smile before. It normally went with his 'help me I'm just a man' shrug.

'What would you recommend?' he asked the attractive young waitress.

She leant in to look at the menu he was holding. 'Beer-battered fish and chips is always popular.'

A3 patted his flat stomach. 'For you, maybe; I've got to watch my weight.'

I gripped the menu and scanned the printed words that marched across the page like an army of ants. A3 reached across and lightly touched the back of my hand. 'Shall we be naughty and share some hot chips?'

What clarity distance can bring. He was a flirt, pure and simple, and he flirted with everyone, spreading himself around so as not to disappoint his audience. What a fool I was not to have spotted that when we'd first met; to have mistaken his flirting for real interest and genuine feeling.

'This is an excellent menu,' he said, smiling at the waitress again. 'I think I'll have chargrilled ocean trout with steamed asparagus on the side.'

'Beer-battered fish and chips,' I said, handing my menu back.

'This is a good pub – you chose well,' he said, watching the waitress's arse as she clipped away.

'Excuse me,' I called. 'Can you add garlic bread to my order?'

I ignored A3's raised eyebrows and reached for the bottle of wine I'd brought from home. It was an expensive bottle and I intended to drink as much of it as I could. I hate noisy pubs.

'So, how's married life?'

It was like winding up a toy. Pausing only occasionally for food or drink, he extolled the virtues of his beautiful bride, the delights of their New York wedding, the breathtaking honeymoon at the Banyan Tree in Phuket – private villa, own pool, butler service – and I settled my features into those of a professional listener.

'Where are you living?' I asked, jabbing another chip into my mouth.

'We bought a house in Croydon. Easy commute to work from there.'

'What does Sasha think of composting toilets and wind-powered turbines?'

'Ah yes. Early days yet. We've got to get a handle on the mortgage first.'

'You must have solar power though.'

He reached across for one of my chips, dipped it into a dish of tartar sauce and pushed it into his mouth. A dollop of sauce dribbled onto his chin. The waitress came back to check we were enjoying our meal and I took quiet pleasure in the sight of a messy eater trying to flirt with someone young enough to be his daughter. 'Yum! Marvellous food,' he said. The blob of sauce held firm.

'You were talking about renewable energy,' I said.

'We had to spend a heap of money on furniture.'

'Solar hot water?'

'It's not that easy in an old house.'

The blob of tartar sauce wobbled and I marvelled that such a shallow academic could ever have impressed me. His special interest in comparative systems of environmental education gave him a credibility he didn't deserve, presenting him as a committed environmentalist, a caring advocate for sustainability, when in reality he was nothing of the sort. He was all talk. Do as I say, not as I do, travelling the world at the expense of others to lecture on a topic that, to him at least, was purely academic. CC's solar panels on the roof of his house in Broken Hill and the rainwater tank in his garden gave him far more credibility than all the degrees and postdoctoral qualifications A3 touted around.

We split the bill and A3 gave the waitress a movie-star smile. 'Thank you, that was excellent,' he said. 'Great service.'

I waited until he had left a large tip before I told him about the sauce stuck to his chin. He grabbed a napkin on the way out. By then it had dried hard enough to require some rubbing to remove.

We walked back along Rowntree Street, past Charlotte's café, the drycleaner's next door and the newsagent's on the corner. I pointed out the bus stop. 'The 441 will take you straight to Darling Harbour.'

'Shall we get the bus in together?'

'I cycle.'

'Oh.'

Actually my cycling had tailed off of late but after all the chips and garlic bread I'd eaten I was going to need the exercise. I opened the front door and dropped my handbag onto a chair in the living room.

'You'll want an early night before your conference tomorrow,' I said.

He pouted. 'But you haven't told me what's going on in your life yet. I've spent all evening talking about me.' So you have, I thought. He gave me the smile that once held so much power and I deflected it with a thin version of my own.

'Plenty of time for that tomorrow,' I said. 'Sleep well.'

As I lay awake (not for long, given the amount of wine I had drunk), I was forced to admit that A3 had never been remotely interested in me. I wasn't that interested in him either, not when I took a step back and looked at him dispassionately. He represented something I wanted that I couldn't have.

How many years had I spent chasing unsuitable men, desperately searching for someone who would make me feel better about myself? Looking back on my dismal relationship record, I realised I had carried a sense of shame about all that meaning-less sex in my early years. The end result was that I didn't believe I was worth loving.

A stranger may have inflicted the first blow at fifteen and Stavros did a good job with the second but I had inflicted most of the damage in the ensuing years myself, locking away the shame and grief and then compounding it with meaningless behaviour that reinforced my lack of self-worth.

Even the long period of celibacy did little to open my eyes because I didn't tackle the real problem. Rather than attempt to communicate, openly and honestly, with someone, it proved easier to conduct fictional relationships than deal with the messy, difficult and ultimately rewarding challenge of true intimacy. I stayed locked up and I was no more willing to accept flaws in other people than I was in myself – nothing short of perfection would satisfy me.

I chased A1 when I knew we had no future, then I lost interest when the battle was won. I fell for A2 partly because he lived fifteen thousand kilometres away, so I could feed my fantasy of the perfect mate without fear of interruption by the real thing, then I grew anxious and fretful when he didn't immediately profess undying love for me. And I pursued A3 because I knew I couldn't have him.

I had never learnt to communicate openly with any of the men I'd been out with. And I had never, ever been honest about how I felt.

What a sorry record.

Looking back, I realised A3 fell for his wife just like CC fell for me and to be loved by someone is a precious gift. A3 had never been overwhelmed with desire for me and he really did come out to Australia for work. He was happily married to a woman he loved and he didn't lie awake at night aching with longing.

Neither do you.

It was true. I didn't. My hurt pride craved the satisfaction of knowing A3 wanted to be with me but if he had made a pass at me I would have run a mile. I had come within a whisker of jeopardising what I had found with CC because I couldn't let go of the fiction that A3 and I were meant for each other. I had written the story in my head, had the outcome all worked out and stubbornly refused to accept that it wasn't reality.

chapter twenty

After four days in Sydney, A3 left to join his beloved Sasha and I closed the door behind him with a sigh of relief. I wasn't sure what pleased me most – getting rid of him at last or finally being free of the tumultuous mix of emotions that had plagued me for so long.

I had behaved like a lovesick loon in a teenage romance. Looking back, I realised it was a role I had slipped into all too often in the past, casting myself as a sad, lonely spinster, forgotten, lovelorn and left on the shelf. I'd been subconsciously punishing myself for all that bad sex and all those failed attempts at relationships by assuming I wasn't worth loving. But what feeble nonsense was this? I was a forty-nine-year-old single woman, relatively fit and healthy, passably attractive and vaguely intelligent.

If there'd been a boot camp for hopeless romantics I'd have joined it. Instead I gave myself a stern talking to, then I confessed all to CC. Well, not quite all. I was too embarrassed to admit I'd spent four years stalking someone who wasn't remotely interested so I just told him that I'd been a fool.

'Are you telling me you had a relationship?'

A phone call wasn't the best way of breaking the news to CC but it would be another two weeks before we met and I wanted to clear the air. 'I'd hardly call it that,' I said. 'It was an infatuation a long time ago and nothing came of it. Anyway, he's married now. I should have told you; I'm sorry, only I didn't want to worry you. And nothing happened, you know. I was glad to see the back of him when he left.' I was talking just a tad too quickly, swallowing my words, unsure of CC's reaction when I couldn't see his face.

'You invited him to stay.'

'Yes, and I shouldn't have.'

CC's voice took on the hard flat tone I remembered from our late-night argument. 'Did you sleep with him?'

'No, of course I didn't! Why would I jeopardise what I've got with you for the sake of a drunken night's passion with someone who's married?'

*

It was a hot November day and the sun was bouncing off the patio. Twenty-four pieces of aluminium piping in three different lengths, several with sprung joints, were strewn across the concrete and a bundle of green-and-white-striped material lay piled in a corner. CC held up a linking piece.

'Where are the instructions?' he said.

'There aren't any. I got it second-hand.'

I was planning to hold a small brunch party in Rowntree Street to celebrate my fiftieth birthday in a few weeks time and, when I saw the picture online, I knew a gazebo would be just the finishing touch I needed. It would be perfect for al fresco dining on the back patio and I could picture it strung with fairy lights and coloured lanterns, ivy twined around the posts, table and chairs set out below.

'Have you actually seen it up?'

'No, but the owner assured me all the pieces are here. It was a bargain,' I added quickly, seeing the dubious expression on CC's face.

'Assuming we can get it up, how do you plan to tie it down?'

The small patio (which was smaller than I remembered now that we had aluminium posts strewn across it) was enclosed by high walls and concreted right to the edge. Clearly there was nowhere to drive in a tent peg.

'Let's not worry about that now, let's just get the thing up, shall we?'

We spent the best part of twenty minutes sorting through poles, most of which looked identical, only of course they weren't. Some were marginally shorter, or fatter, depending on where they sat in the overall structure.

'Why didn't they just number them?' CC grumbled.

Sydney was sweltering through a heatwave and the task was made more difficult by the fierce sunlight. His shirt was soon stained with sweat.

'Do you want a cold drink?'

'Let's get this done, shall we?'

'What about a hat?'

'No, thank you. That's a jointed piece; here, put that over there.'

'How many corner pieces have you got?'

It took an hour and a half of sweaty work to assemble the gazebo and we needn't have worried about tying it down because it had to be shoehorned into place. The back door would only just open without hitting the frame and the poles were jammed up against the walls. Conversation had been lacklustre while we'd been working but that didn't surprise me: it was hot, the poles were fiddly and twice we'd had to dismantle half the struc-ture when we spotted an infinitesimally small difference in pole length, barely noticeable on the ground yet critical when six feet up in the air. We pulled over the cover, hoisted the jointed legs and stood back to admire the finished result.

'Shall we discuss it?'

I assumed he meant the dinner party.

'I was thinking about salmon, I could get a whole one from the fish market and slow cook it.'

'No, I meant the phone call. Why did you do it?'

'Do what?'

CC bent down to clip a flap of fabric to the bottom of a pole. He spoke calmly and quietly, with his back to me. 'Why did you sleep with him?'

There was silence.

'I didn't,' I said, just as quietly.

CC didn't answer at first. I was puzzled, unsure what was happening. Why was he accusing me of sleeping with A3 when I'd explicitly told him I hadn't? CC straightened up. 'You said something about a drunken night of passion. You said you realised it wasn't worth jeopardising our relationship for. So why did you do it?'

I tried to remember my exact words.

'I didn't say I slept with him. I said it wouldn't have been worth it if I *had*. It would only have been a drunken night's passion. Only it wasn't, because it didn't happen.'

Was it jealousy that twisted his interpretation of what I'd said? Insecurity? Or was it because I was stupid enough to invite A3 to stay?

'So where do we go from here?'

'What do you mean, where do we go? Nothing happened! We agreed, we promised . . . I didn't . . . nothing happened.'

Before I could say anything else his mobile phone rang. He flipped open the case and checked the number. 'Excuse me, I have to take this.'

Snatches of conversation drifted through the open window as I sat under the gazebo. I couldn't hear what was said but there was unmistakeable warmth in his voice, even a suggestion of laughter. Up until that moment I'd thought that kind of warmth had been reserved exclusively for me (not that I'd seen too much of it recently).

*   .

It took less than a week for CC to turn into a bitter, jealous, quietly enraged lover. He tried hacking into my phone to check for messages, grilled me endlessly on tiny details, twisting and turning them until they became bitter black stains on my character. It was a relentless process of accusation and suspicion, certain to kill our fledgling relationship if it continued. CC was in the grip of something he couldn't control and all I could do was tell him, over and over again, that I hadn't slept with A3.

'I haven't cheated on you, I'm not cheating on you and I won't cheat on you.'

'I have evidence,' he muttered darkly.

'Evidence of what?' I shouted. 'Nothing happened!'

CC's forensic examination was not unlike the intense scrutiny I used to turn on any potential new relationship, analysing it until there was nothing left. Turn a magnifying glass on a butterfly, examine it too closely and the sun will scorch its wings until it shrivels up and dies. And there ain't *no* way you can resurrect a dead butterfly.

'Have you seen *Othello*?'

'What's Shakespeare got to do with anything?'

'Because I feel like bloody Desdemona right now!'

But I was no butterfly and no innocent Desdemona. You don't have to sleep with someone to be unfaithful and I had jeopardised my intimacy with CC by inviting A3 into my home. That put a man like CC through an agony of jealousy and suspicion.

'Surely if I was going to cheat on you I would have kept it quiet?' I reasoned.

'Maybe you felt guilty. How can I trust you?'

'Trust is like faith,' I reminded him, not knowing how else to counteract his suspicion. 'You either have it or you don't.'

'You should believe your own eyes. Trust what you can see,' he countered.

'But what can you see?'

'Evidence,' he said, refusing to be drawn on what that evidence was.

*

'This is the point when you would normally head for the hills.'

I was with Kate and Hanne, flicking through racks of clothes in a bid to find something special to wear at brunch. Hanne had suggested we look in Just Jeans (somewhere I hadn't thought to try, can't think why) and she and Kate had listened patiently as I'd told them a little about the tension with CC that had built up over the past few days. Kate's comment about heading for the hills took me by surprise. I'd been expecting sympathy.

'I don't do that, do I?'

Kate raised her eyebrows.

'Hanne, do I do that?'

I looked across at Hanne, who was calmly inspecting scraps of material that passed as dresses and barely covered the hangers.

'Maybe. A bit,' she said, diplomatically.

'What about this one?' said Kate, holding up a maxi dress with thin plaited straps. The flimsy concoction of pale blue, dusky pink and ochre chiffon had a plunging neckline and a frilly hem (it looked a lot better than it sounds).

'Seriously, I'm turning fifty, not thirty.'

'Try it on.'

I emerged from the changing room, tugging at the neckline.

'Are you sure about this?' I said.

'You look gorgeous!' said Hanne.

'Come on,' said Kate, 'it's perfect. Get a wriggle on, I'll be late for Inga.'

I paid for the dress, arguably the cheapest and prettiest dress I'd ever bought, and thanked Kate and Hanne for coming with me.

'See you Friday,' Kate said. 'And wear the dress!'

I went home, clutching a featherweight bag of coloured froth, wondering how many relationships I had run away from at the first hint of trouble. The answer was probably quite a few.

*

The gazebo was decorated with fairy lights and flowers. There were hot croissants, fresh fruit salad, Greek yoghurt, homemade muesli, French champagne and freshly squeezed orange juice. There were bouquets of flowers from friends in Sydney, more from family in England and still more from friends in London. I floated through it in my flimsy maxi dress, clipping on high-heel shoes, waving painted fingernails.

'Happy birthday!' said Kate, as she and James squeezed under the gazebo (which trapped an obscene amount of heat under its plastic cover even at seven thirty in the morning).

There was a shout from upstairs. 'Anyone home?'

'We're out the back,' I called.

'Happy fiftieth, sweetheart, love the dress,' said Andrea, fanning herself as she joined us on the patio. I poured champagne and handed out glasses. 'Here's to ageing disgracefully,' Andrea called. 'Cheers!'

The day passed in a blur. There were cards and gifts, and calls from family in England, followed by a girls' trip on the harbour from Balmain to Chowder Bay for lunch at Ripples. The champagne flowed, the sun shone and I couldn't have wished for a better day.

If only CC had been there.

He'd done all the right things, sent a card and flowers, phoned to wish me happy birthday, said he was sorry he couldn't be there, said he'd try to get down to Sydney again as soon as he could, but we both knew something had shifted. He was convinced I had slept with A3.

*

I know how powerful a trickster the mind could be. It had been easy for me to believe that A3 was interested in me and I had seen 'evidence' where none existed. It had been enough that, after bombarding him with calls and text messages, he had occasionally picked up the phone in exasperation when I rang, or answered the odd email weeks after it had been sent. The stalker in me had taken that as evidence that he was burning with desire to be with me. He hadn't been.

Unfortunately, that didn't make me any more understanding of CC's behaviour now. I was offended and hurt by his constant questioning. Did he have an Iago dripping poison in his ear? Nothing good would come of it if he did. I thought back to something Metro Mike had said, how there were three women around CC and any one of them would have made a suitable partner. Was he now reconsidering his options?

The phone calls got worse, terse question and answer sessions that led nowhere, and we lost the easy rapport we'd once had. I knew it was partly my fault for inviting A3 to stay but I was furious that CC wouldn't accept my word when I told him, repeatedly, that nothing had happened.

The relationship with CC seemed to be going nowhere, which disappointed me more than I was willing to admit. My stint in Australia had served its purpose. I was over A3, finally and definitively, and I'd learnt a hard lesson: stalking any man was pointless and counterproductive. Kate's comment about always heading for the hills at the first sign of trouble had stayed with me. It rankled because it was true, but surely now it really was time to leave? It made sense to pack up the few belongings I had brought with me, and head back to England. The short-term contract at the RFDS had turned into something more permanent but working in a marketing department, even for an organisation as prestigious as the RFDS, wasn't really what I wanted to do.

I rang my close friend Helen, who worked in the HR department of a large fund manager in London. 'It's not good,' she said. 'We're making 150 people redundant.' She faced a nightmare few months herself that would culminate in her turning out the lights and making her own job redundant.

The event management team another friend headed, where I had worked before leaving England, had been slashed from a team of seven down to just two, and they'd been forced to let all of the contractors go. That would have been me if I'd stayed.

Prospects in the UK looked bleak but were they any better in Australia? It had been a long time since I'd worked as a freelance journalist and my contacts were few and far between. I thought back to what Metro Mike had said about writing. How, though? The lease on the house in Birchgrove was coming to an end and, without a job, I wouldn't be able to afford to rent anywhere, never mind a place in Balmain or Birchgrove. It made sense to go back to England, where at least I had family. I felt unaccountably gloomy at the prospect of leaving Australia.

In all the swirling indecision I couldn't get CC out of my mind. There had been something about him – respect, kindness, laughter, fun, consideration – that made me wish we could have spent more time together. I missed his lean body and his sense of humour. The realisation that it was too late left a hollow feeling where once there had been joy.

He used to call every day, sometimes several times a day, and now my phone was silent. I missed him.

chapter twenty-one

'Casper likes people making a fuss of him, don't you, darling?'

The terrier lying on my lap gave a surprisingly loud snore as I stroked his overweight body. Pale hair clung to my black trousers, stuck to my fingers and floated in the air around my head. 'He's a delightful dog,' I said, plucking hair out of my mouth.

The owners smiled indulgently at the snoring creature spread-eagled on my knees. 'We think so. The cats are a bit highly strung but you'll get used to them.' I silently hoped I would. I needed this house.

Unemployment in the UK was rising and the economy had been officially declared in recession. Redundancies were rife and thousands of jobs were being shed each week; no one knew who could be next. Friends in the UK had counselled against going back.

I took a chance and negotiated a deal with the RFDS to continue working on their quarterly newsletter, which would pay me a salary for one day a week and bring in just enough money to cover food. All I had to do was find somewhere to live.

There are people who never pay rent, moving from one house-sit to another, and it seemed like the perfect solution to cover the shortfall in salary until I could find more work. So I joined 8500 other registered house-sitters and I started searching. I had a clear notion of what house-sitting would be like: a prolonged summer holiday on the island of Santorini perhaps, or maybe high-rise apartment living within easy reach of Sydney Opera House. There was always the chance I might luck upon a Glenn Murcutt classic surrounded by swaying eucalyptus trees, or perhaps I'd find a glass-walled apartment perched on the edge of a cliff overlooking the ocean. I wasn't fussy; any of those would have been fine. My ideal was somewhere near the coast, a haven of uninterrupted bliss that would supply me with a calm, orderly existence (unlike my own life) where I could embark on my plan to write a bestselling book and learn to meditate.

It soon became apparent that there were alarmingly few houses to go around the thousands of people looking, and most were for properties in rural Queensland, inland Victoria or remote farms in Tasmania. I could have spent ten days in a flat in Marrickville, four days on a 500-acre property in outback Queensland or two weeks in a unit in Cremorne next to a busy main road, but where was the six-month stint in a villa overlooking the Pacific? Where was the glass-walled apartment close to Sydney Opera House? And house-sitting was a misnomer. No one really cares about an empty house. They care about pets.

Every advertiser had pets, and lots of them. There was a man with four dogs and two cats in Fountaindale; a woman in Tasmania with two cats, a Siberian husky and six chickens; and another poor soul in Miriam Vale with seven dogs who wanted a weekend away. Who could blame her? If I'd known how to ride a horse or milk a cow I could have applied to spend three months looking after a stud farm but even I knew there was no point lying to that extent.

After two weeks of scouring ads, with the end of my lease fast approaching and the perfect property no closer, I gave up on the idea of perfection and applied to house-sit for a young couple in Coogee, a trendy beachside suburb just south of Bondi. They wanted someone to mind two cats and a dog while they attended a wedding in Canada, followed by a two-month tour from east to west.

'I'm an art teacher,' Miriam said with pride, her pale face hidden behind a dark bob with a long fringe. I'd worked out it had to be something creative; her fingers were splashed with paint and wide bracelets jangled on her wrist. She was as dramatic as some of the pictures on the walls – unlike her husband, Jack, who radiated peace, his bald head as smooth and white as a Buddhist stupa. Their house was gorgeous, an old weatherboard perched high above the beach, full of books, prints, water-colours, patterned rugs and quirky furniture. It was spacious, free-standing and quiet.

By that stage I had worked out that good house-sits were hard to find and getting an interview was even harder, so I was doing everything I could to impress. I had struck house-sitting gold.

I sat primly on the edge of their worn leather sofa, stroking a warm bundle of sharp claws and wet snuffles. Miss Prissy Knickers took the floor to talk about housekeeping (there are some benefits to having her around) and the owners were impressed. They showed me around the place I was hoping to call home for the next two months and I gushed with enthusiasm at every opportunity. 'Gosh, three litter trays indoors. That's a good idea. I suppose you can't have too many.'

'There's another one in the ensuite bathroom,' said Miriam.

'That's handy,' I said, wondering why any cat would need four litter trays. And who in their right minds would put a smelly litter tray in an ensuite bathroom? I said nothing. I wasn't about to jeopardise my chances by showing any sign of discontent. Miriam opened a cupboard in the kitchen crammed full of tiny cartons of premium cat food, stacked up like gold bullion. She popped open a foil tray of tasty paté with chicken and turkey and scooped the contents into a pink plastic dish.

'Itsy Bitsy! Tania!'

A wisp of smoke from Harry Potter leapt onto the counter, closely followed by the feline equivalent of Beyoncé after a bad blow-dry.

'Hang on, Princess,' said Miriam, as Beyoncé pressed herself shamelessly against Miriam's ample breasts. I expected her to sweep the cats off the counter, scold them for daring to jump onto a surface used to prepare food, but instead she popped open another foil carton and tipped the contents onto a gold-rimmed plate. She placed the meals side by side and Itsy Bitsy and Tania settled down to eat, on the kitchen counter.

'Ah, so you actually feed the cats . . . on the . . .' I let the unfinished sentence drift away. I needed this house.

The magic words 'Royal Flying Doctor Service' clinched the deal and I thanked my lucky stars that they asked my boss for a reference, not the owners of the house I'd been renting in Birchgrove. I'm not sure they would have given me one, not after the accident – although before we go any further, let me just say it could have happened to anyone and the insurance will pay, I checked.

I'd been giving the house a decent clean before I moved out and the flimsy bedroom curtain kept getting sucked into the nozzle of the vacuum cleaner, so I did what anyone would have done. I looped the curtain over a floor lamp. What I didn't appreciate was that the lamp faced upwards, exposing the halogen bulb. Halogen bulbs get very hot. Exceptionally hot. I went downstairs to mop the floors and forgot about the curtain until I smelt smoke. I raced back up to the bedroom and found a sheet of flame about to set fire to the window. I acted swiftly and decisively. First I tried beating the flames out with my shoe but that sent burning embers flying around the room, setting off smaller fires on the expensive-looking rug. So I raced downstairs, grabbed the bucket of water I'd been using to mop the floors, ran back up and threw it at the window, then stamped on the burning embers to limit the scorch marks. It's fair to say it left a bit of a mess.

Like my life really.

*

So there I was, installed in a large house overlooking the beach in one of the most desirable suburbs of Sydney, pouring over six pages of closely typed notes on how to look after two cats and a dog. It was a dream house, I was lucky beyond words and I should have been grateful – I *was* grateful – but it felt unexpectedly lonely to step into someone else's life and pick up on their daily routine, surrounded by family photographs and mementos of important events that mattered to other people, not to me. I missed CC. A mood of despondency settled like mist hovering on the Yorkshire moors in winter.

I turned to the animals, hoping for solace. Casper, the terrier-type with a shaggy pale coat and black button nose, was an elderly good-natured sloth. He ignored a lead shaken enthusiastically in front of his face, closed his eyes at the word 'walkies' and wasn't remotely interested in chasing a ball. Open a packet of biscuits and it was another story. When that happened, Casper was instantly by my side, tail wagging, tongue lolling out of his mouth. Without the prospect of food Casper was content to slump on my lap, snoring loudly. I liked Casper.

Itsy Bitsy was something else. A coal black Siamese shadow of uncertainty, she hugged the walls and avoided all contact, slinking behind the sofa, mistrusting any attempts at friendship. She would take some coaxing. Then there was Tania, the pink Persian Princess with baby blue eyes who looked like she had recently climbed out of bed and was disappointed to find no one willing to comb her hair. The world was fortunate to be graced with Princess Tania's presence.

On the first night, I encouraged Casper into the laundry with soothing words of welcome. According to the notes, he was meant to sleep in the laundry with Itsy Bitsy. I thought it seemed odd to shut a cat and dog into a small room together for several hours each night, but that's what the notes said so that's what I did. I was taking my responsibilities seriously. Casper eventually succumbed to a treat left in his basket but Itsy Bitsy looked at me as if to say, 'The laundry? I don't think so.' She stalked away, tail swishing, her body language suggesting this was the first she had ever heard of sleeping in the laundry and she wasn't best pleased with the idea. I double-checked the notes. *Itsy Bitsy must be shut into the laundry each night with Casper.* He was already there, lying docile in his bed next to the washing machine, so I soothed and stroked the Siamese in an effort to allay her fears. 'There, there, little kitty, it's all right Itsy Bitsy, time for bed.' She bit me.

I wrenched my hand out of her mouth, mopped up the blood, dabbed tea-tree oil onto my swelling finger (well, it worked in Bali) and tried again, this time coaxing her into the laundry with morsels of fresh meat, dangled just out of reach. The smell of raw flesh did the trick and the vicious beast was soon locked up for the night. Sorry, Itsy Bitsy was soon safely ensconced in her cosy bed in the laundry.

That just left the Queen of the Fairies. According to the notes, Tania was allowed to go anywhere; she had the run of the house, any time of the day or night, which included sleeping on the owners' bed. Not under my watch, it didn't. I checked that the various litter trays were clean and accessible, positioned one immediately outside the bedroom door and left her to roam.

Battlelines were drawn the next morning when I opened the bedroom door and found a stinking swirl of cat shit sinking into what looked like a horribly expensive floor runner. The litter trays Tania could have used, including the one I considerately placed right outside the bedroom door, were untouched. I stepped over the stinking pile, opened the laundry door and Itsy Bitsy shot past, leaving behind the acrid smell of cat piss mixed with old wool and wet dog. Casper was lying in his bed, no doubt waiting patiently for the sound of a packet to be opened, and I knelt down to sniff his coat. The stench had me scrabbling to my feet. At some point during that long night Itsy Bitsy must have peed on Casper and he and his bedding now stank of cat piss. When he did finally rouse himself, Casper reacted to this indignity by trotting into the lounge room and crapping on another expensive carpet. I reached for the disinfectant. It was a mistake to turn my back because while I was cleaning up the mess, Tania sneaked into the bedroom, peed on the mat in the ensuite bathroom and squatted beside the litter tray – not in it – to deposit another evil-smelling mess on the tiled floor. She skipped away as I approached, innocent of all wrongdoing.

The house was like a war zone, with stink bombs the main weapon. If I'd dragged a doggy bin into the corridor and upended it there would have been less mess, and at least then the shit would have been in those neat little plastic bags. I tried not to panic and spent the day frantically washing the dog, hosing down the laundry, spot-cleaning the carpet, swabbing the floors and disinfecting dog blankets. Itsy Bitsy was sprawled on the floor in the lounge room, watching me from a distance. She stared malevolently through the narrowest slit in one eye, a splinter of black running down the centre of her green iris like a dribble of blood.

As the day wore on I brushed Casper, combed Tania, avoided Itsy Bitsy, emptied *all* the litter trays, fed the cats, failed to coax Casper into taking the walk he was meant to have every day and shuddered at the thought of the amount of excrement three animals might deposit on the owners' expensive carpets over the next two months. I also discovered Princess Tania had a delicate stomach. Judging by the size of the fur ball she coughed up that afternoon I assumed she must have been saving it for weeks. Wrong. She could part her miniature teeth, give a delicate cough and produce a slimy fur ball at will. It was her party piece, like a magician pulling a rabbit out of a hat (although in her case the rabbit was slippery with mucus and smelt of undigested cat food). Given the amount of hair Princess had, and her propensity to groom herself in a desultory sort of way like a sulky teenager checking for split ends, I had a feeling there would be a lot of fur balls.

I made a mental note to buy rubber gloves and more disinfectant the next time I went shopping.

I woke up on Monday morning and consoled myself with the thought that I had free lodging for the next two months as well as a tranquil spot in which to write the bestselling novel Metro Mike had spoken about (although admittedly he had never actually used the words 'bestseller' – or even 'novel' come to that – which means he could have been talking about marketing brochures). I'd been trying to write a book for a couple of years, scribbling notes about the life of a courageous woman in her mid-sixties who overcame huge obstacles to create a new life for herself in France. Her determination to follow her dream had been a source of constant inspiration for me. I lay in that sweet spot between sleep and wakefulness and let my mind wander back to the last time we had met.

The dream-like state I drifted into was interrupted, not by the alarm clock, but by the reason Miriam and Jack went away for two months. At seven o'clock on the dot the building next door exploded into life. The terrifying screeching sound gathered pace and volume until there was a veritable Dickensian symphony of wrenching, grasping, creaking, scratching, grinding, hammering, sawing and sanding rage that shattered the peace and quiet of my secluded house-sit haven.

Legions of sparkies, brickies, carpenters, tilers and labourers had descended and they all seemed to be at work simultaneously. They had to shout to make themselves heard above the constant thump of music (played at high volume so they could hear it above the shouting) and when the floor sander, jigsaw and jack-hammer joined in they were forced to shout all the louder. The thudding bassline that accompanied the music was a machine that slammed outdoor pavers into place and the treble was a concrete saw. Not surprisingly, there was no one living in the half-finished house emerging out of the ground on the adjacent plot – a house I had failed to notice and which the owners had failed to mention during the interview (which, now I remember, took place on a Sunday), so the builders had free reign to make as much noise as they liked.

I found the quietest spot in the house and sat down to concentrate on writing copy for the next Flying Doctor newsletter. Casper fell asleep at my feet, snoring like a drunken Falstaff. So much for the peaceful stint in Santorini.

When I couldn't stand the noise any longer I walked the streets of Coogee with Casper, trying to shake off my bad mood. Every second car seemed to be a 4WD or an SUV, most of them with stickers in the back proclaiming there was a baby on board. Were they boasting to make the rest of us who didn't have children feel inadequate? Were they telling other drivers to take extra care, so if I was driving behind one of those yummy mummies (that's if I had a car, fat chance) I would see that sign and think, 'Ah yes, I'd better not crash into that car, there's a baby on board; I'll crash into someone else instead.' Maybe the sign was meant to face the other way, to remind the driver not to leave the baby in the car or to remember to go back and get it from the supermarket.

Baby on board. Bun in the oven. Up the duff. The signs irritated me beyond belief and I wanted to shout at the smug-looking drivers. 'I was fertile and fecund once too, you know!'

If ever I was, it was a long time ago. There was no point regretting what might have been; I hadn't been mature enough to handle relationships so what hope would I have had as a mother? The thought that I could probably add CC to the list of failed relationships made me jam my hands into my pockets and dig my fingernails into the palms of my hands to stop the tears that could so easily have fallen. I trudged back to the house, dragging the recalcitrant Casper behind me.

Noise levels dropped at lunchtime and the radio jingles were interspersed with snatches of conversation.

'Haven't seen Mick around for a while.'

'Nah, he's taken a couple weeks off. His missus just had a baby.'

'Good man.'

'Yeah but she's got a problem with her utopian tubes. They reckon she's suffering from post-natal dementia.'

Poor woman. Fertile and fecund she may have been but utopian dementia beckoned.

*

My nephew Tom arrived from England, for what would probably be his one and only visit to Australia. Instead of the exciting

Sydney experience he was hoping for, he found himself sharing a house with three incontinent animals and an irascible aunt who was growing more like Itsy Bitsy by the day. From a long-term single to head of a household of five souls, it felt like I was trying on family life for size, seeing how it fitted. I wasn't sure it did.

And CC still hadn't called.

By the end of the second week Casper wouldn't stop scratching. Tom rolled him over to see if his skin was inflamed and we found a large lump. Cancer? A boil? A tick? I checked the closely typed pages of notes and learnt ticks could kill dogs. *They're often found in the nature strip at the end of the street.* Hang on, though, that was where they told me Casper liked to walk (on the rare occasions he could be persuaded to go for a walk). Half an hour before the vet closed for the night, we were waiting anxiously to be seen, the snorting, scratching Casper lying at my feet.

'Fleas,' the vet said. 'This animal has fleas, and a bad case of them too.'

'There are cats in the house,' I said. 'Will they have fleas too?'

The vet laughed. 'That's probably where he got them from,' he said.

We went back to the house to check and it was true: the cats were riddled with microscopic black specks that leapt into the air as soon as they were exposed.

We treated Crapper, Witchy and the Pissy Princess (sorry, Casper, Itsy Bitsy and Tania) for fleas and a frenzy of washing followed. Ever since Tania's tantrum on the first night, she had slept on the bed (the nightly consequence of shutting her out was too gruesome) so everything had to be flung in the wash: doonas, doona covers, pillows, pillowcases, clothes, dog blankets, cat beds. Only when the washing line was full of flapping sheets did I think to google, 'how to rid a house of fleas'. Washing wouldn't kill them, apparently. Several cans of flea spray later I read the warning on the side of the can: 'May cause an allergic reaction.' The round of washing started again.

By week three I was a bag of nerves. Close scrutiny of the notes revealed nothing about fleas or flea treatment but it did reveal that Tania was **on no account to go out unaccompanied**. What is it about words underlined in bold print? The thick black type is meant to make you sit up and take notice but that's the bit I always skip. Tom had been retrieving Tania for the past week, thinking she'd escaped, whereas I had simply been letting her out, **unaccompanied**. I was suddenly terrified she would go missing. But how are you meant to accompany a cat that can leap tall fences, squeeze under gates, run faster than an Olympic sprinter and disappear in the time it takes to trip over a fur ball?

I compromised and accompanied Tania as far as the patio, then I watched her disappear, hoping she would come back. There was no point keeping the doors and windows shut because according to the notes, Itsy Bitsy **had to** be allowed out, whenever she wanted. That was normally via the laundry door and she couldn't possibly come back in the same way (something to do with not retracing her steps – some secret Witchy black cat business no doubt), so each time she was let out she would walk to the other side of the house and bang on the screen door to be let back in. She performed that exact manoeuvre at least a dozen times every day, and a dozen times a day I got up to let her in.

One day I got tired of the whole business so I let her bang on the screen door for a while without responding. Before long there was a different noise. I got up to check and there was the silhouette of Itsy Bitsy, halfway up the screen door, legs splayed out like a cartoon cat, claws gripping the mesh like a lizard. Having successfully scaled the screen door, she was trying to push the handle with her front paw to open it, which was an extremely clever trick and made me even more convinced she was a witch.

My stress levels rose to match the decibels being produced next door.

The evidence of fleas led to Tania's renewed banishment from the bedroom and once again the Persian Princess exacted the usual punishment, refusing to use any of her litter trays. What is it about cat shit? Unlike dog shit, which seems designed to be easily disposed of, the mess cats excrete has a different consistency, especially when deposited on a shag-pile carpet. I scraped up the mess, spot cleaned the carpet and covered the entire corridor in newspaper. That worked until I went out one morning and forgot to close the bedroom door. Not only did Tania sleep on the bed while I was gone – the long strands of Persian Princess hair were unmistakeable – she also peed on it. There were four perfectly clean litter trays scattered about the house and Tania left a stinking yellow stain of such magnitude that it soaked right through the doona as well as the top and bottom sheets. CC would have been horrified. He would have booted the cat out of the bedroom and then sent the owners an email suggesting their cat had met with a mysterious accident, and we would have had a good laugh about it. But CC wasn't there. In all likelihood he was courting someone else by now. Courting. What an old-fashioned word. I had never used that word about a lover or a boyfriend before but looking back, I realised that's what it had been. I had been courted by CC, and I missed him. I pulled the bedding off and jammed it into the washing machine.

The final straw was when funny, fat lazybones Casper, the friendly companion whose tiny head and warm body were designed to rest comfortably on a lap like a stuffed pyjama case, decided he'd had enough of being dragged outside for a walk and took to crapping behind the sofa. The whole house was beginning to resemble a giant toilet.

Tom decided to go back to England and I couldn't blame him. For a young lad in his early twenties he was surprisingly mature. He didn't get too worked up about life and he knew what he wanted and what he didn't want. He certainly didn't want to be living with his aunt in an oversized toilet, that's for sure.

chapter twenty-two

Something about the light filtering through the vertical blinds made me want to stay in bed. In England I could wake up and know instantly if snow had fallen outside; it was something about the translucency, a kind of hushed, expectant silence and a thicker than normal atmosphere. Pulling back the curtains on a snowy morning would reveal a blanket of white covering the ground, fullness pressing against the windows. This morning here in Sydney the light wasn't white. It was orange.

I got out of bed and lifted the blinds. A thick haze of orange fog hung in the streets. The sun looked like the circle on a Japanese flag. An eerie orange glow pervaded the whole house and my first thought was bushfire, but there was no smell of burning, besides which late September wasn't bushfire season. I fed the animals, cleaned up the nightly mess and switched on the radio.

'Those with asthma and heart conditions are being warned to stay indoors. Flights in and out of Sydney airport have been cancelled and all ferries have stopped running.'

What the hell had happened?

I switched on the television news and saw images of Sydney Harbour Bridge enveloped in a red haze so thick it was impossible to see from one side to the other.

'Some Sydney residents are reporting birds falling out of the sky, with reduced visibility across the city and widespread disruption to travel. The Bureau of Meteorology has issued a severe weather warning for damaging winds in Sydney and across parts of New South Wales,' said the presenter. 'Just to recap on this morning's news, residents of Sydney have woken to what some have described as a "Red Dawn", a dust storm so vast it can be seen from space. The huge storm travelled overnight, at speeds of up to 100 kilometres an hour, reducing visibility across the city and forcing the cancellation of hundreds of flights and ferries. The choking clouds of dust have wreaked havoc across much of the state.'

The only good thing about the storm was the shut down of all major construction work. For once the house next door would be silent.

Later that morning a friend sent me a link to a video clip on YouTube. It had been taken the day before, in mid-afternoon, and I watched a shaky camera film red sky and rooftops, not dissimilar to the sky I'd seen that morning in Sydney. Moments later a cloud of dust rolled across the screen and it darkened, turning black so quickly I thought the person filming must have dropped the camera. The only indication they hadn't was the soundtrack. 'Oh wow. Shit, that's black. We'd better go inside.'

The video clip had been taken in Broken Hill.

The CSIRO estimated sixteen million tonnes of dust had been picked up from the deserts of central Australia and swept towards the sea. The dust reached as far as New Zealand. The storm had travelled at over 100 kilometres an hour and it slammed into Broken Hill before anyone could prepare for it.

People were stranded in their cars and electricity to the entire town was cut.

I rang CC, heart thudding as I waited for him to pick up.

'I saw a video clip of the dust storm. Are you OK?'

'We'll live.'

'I was worried about you.'

His voice softened. 'I heard it was bad in Sydney as well.'

'At least we could still see.'

'The worst of it's over. The aircraft were grounded and there's a lot of clearing up to be done but it was only dust.'

'That was a lot of dust.'

'It's the graziers I feel sorry for.'

'How come?'

'People on properties have been doing it tough. The drought's been with them ten years now and that dust storm was the last straw. What sheep they had left were struggling anyway, and sand from a storm that big gets caught in their wool. Some of them just keel over with the weight of it and they can't get up again. They get buried alive. Those that do survive will be impossible to shear. The dust blunts the shears. Hang on a sec –'

CC put his hand over the mouthpiece and I could hear phones ringing in the background. He mumbled something I couldn't catch, then reappeared.

'I have to go –'

'How are you? How's work?' I asked, not wanting him to hang up.

'Busy. I've got a meeting in Tassie next week . . . the usual.' There was a pause and I wondered if he was still there. 'The week after, I'm in Sydney.'

His words hung in the silence between us, so I took a deep breath and plunged in.

'Would you like to meet up?'

I'd had plenty of time in the preceding weeks to reflect on what had gone wrong and I realised I had survived a storm of my own making. I'd been unable to see through a haze of smoke left over from a fire that had burnt out long ago, and I hadn't appreciated being with CC.

I'd been foolish (and more than a little insensitive) in inviting A3 to stay when CC wasn't there, and I had failed to appreciate his point of view, stubbornly digging in my heels and stoking the fires of moral outrage at his lack of trust. When I stopped to consider how I might have felt if the circumstances had been reversed, I had to acknowledge that I would have felt jealous and suspicious too, perhaps not to the degree CC had, but that was just a function of personality types.

I'd also had time to reflect on what Metro Mike had said, about there being three women around CC, all of whom would make suitable partners. I hoped I wasn't too late.

We arranged to meet on the steps of the Opera House. I was there half an hour early so I spotted him well before he saw me, picking him out by the myriad tiny details that were uniquely his – the slim frame, the slight forward stoop of his shoulders and the way he sometimes closed his fingers on his hands when he walked with purpose, like he did now. In place of the usual tracksuit pants and rugby jumper, he wore jeans and a pale blue fitted shirt, and I have to say he was drop-dead movie star gorgeousness personified, from the top of his silky white hair to the tips of his RM Williams boots.

I knew then that I wanted to be with him; how long for, I couldn't honestly say and I didn't care either, because for once in my life I wasn't thinking about outcomes or happy ever after endings. It was the here and now I cared about. I cared about CC. He was the most considerate, attractive man I'd ever met and in all the time we'd spent together I'd never once had to pretend to be smarter, fitter, sexier or better read than I really was. I hadn't worried (no more than I would normally) if the outfits I wore weren't slimming and I could wear sandals without thinking, 'Do my bunions look big in these?' (The answer was yes, they always did.)

'Hello, Frosty.'

'Hello.'

It was no *Gone with the Wind* reunion – we had too much talking to do first – just a smile and a simple peck on the cheek.

'Shall we walk in the Botanical Gardens?'

I'd always been able to talk to CC, from our very first date, and it was a relief to find a quiet spot among the Moreton Bay figs and unburden the ugly truth I'd been hiding. I confessed the whole sorry stalking business and felt lighter with each sentence.

'Yes, I loved him but that was a long time ago. I worshipped the ground he walked on,' I said, 'and he didn't love me. I'm sorry I invited him to stay; I shouldn't have done that, but please believe me when I say that nothing happened. Even if he had made a pass at me – which he didn't, by the way – nothing would have come of it. It's been four years now, I've seen him many times and nothing has ever happened. He hasn't shown the slightest interest in me and I've always known in my heart that we weren't right for each other.'

'You should have told me.'

'I know, and I'm sorry I didn't.'

In return, CC offered his own confession about a relationship he'd had that didn't surprise me.

'It was over before you and I got together,' he said. 'Both of us knew it wouldn't last.'

'Would you go back to it, even if you and I –?'

'No.'

We walked for a while, following the foreshore path towards Mrs Macquarie's Chair, then we climbed a flight of steps to find another shady spot.

'What about the third woman?' I asked.

He picked a blade of grass and rubbed it between his fingers, looking into the distance. 'That's harder,' he said. 'That could be one of several.'

'What?'

The shock must have shown on my face because he laughed. 'Lighten up, Frosty, I have no idea who that might be. You'll have to keep your eyes open.'

And I laughed too.

'What's the house-sit like?' he asked.

'You can come and see it if you like; that's if you don't mind a dog that's got fleas or cats that crap on the carpet or —'

'I'd like that.'

We caught the bus to Coogee. In spite of the immaculately maintained house he was accustomed to living in, CC professed not to care about the cat hairs on the kitchen counter and the smell of cat pee on Casper's coat, or the cat litter trays in the lounge room. If he did object, he sweetly said nothing and we were reconciled, with kindness, good humour and quiet grace on both sides.

*

Over brunch in a local café the next day we agreed that when the house-sit finished, as it would soon, we should try living together. That would mean me moving to Broken Hill. We both wanted to make it work and my biggest fear . . . actually I didn't have a single biggest fear, I had a snake pit full of them. I was afraid our relationship might not work (an oldie but a goodie) and I worried I might not cope with life in a mining town in the middle of the desert. With no friends in Broken Hill, and very little paid work, not only would I be financially dependent on CC, I'd also be reliant on him emotionally. For a lot of the time it would be just the two of us. Then I worried I'd be a rubbish writer, afraid of snakes, terrified of spiders, allergic to sand, scared of pink velour. You get the picture.

'There's one other thing,' said CC.

'What's that?'

'A pre-nup.'

My notions of what constituted love and romance (which by that stage were about as threadbare as Casper's blanket after endless washing cycles to remove the smell of cat pee) were threatened by the idea of a contractual agreement. The only people I had ever borrowed money from (I hope) were my parents and my friend Jane, who once lent me £250 to get to France. Since leaving home I had been financially independent; I hadn't always made the wisest financial decisions (I can hear the hollow laughter of friends and family now) but I had made those decisions and I had suffered the consequences. Buying and selling flats in London had generated and subsequently obliterated significant amounts. If pressed I would have said I didn't have much financial acumen – you wouldn't expect me ever to win at Monopoly – but I had always survived and I had *never* been financially dependent on a man. I considered myself a pretty decent person and if anything were to go wrong with our relationship, I would simply walk away (woah boy, there goes that high horse again).

So I had to put myself in CC's shoes. He'd fallen in love with a woman fifteen years his junior, who constantly kept saying I like you, not I love you, and maybe a binding financial agreement was his equivalent of standing on the bank. He had assets and he didn't want them to be swept downstream if the relationship failed.

If I'd thought CC had been unromantic before the topic of pre-nups came up (sorry, binding financial agreements, BFA, let no one think we were about to get married), then once the subject was on the table CC's actuarial approach made his previous behaviour seem positively Mills & Boon.

'Never confuse love and money,' said CC. 'I'm very careful when it comes to the latter.'

And he was. I was far more cavalier, which is probably why he had so much of the stuff and I had so little. In a funny way, that gave me a certain freedom; having so little to lose, it was easier to contemplate embarking on a crazy project at the age of fifty. Leaving aside the whole question of living with CC, I would be moving to a mining town in the middle of the outback in order to write the biography of Jane, a woman I'd met in London who had subsequently moved to a cottage in France. The thought did cross my mind that an old barn in the Loire Valley might be more conducive to writing Jane's story but beggars can't be choosers and I was, when all was said and done, extremely fortunate that I would have CC's support while I battled to finish the book.

The final hurdle was crossed after a tetchy few weeks with an aggressive lawyer, until I ditched him and found a woman who completely got that I didn't want anything from CC if the relationship hit the rocks: I was signing the BFA to give him peace of mind, not me. I came with nothing and I fully intended to leave that way if it didn't work out. As soon as the agreement was signed, CC went back to being his usual calm, considerate self.

That left me to do all the fretting. It didn't help that any time I mentioned the words 'Broken Hill' to friends in Sydney they would invariably reply with something along the lines of, 'Don't worry, it won't be forever, you can always come back if it doesn't work out.' Often they simply looked blank and said, 'Where?' The answer provoked a look of anxious concern. Not one person said, 'Hey, fantastic!'

Miriam and Jack eventually came back from Canada (I'm sorry about the carpet) and I handed back responsibility for their precious pets with a huge sigh of relief. Broken Hill beckoned.

I was jumping in at the deep end and it didn't get much deeper.

chapter twenty-three

I moved to Broken Hill in autumn, my favourite time of year in England when apple trees laden with fruit bend heavy branches to the ground and long drawn-out evenings are filled with the sound of bonfires crackling in the chill damp air. 'Season of mists and mellow fruitfulness,' according to Keats. Not in Broken Hill it's not.

Excuse me for saying this, but the weather in Broken Hill arrives like a whore on a weekend trip to an oil rig. It slams into town, gets the job done and then shoots through. Dust storms can turn day into night in seconds, rare cloudbursts have been known to dump six months' worth of rain in a few hours, and forked lightning can start bushfires that rage for days. Most of the time, though, it's hot and dry in summer and cold and dry in winter.

The epic dust storm that slammed into Broken Hill and then raged across the southern half of Australia in September marked the end of a decade-long drought. Rain fell in torrents across most of the eastern seaboard as well as many inland areas. Drenching, flooding rain. In the sweaty, steamy months that followed, nature did its thing. Grass grew in the desert, crops flourished further south and insects multiplied. Like specks of dust in a haze of smoke, the insects went on the move – mating, eating, moving, mating, eating, moving out on those vast empty plains – and the only thing that got in their way was Broken Hill. The locusts arrived with explosive force, erupting like the forces of evil from Pandora's box.

I arrived at about the same time.

'I've got a spare bicycle you can use to get around town if you like,' said CC.

Cycling to the post office that first day was like riding through a series of puddles, brackish water splashing up to my calves, only it wasn't water, it was locusts. The fluttering, clacking noise of a swarm of insects shooting into the air as I rode through them conjured up childhood memories of pegging pieces of cardboard onto the spokes of our bicycle wheels for the joy of hearing it flutter. That was fun. This was frightening.

The roads were thick with squashed insects, and windows were plastered with them. Shopkeepers had to sweep a path through piles of dead bodies – locusts that had crawled in and died overnight – before early morning customers could reach the checkout. Swimmers at the pool ran the risk of swallowing mouthfuls of locusts on each inward breath; only a hardy and committed few ventured in. CC was among them. Was he trying to show me that it didn't matter? That a plague of locusts was nothing to worry about? I'd never experienced anything like it. Children playing on the grass at the edge of the pool ran screaming with delight through carpets of insects that rose in a noisy black cloud before settling back down to the job of mating and eating.

I retreated indoors and read the *Barrier Daily Truth*, Broken Hill's local paper, watching insects flinging themselves at the screen door. According to the paper, this was the start of what

234

might lead to a major infestation. Might? How did this not *already* rank as a major infestation? The article pointed out that 'one female can lay between 250 and 300 eggs'. Apparently Broken Hill and the surrounding area was where those eggs might hatch the following spring.

CC's house was a welcome fortress against the locusts, moths and crickets that swarmed around any available light source so I shut the doors and windows and stayed in until the infestation passed. The evaporative air-conditioner was set to maximum. The system blew air across a curtain of water trickling down vertical panels on a box outside then circulated that 'wet' air inside. It was a neat system but it could only reduce the temperature by three or four degrees so it was still hot, thirty-two degrees of hot, and it wasn't even summer.

A more effective defence against the heat were the trees that CC had planted on all sides of the house, and several grape-vines smothering the walls. The garden looked prettier than I remembered (even when viewed through windows smeared in dead locusts). Six old-fashioned standard roses bloomed near the back fence and the lawn was surprisingly green (my father had exacting standards when it came to lawns and CC's would have passed with flying colours). There were daisy bushes and fruit trees and a near empty bed to one side that, given the amount of sun there was in Broken Hill, could do quite well as a vegetable patch.

The plague of locusts left as quickly as it had arrived and by the weekend all that remained was a mass of dead bodies and a bad smell.

The older I get, the more I like gardening. It can put colour in your cheeks, it's mucky and you can do it in front of the neighbours, according to the folks at the BBC. Gardening's the new sex, didn't you know? All I knew was that I never really felt at home in a new place until I got a garden sorted.

CC's shed was a gloomy storeroom holding thirty years of someone else's story, cloaked in red dust. Furniture, cartons, trunks and boxes were all closely wrapped in plastic – and coated with a thick layer of dust. I moved slowly through the dark heat, looking for tools and compost to fork into the sandy soil.

I found the compost beside a delicate mess of spiders' webs. I dragged the bags into the light, brushing away the remnants of brittle webs that crumpled like ancient paper doilies.

Having read stories of spiders biting bushies on the bum when they spent too long in the dunny (it hadn't taken long to knock the edges off my English grammar school education), I thought it best to play safe and I hauled the old compost bags towards the house.

CC looked up from his computer when I tapped on the study window.

'Do I need to worry about spiders?' I asked, indicating the bags of compost at my feet. CC shook his head and I started shovelling compost onto the sunny strip of garden that might one day be a veggie patch. Closer examination of one of the bags revealed a tiny speck of spider clinging to the plastic, half the size of a small fingernail. I went back to the window.

'What if I find a really small spider with a dash of red on it?'

The sound of the screen door slamming against the wall was like a sonic boom – I swear CC reached me before I'd finished the sentence.

'Show me,' he said.

I pointed to the small spider and CC grabbed a stick, knocked the unassuming creature off the bag and stamped on it with his RM Williams boot, grinding it into the dirt for good measure.

'Oh, so, "Spiders aren't something to worry about," you said. "Perfectly harmless creatures, not worth bothering with," oh no, what a lot of fuss over noth –'

'Frosty.'

His voice cut through the sarcasm I couldn't contain. It was the look on his face that spooked me.

'That was a red-back. If you see any more of those, you should kill them.'

How could something so tiny be so venomous? Like everyone, I'd heard of red-back spiders but I'd never actually seen one before. It must have been a while since CC had spent any time in his garden because by the end of the afternoon I'd found nine more. There were red-backs behind the brick barbecue, under the rim of a pot plant, hidden in the handle of the hose reel and one even tucked into a corner of the aluminium frame on the bathroom window. The webs were easy to spot – messy and strung low to the ground – so at least they gave the game away, but each new discovery put a dampener on my enthusiasm for growing vegetables. Especially when several days later I found one of the telltale webs stretched between my side of the bed and the bedside table. CC was away so I slept on the sofa. (The spider was long gone but the toxic fumes from a full can of fly spray took a while to clear). 'It must have come in on your clothes,' CC said when he got back. That didn't reassure me.

Most of my ideas about Broken Hill were based on Kenneth Cook's brilliant novel *Wake in Fright*, made into a film in the early 70s, that depicted Broken Hill (called Bundanyabba but everyone knew it was the Hill) as a lawless place of excessive drinking, out-of-control gambling, alcohol-fuelled violence, inescapable dust and searing heat. The main character (a prissy young man from Sydney, no less) gets sucked into a game of two-up, loses all his money and slides into a swampland of moral turpitude, gratuitous violence and self-degradation – not the best book to have read before I moved to Broken Hill. Maybe I should have watched *The Adventures of Priscilla, Queen of the Desert* instead.

As if to reinforce the extensive research I'd done, on my first shopping trip to Woolies a sunburnt grizzly in leather chaps, Akubra hat, cowboy boots and grubby denim work shirt joined the queue. He had a hunting knife tied to his belt that would have made Crocodile Dundee weep with envy.

I was ready to hate the place, prepared to grit my teeth and get through it, all the time secretly thinking I'd give up after a few months and flee back to Sydney. (I wasn't the only one; CC has since admitted he gave me six months, at most.)

*

'You know what? You're not getting the full Broken Hill experience.'

'What am I missing?'

'A creek-bed barbecue. Come on, it won't get dark for a couple of hours.'

We found a battered old saucepan in the shed, its handle replaced by a length of twisted wire looped over the top. I stood back, worried about red-backs.

CC muttered as he searched. 'It's in here somewhere.'

'What is?'

'The frying pan.'

Worryingly, he found the frying pan in a kitchen cupboard: a blackened, barely recognisable thing encrusted with layers of carbon.

'Did you know burnt food causes cancer?'

'Live a little, Frosty.'

He was right, of course. I should stop worrying about snakes and spiders, and the isolation and open space, or I wouldn't get the full Broken Hill experience. The problem was, I wasn't sure I wanted the full Broken Hill experience. The prospect of heading out to a lonely creek bed for a barbecue in the dead of night (sorry, early evening) was the inland equivalent of swimming in Sydney Harbour, something I've never liked doing. Even in a sheltered bay, you don't know how deep the water is or what's circling unseen under the dark, glistening surface. The desert gave me that same feeling. There was something unnerving about being surrounded by so much empty space.

Fifteen minutes later the boot of the car was crammed with camping chairs, an axe, a shovel and an esky with water, steak, eggs, bread and oil. A cardboard box held a frying pan, a saucepan and the makings of tea and coffee, and before you could say 'drover's dog', we were on a dirt road heading out of town, with no mobile signal and not another car in sight. It all happened very quickly.

'You know, it's odd, I dreamt we went out to the desert last night,' said CC.

'That's weird.'

'And a bunch of thugs attacked us.'

'Not good.'

'I shot one of them to stop him attacking you.'

'Ah.'

'I would, you know.'

'What?'

'Kill someone to protect you.'

That was the closest CC got to romance. I think he thought it would reassure me. It had the opposite effect and silence seemed the only appropriate response. Moments later we veered off the dirt road onto a barely recognisable track, heading for a line of trees in the distance. The sand grew softer as the silence stretched on. CC stopped the car a short way from the trees and the silence settled around us like a shipwreck. The only signs of life were occasional sheep droppings.

'We'd better walk from here. We don't want to get bogged.'

No, we don't, I thought, especially as we have no mobile phone signal and you're a potentially murderous driver armed with an axe and a shovel in the back of the car. You could kill someone with that axe and then dig a grave in the sand with the shovel and no one would be any the wiser. See what I mean? Empty space made me nervous.

The creek bed was about fifteen metres wide and there were clear signs that water must have cut through this section of desert once, carving out clean walls of sand over a metre high. 'Waltzing Matilda' coolibah trees lined the creek bed, looking more dead than alive with their twisted, spindly limbs and elongated leaves. In the height of summer, you'd be glad of any shade you could get out here, and as we drew closer I could see there was life in the ancient trees yet, which was more than could be said for the rusting heap of metal just visible around a bend in the creek. Finding an abandoned car in an otherwise pristine environment, with no other sign of human intervention, was bizarre.

'Probably got washed down here in the last flood,' said CC.

'Flood?' I spun around and scanned the horizon. 'What's to stop it flooding now?'

'Relax, Frosty. The water that's on its way will take weeks to reach us.'

We found a suitable spot to make camp and settled our small blue camping chairs into the bed of soft sand, their backs against the carved wall opposite the trees. The chairs looked insignificant in such a vast landscape, like specks of ink mistakenly dropped onto a sheet of white paper.

'Hang on.'

CC climbed the bank and disappeared towards the car, leaving me alone with the flies in that hot, silent evening. I was instantly intimidated by the silence and empty space: fearful of embracing it, yet sensing that if I could, my soul might expand and grow.

A quiet, natural beauty resonated out there. 'Beauty is truth, truth beauty. That is all ye know on earth, and all ye need to know.' If I could just breathe deeply I might glimpse the harmony there was to be found within that silence. Was that why white space in a painting or silence on stage could sometimes feel so satisfying?

CC reappeared carrying the shovel. 'Is that for protection?' I asked. Sometimes I like winding him up.

'Frosty!'

He dug a shallow hole in the sand to form a fire pit and we collected wood, dragging dead branches thick as our thighs over the soft sand. We filled the depression with leaves and twigs and held a single match briefly to the dry leaves, which ignited with a whoosh of combusting eucalyptus oil. It was a reminder of the deadly potential of bushfires. There was no danger of that out here, though. We stoked the fire, lay a heavy branch across the middle and settled into our camp chairs, watching it burn through as the sun sank lower in the sky behind the line of coolibah trees.

A kingfisher made a brief appearance, making me wonder about an imminent Noah-like flood but it was too silent for that. We were alone apart from him, a clutch of galahs and a squawking cockatoo. Blackened tree branches stretched against an ink-splashed sky as charcoal smudges of cloud appeared, streaked in pink, yellow and orange.

Soon the glowing embers of the fire were perfect for frying steak and eggs so we settled the carbon-encrusted frying pan onto the fire and CC poured water into the battered saucepan, poking a stick through the wire loop to rest it on a glowing log. We were brewing the billy, Broken Hill-style.

Flies were a constant irritation – we must have looked like cartoon campers, heads enveloped in a cloud of flies, bodies and legs just visible underneath – yet I wasn't remotely tempted to suggest we go and sit in the car. With CC by my side, the emptiness wasn't intimidating, it was beautiful.

We ate quickly, outsmarting the flies that clustered at our lips. An egg sandwich had never tasted so good. The flies disappeared as soon as the sun did and when the first clutch of stars appeared I marvelled at how clear they were. It was just the beginning. Over the next twenty minutes the sky darkened and the Milky Way revealed itself in a dusting of stars that looked impossibly numerous, like fine powder thrown across the face of the universe, as clear as a child's breath on a cold winter morning. The pinpricks of light surpassed any dazzling firework display I'd seen in Sydney.

As the fire died down, we packed up the cooking gear, folded the chairs, doused the embers and stood together in silence, arms wrapped around each other, heads craned back to take in the beauty above us.

We both saw it, a shooting star, and without thinking I made a wish. *I wish I could spend the rest of my life with CC.* The words were in my head before I had time to judge or retract them.

chapter twenty-four

In the cold light of day the thought that CC and I might spend the rest of our lives together vanished, and the same old questions came flooding back. Did we really belong together? After so many years of desperately yearning to be with someone (usually someone unattainable), was this it? I was with the lovely CC and I felt scratchy and irritable. Why? Leaving aside the fact that I was living in a bungalow in Broken Hill, largely furnished in the equivalent of a pair of crimplene trousers, there was nothing wrong with our relationship. The heady rush of passion I'd been addicted to in the past had been replaced by a pervasive sense of wellbeing and peace: emotions so alien they made me feel anything but peaceful. CC picked up on my unease.

'Do you want your money back, Frosty?'

'Oh don't be silly, of course I don't.'

But did I? I felt isolated and alone. Broken Hill was a two-day drive from friends in Sydney and I was struggling with that sense of isolation. Yes, it gave me time to write, but it also made me totally reliant on CC. I'd never been in that situation before and

I wasn't sure I liked it. I hid my confusion in the *Barrier Daily Truth*, where an ad in the classified section caught my eye.

Layer pullets, commercial crossbreds, not debeaked, 12 wks (red, black, white) $14.00.

'What's a layer pullet?'

'A chook. A young one.' CC looked up from *The Australian*. 'Hens,' he said helpfully and went back to reading the paper.

Eggs were one of the few sources of protein we could agree on. I liked the thought of chickens roaming free in the back garden, scratching in the dirt or pecking at the grass, stopping occasionally to ruffle their feathers or lay another egg. Maybe this was the romantic dream of outback Australia I'd been searching for? I had a sudden picture of me in a straw hat with a basket on my arm, collecting fresh eggs every day. Chicken manure would fertilise the vegetable beds and we'd have freshly laid eggs with creamy yellow yolks for breakfast every day. Such an idyllic picture of rural bliss lifted my spirits instantly. Maybe chooks would help me survive the rigours of Broken Hill.

*

I'm a tip tragic, into waste in a big way. Not the junk CC worries about (if a bond's junk, why buy it?); I'm into the real thing, and there's plenty of it in Broken Hill. When it came to building a chook shed I drove straight to the tip, a fly-blown, fetid waste-land on the edge of town.

Residents of Broken Hill simply empty the contents of their trailers, trunks and pick-ups straight onto a patch of dirt bordered by chicken wire about two kilometres out of town, not far from the cemetery. Clouds of black crows circle overhead in ominous herald of unnatural deeds, barely waiting until the drivers have hurried back into their cars and slammed the doors before they swoop. It's like the end of the world, a post-apocalyptic nightmare rivalling anything you might see in *Mad Max*, with piles of rubbish strewn across the desert and no visible means of preventing it being blown all the way to Adelaide.

I loved it.

To be fair, the bit I loved was a shed the size of a small aircraft hangar that was perched at the entrance. Inside it, and stretched beyond it on the hard-packed earth out the back, were treasures worthy of *Steptoe and Son*, a rag and bone man's delight, plentiful enough to satisfy any junkie into serious junk. Someone – God knows who or how – had fought off the circling crows, picked their way through the detritus that other people had discarded and separated out the bits that could be salvaged. They'd even sorted them into categories. The result was an emporium of waste, laid out on the baked red earth under an intense blue Broken Hill sky. It was beautiful.

I picked up chicken wire, corrugated iron and bits of old timber, paid my five dollars and drove home to build a chook shed.

'Who threw that rubbish on the lawn?' CC remarked when he got home from work that night. I hadn't got around to assembling the shed as yet and its parts were displayed on the lawn.

'That,' I said proudly, 'is the makings of a chook shed.'

'We've got a perfectly good one already.'

'Where?'

'Behind the rose bushes.'

What I had thought was a makeshift storage area for logs and old timber turned out to be a chook shed. Several sheets of corrugated iron tacked against the fence formed a back wall; the sides were chicken wire and more sheets of iron on top formed a roof. (I hoped CC hadn't paid for the materials; there were plenty out at the tip.) About a metre wide by two metres long and almost tall enough to stand up in, it had a soft floor of red earth.

In short, the perfect chook shed. CC seemed pleased with the idea of getting chooks.

'We used to keep them years ago,' he said.

'Did you?'

'As long as you know they'll take a bit of looking after,' he added.

'Well I wasn't expecting them to look after themselves,' I said, slightly miffed at the idea his ex had also liked to keep chooks. I ordered four Red Leghorn crosses, to be delivered in three weeks' time, along with a feed bin and a water container.

A quick search through the second-hand section of Browzer's bookshop on Argent Street — it rivalled the tip in its collection of treasures — revealed a section on animal husbandry and I paid $2.50 for a slim pamphlet on how to care for chooks. 'They need somewhere safe to perch, nest and roost,' I declared, already an expert on the dos and don'ts of chook husbandry without the faintest clue what the difference between perching, nesting and roosting might be. CC nodded. He probably knew it all anyway but it was worth reminding him. 'And healthy, happy chickens can fight off disease,' I said.

'That makes sense.'

'So they should be free range.'

CC frowned. He looked as if he was about to object so I pointed to the booklet. 'It says chickens like to roam.'

'You're the one who likes gardening.'

I wasn't sure what he meant and I got the sense there was more he could add so, before he could say anything else, I turned the page. Our chickens would be free range and I would brook no argument. 'It says here that the more space chooks have, the happier and healthier they will be. And healthy, happy chooks lay more eggs.'

'Whatever you think, Frosty.'

The chook shed was (apparently) where the girls would perch during the day when they wanted a rest from all that free ranging, so having cleared the chook shed of old logs and dug over the dirt floor, I went in search of something they could perch on. The vast quantity of rubbish I'd dragged back from the tip contained nothing suitable (which was a surprise, given how much there was).

'There's an old broom handle in the shed,' said CC. 'They can perch on that.'

He retrieved the broom handle from the rafters and rammed it diagonally through the wire mesh sides. I was willing to concede CC had more practical experience than me in the whole business of chook husbandry but I couldn't help feeling there was a flaw in his plan. I pictured four chooks flying up to perch (or nest or roost; I was yet to work those out) on a circular broom handle, then I pictured them trying to grip the smooth, circular surface as it started to revolve. I could see them scrabbling for purchase as the broom spun faster and faster until the inevitable happened and all four chooks were flung into a heap in the far corner.

'Are you sure this will work?' I asked.

'Why not?'

'Look,' I said, spinning the broom handle and hoping he could visualise the problem.

'We need to fix it in place,' he said, heading for the shed and emerging moments later wearing safety goggles and carrying a drill.

'I'm not sure a round pole is the answer,' I said diplomatically. 'Won't they be happier on a flat piece of timber?'

CC started drilling. I deduced (correctly) that his mission was to get the chook shed set up as quickly as possible so he could get back to the tennis on television. I tapped him on the shoulder and shouted above the noise of the drill.

'Is this what you used before? A broom handle?'

He didn't answer, which meant no. Even if he did manage to fix the broom handle in place it looked alarmingly thin, more suited to a budgie than a fully grown chook. I rummaged through the rubbish I'd rescued from the tip again and found a flat piece of timber the right size, which I jammed into place on the opposite corner. 'Just so they have an option,' I said brightly, not wanting to discourage CC's efforts. We still had to sort out roosting and nesting and he was itching to get back to the tennis, I could tell.

'Now, what about roosting?' I said.

'Frosty, they'll roost in there,' he said, pointing to the chook shed.

'OK,' I said, still none the wiser. 'That just leaves nesting then.'

'That's what the crate was for,' he said, retreating back inside to catch the last of the tennis.

I retrieved the crate, which I'd thrown into the trailer-load of rubbish that was going back to the tip (against my better judgement), filled it with straw and placed it on its side in the chook shed. It was all so marvellously rustic and makeshift in a laid-back Aussie outback kind of way. I was starting to fit in, starting to belong in Broken Hill. The chooks wouldn't lay eggs for another ten weeks but that didn't matter; while we waited we could enjoy the sight of their beautiful brown feathers and red combs as they wandered through the garden. I charged my camera, ready to take photos of the flock quietly pecking at the lawn, and googled Hugh Fearnley-Whittingstall's recipes for eggs. I was feeling quietly pleased with myself. Food scraps wouldn't go to waste anymore and people who came to visit would say, 'Oh look, you've got chooks,' and I'd smile and say, 'Yes, free range, of course.'

The image of rural bliss lasted until lunchtime on the first day the chooks arrived, which was as long as it took for them to discover that tender young vegetables tasted better than grass. I spent most of my time slamming through the screen door, sliding across a patio smeared with chicken shit and racing across the garden to stop them eating the sweet peas, broad beans, beetroot, lettuce and cabbage I'd been nurturing in the newly planted vegetable plot.

Chooks are voracious feeders. Once they discovered there were baby vegetables on the menu, they ignored the lawn and got stuck into the leafy greens, producing vast quantities of manure as a result. There was crap everywhere, mostly outside the back door because the canny chooks worked out that food scraps occasionally emerged from there. When they weren't destroying the vegetable garden, they hung around the back door, crapping on the patio as they waited for me to emerge.

'Happy, healthy chooks lay more eggs,' CC said, standing at the window with his coffee and surveying the damage.

I rigged wire mesh around the broad beans and the chooks pushed their beaks through it, pecking the young plants until they were nothing but bare stalks. I tried finer mesh and the chooks worked out how to get under the barrier but not back out so they had to be rescued before panic set in and they trampled the plants they hadn't got round to eating. Once the chooks had worked their way through the broad beans, they turned their attention to the sweet peas – an old-fashioned variety, the seeds bought online at some considerable expense and nurtured in a pot for the past two months. Daily watering had encouraged tendrils to twine their way through a painted lattice nailed to the side of an old dog kennel. It was all looking oh so *House & Garden* magazine. I had swathed the sweet peas in fine white fabric, which kept them safe until sliding across the patio one morning I noticed the fabric was bulging and writhing. Four plump birds were concealed underneath, gorging themselves on every sweet pea I'd raised from seed until they were nothing but stalks too.

Strewn with wire mesh and covered in crap, the garden looked like a battlefield, the plants half eaten and the ground scraped into craters. Chooks can dig deeper than dogs. I spent my days scraping chicken shit off the patio, hosing down the paths and running round the vegetable beds, clapping and waving my hands, shouting 'Get off there!', causing the chooks to scatter in a flighty bundle of feathers, waddling and squawking until they settled back down to peck at the lawn. The minute my back was turned they were under the wire again.

Naming them was futile as they looked identical; even counting the pointy bits on their combs didn't help. One had a smidge of white on her feathers and she hung back when the others rushed the back door, so the chooks were dubbed Chook, Chook, Chook and Lonesome.

The girls were happy, relaxed and carefree and I was a bag of nerves. Ticks were a potential problem in that part of northern New South Wales so I had a routine of dusting and de-worming. I was on the lookout for fleas and signs of coccidiosis too; according to the pamphlet it could cause anaemia, depression, low production and mortality.

Depression? I don't think so. By now the chooks were surprisingly choosy about what they would and wouldn't eat. Of the giant smorgasbord of treats laid out in front of them, they ignored celery, parsley and radish but everything else in the vegetable patch was fair game. They liked cheese, meat, bread, salad and all the yellow and black seeds from the chook feed, but they wouldn't eat the grey or brown pellets (boring bits that made up eighty per cent of the feed).

And low production? The chooks were meant to start laying any time from twenty weeks so I made a note on the calendar and weeks twenty, twenty-one, twenty-two and twenty-three passed without any sign of an egg. I skulked close by whenever one of them settled into the dirt under a bush, aware I was in danger of re-awakening my stalking tendencies. CC was quietly amused by the whole palaver and wisely said nothing.

Early one morning we got a call from a man a few doors down. 'Have you lost one of your chooks?' he asked. I looked out of the window and counted the number of fat feather bundles, partially hidden in what remained of the vegetable patch.

'No,' I said, somewhat wistfully. 'They're all still here.'

'One turned up in my garden and I think it might be a stray. Do you want to try to incorporate it into your flock?'

I'm a soft-hearted pushover when it comes to a stray looking for a good home so I put my hand over the mouthpiece and explained the situation to CC. I was relying on him to shake his head and say no. 'Sure,' he said. 'One more can't harm.' There was a suggestion of a smile on his face and it looked like he might be about to remind me that happy, healthy chickens produced more eggs. I could tell he was weighing up the consequences. In the end he played safe. 'Shall I fetch a box?' he said.

Given the Christmas turkey-like proportions of our well-fed chooks we took a large cardboard box but the stray turned out to be half the size of a dove, a small white bird with patches of blue grey feathers under its scared-looking eyes, trapped under a net that the neighbour had thrown over it. There was no way I could refuse to take it (although how such a small bird would cope with the four buxom beasts in our back garden was less certain).

'It's a bantam,' said CC as we drove home with a small scared bird inside an overly large box. 'It will hold its own; bantams are fiery creatures, you watch.'

We fed the little bantam bits of bacon and debated how best to introduce it to the Red Leghorn crosses, all of which were more than three times its size. CC favoured the direct approach – shut them in the cage together – and I advocated a more gradual 'getting to know you' program. The compromise (although goodness knows why we thought this would work) was to shut the bantam into the girls' quarters and leave them on the outside. They went wild, enraged that their personal quarters had been so brutally invaded. Standing outside the coop, they tried to attack the bantam through the wire mesh and the little bird immediately dropped a wing to one side, as if it was wounded.

'See that?' said CC. 'Male bantams do that when they want to mate. Not even half their size and he wants to mount them,' he added with pride.

I wasn't so sure. If the little bantam did want to mount the girls I doubted he would get very far; they looked like they wanted to rip his head off. We let the bantam out, protected him as the girls went in for the kill and he flew over our heads to hide in a vine growing over the pergola. At least if he could fly he might survive. The girls kicked around the dust inside the cage, squawking and scratching with noisy displeasure, so we left food and water where the bantam could reach it and shut the girls in. 'Bertie the Bantam, what a guy,' said CC, staring up at him.

The arrival of a fifth bird meant reinforcements were needed. What was left of the broad beans and sweet peas were already ring-fenced with wire mesh and tightly encased in shadecloth but the main vegetable patch was still vulnerable. I had a solution.

'Hold that and don't move,' I said to CC. He was holding a spool of wire, which I unrolled and fixed to the shed at one side of the garden and the carport at the other (high enough so neither of us would slit our throats when pulling up a radish). I threaded fifteen metres of expandable bird netting along it.

The white curtain cut the garden in half, with the protected vegetable patch on one side and free-range grazing on the other. The garden looked like a giant stage set.

There was a hushed silence, not unlike the stillness that settles on a theatre audience before a performance begins.

The chooks hesitated, clearly mystified by the curtain. The suggestion of a breeze whispered through the grass and the flimsy netting lifted into the air. *Curtain up!* The chooks rushed the stage, pushing into the limelight like born performers. I shooed them off and pegged the curtain with rocks and old plant pots until Bertie worked out how to squeeze under the pegs. His lone achievement sent the girls into a frenzy of jealous rage and they pecked and scratched at the line of rocks and stones as I rushed back and forth, like a general on the front line, checking defences, plugging holes and extracting the chooks that managed to squeeze through the gaps at the side.

When all that remained of the garden was hidden under bent wire mesh, torn shadecloth and muddy white netting, I finally admitted defeat.

'I thought you said free range –'

'Shut up and pass me that hammer.'

CC helped me fence off a ten-metre square section of the rose garden, effectively ending the fantasy of chooks roaming free. And still we didn't have a single egg.

*

The girls waddled through the rose garden in a clutch, Lonesome never more than a couple of feet behind. Bertie made no attempt to mate with them but he did desperately want to be friends. The girls wanted nothing to do with him. They saw off any attempt at friendship with ferocious stabs to the top of his head and he fluttered away, only to repeat the attempt moments later.

The fence was high enough so the girls couldn't get out, and low enough so Bertie could fly in and out at will, which was probably the only thing that saved him from certain death.

Several times a day the chooks rejected his overtures and several times a day he went back for more, until he had a permanent scab on top of his head, none of which deterred him from trying again. No matter how often he tried he never succeeded. I felt a certain affinity with Bertie the Bantam.

The chooks weren't Bertie's only problem; a greater risk to his safety was next door's cat. At night Bertie roosted in a tangle of branches underneath the pergola, high enough to be safe from predators. At dawn each morning he fluttered down to the chicken coop and hung around outside, waiting for another attempt to make friends with the girls when I let them out. Several times I'd got up to let the chooks out and discovered next door's cat peering over the roof at the unsuspecting Bertie. It was only a matter of time before the cat pounced.

I had a plan.

Dawn hadn't broken when I nudged CC awake. 'It's time,' I whispered. We pulled on slippers, shrugged on dressing-gowns and eased open the back door, being careful not to let the screen door bang. I pointed at the tap and CC nodded, padding across the dew-soaked lawn as I reached for the hose I'd left uncoiled the night before.

'Is he there?' CC mouthed.

I risked a peek around the corner. Crouching low in the pre-dawn light, silhouetted on top of the chook shed, was an outline of black fur. We weren't a moment too soon – poor innocent Bertie was scratching in the dirt below. I gave CC the thumbs up, picked up the hose, positioned myself at the corner and raised my arm. When I let it fall that would be the signal for him to turn on the tap.

I signalled, he turned the tap and with straight arms and a strong grip (I haven't ever seen a Quentin Tarantino movie but I know the drill) I leapt around the corner and squeezed the trigger. The water pressure was high and I was firing at close range; that cat would be flung in the air and shot back where it belonged. Take that, you mangy, stalking intruder, get back over the fence where you belong, you dirty murdering son of a . . . A gentle drift of rain fell from the gun, misting the ground at my feet. The cat yawned, arched its back and disappeared across the neighbour's roof with a dismissive flick of its tail. CC appeared at my side and stared at the spray gun in my hand, set to mist instead of stun. 'Flaw in the plan there, Frosty,' he said.

My frustration with the lack of egg production mounted until I heard the story of an Aboriginal couple trying to get pregnant. They succeeded only when an older, wiser woman slipped a ceramic egg with magical powers under their bed. I had an egg-shaped souvenir from the Daydream Mine near Silverton so I nestled the fake egg on a bed of straw inside the chook shed. Two days later there was a perfect replica lying on the straw, an unblemished, still-warm gift from one of the girls. The laying drought was broken in spectacular fashion and before long they were all at it, squawking loudly to announce the arrival of that day's batch. It was unexpectedly moving and I marvelled at the magic of it. The daily egg collection was worth all the disruption and mess.

Then something happened that filled me with wonder – a surprise I could never have anticipated. It was a simple but startling discovery that made me stop and realise something: if I think I know what to expect, how can I ever be surprised? If I cleared my mind of pre-conceived ideas, a whole new set of possibilities opened up, like the possibility that CC and I might be meant for each other, or that Broken Hill was a beautiful place and I just hadn't been able to see it.

Weeding one of the garden beds early one morning, in a corner of the garden I rarely visited, I pushed aside a thicket of lavender bushes and found Bertie sitting on a nest of squashed daisies. He didn't flutter away as he normally would when I approached and I was able to pick him up. He was a soft, featherweight bundle, lighter than I thought he'd be, but the real surprise was what he'd been hiding. Lying on the ground underneath him, gathered into a small neat mound, were seventeen tiny white eggs, so delicate and unlike anything the girls had laid that they clearly belonged to him. Her. I carefully put Bertie down and gathered the warm eggs one by one, cradling them in the fold of my shirt to carry them indoors. The next day, in exactly the same place, I found Bertie sitting contentedly on another small white egg. Bertie wasn't a boy at all.

He was a girl.

*

The arrival of chooks settled me into a daily routine that included a couple of hours tending the vegetable patch, where basil, rocket, mint, chives, coriander, parsley, rosemary and thyme quickly filled the bare patches of sun-baked earth. When I ran out of room, Joe, who normally cut the lawn and tended the trees and roses (which explained why they did so well), helped me clear another patch and together we removed five wheelbarrows of heavy stone, adding compost and manure to the sandy soil that was already rich with minerals and crawling with worms. Not as barren as I thought, then. I planted onion sets, capsicum, melon, tomatoes, beetroot, peas, broad beans, pumpkin, zucchini, cabbage, radish and lettuce. Once the chooks were safely penned, it all grew with astonishing speed. There's no shortage of sunlight in Broken Hill and no lack of water either; the Menindee Lakes system (three times the size of Sydney Harbour) supplied the water and since it evaporated faster than it could be used, the only restriction was cost (sorry, CC).

Broken Hill had welcomed me with unexpected generosity. Lynne Gall, a member of the Broken Hill Women's Auxiliary, whose husband, John, is a grazier and long-standing RFDS board member, brought me a box of produce from Langawirra Station: jars of homemade jam and relish, honey from bees fed on red gum and black box at Coogee Lake, ripe tomatoes and clumps of strawberry plants dug up from her garden, ready to be transplanted into mine.

I came home one day to find two jars of homemade apricot jam on the doorstep, like liquid amber held in glass. I kept expecting a phone call and tried calling a few people to see who might have deposited the jars but it was an unsolved mystery. A gift that looked for no reward. Isn't that the sweetest gift of all? When I opened one of the jars it was like releasing a genie and I inhaled the scent of summer in those sun-ripened apricots. Weeks later, Joe asked for the jars back and I found out his wife, Marlene, had made the jam.

Broken Hill felt like a town that wasn't stopping when I first arrived but that's because *I* wasn't stopping. I was planning to shoot through and get out at the first opportunity, and what a mistake that would have been. I would have missed the beauty of jaw-dropping sunsets and changeable weather that had me leaping to my feet like a ticket holder at a Rolling Stones concert, applauding the audacity, the bravado, the noise and fury. When weather blew through it left behind blue skies that went on forever and a silent sense of belonging to something big.

Once I got over my fear of the unknown, I grew to love the desert too. An elemental place of earth, stone, heat, light, dust and sky, it could be fierce and brutal in forty-five-degree heat, and utterly beautiful when the heat dissipated and evening light softened the landscape. There was a weight and shape to the silence out in the desert. On winter afternoons the coming night lurked behind the hills, shadows lengthening on the ground as the sun slid towards the horizon. On still days you could feel the air give way as you stepped through it, gravity pressing close.

In my first year in Broken Hill Sturt's desert peas sprang up on the sandy hills in great clumps, like alien characters from *Doctor Who*. They stood upright on runners, tall and erect with watchful red and black eyes: meerkats on sentry duty. Word went around that another batch had sprung up off the road that led to the Living Desert and Sculpture Park; turn left after the first dirt track, someone would say, and they're just over the hill, or try beyond the rise where the mountain bike track meets the road to Menindee. The location changed each time, as if desert peas had the ability to uproot themselves at night, march silently across the moonlit landscape and settle in a new location. By morning they would be standing ready to meet the dawn, watchful and, quite frankly, weird. If Dick Turpin were to be reincarnated and come back as a flower he'd be a desert pea, no question.

Viewed from a distance, Broken Hill was a dirty brown smudge surrounded by desert. Up close, it dazzled. In early November, jacaranda trees lining Morgan Street traced a lacy pattern of lilac against a whip-cracking blue sky, blossoms piled into drifts below. At other times of the year there were saturated blooms of magenta bougainvillea, gum trees flowering in candy floss bunches of salmon, rose, snow white and burnt ochre, pink peppercorn trees in Sturt Park, while roses bloomed practically all year.

Summer was a challenge; there was no point pretending otherwise. I left the secateurs in the sun one day then picked them up and tucked them under my arm while I reached for a weed. I bore the burn marks for days. Only the arrival of shadecloth to protect the veggie garden, coupled with kindly shadows cast by a majestic lemon gum tree, stopped the tender plants from scorching in forty-five-degree heat that could sometimes last for days.

I had missed Sydney when I first arrived, but if I was honest, life in a big city often gave me a sense of being left behind, of not doing enough or seeing enough, uneasy at a pace that allowed no time for reflection and no pause in the frenetic dash to get somewhere and be someone. Broken Hill didn't expect anything of me; it simply accepted me, which meant I didn't expect too much of myself. I learnt to relax.

I'd always thought routine was boring, an indication of a life that lacked interest, but in Broken Hill I learnt what comfort and reassurance routine can bring. Weekends were slow and measured: fish and chips on a Friday night, brunch with friends on Saturday, a swim in the pool, reading the papers, catching a film, watching the footy, a spot of gardening, a barbecue in a creek bed if the weather allowed, then back to work Monday morning and do it all again the following weekend. It was a quiet rhythm I grew to love.

The peace and the space were just what I needed to complete the book about Jane. Although far from being the backwater I was expecting, Broken Hill turned out to be a vibrant hub of activity. There was no shortage of workshops I could (and did) attend – throwing pots on Wyman Street, polymer clay jewellery making with Wendy Moore, figure drawing with Robert, creative writing with Rae and play writing, acting and directing with Short + Sweet. I could have learnt to play the ukelele like Sue and Lisa, joined a bush walking group with Ann, taken quilting lessons, photography classes, learnt lead lighting – there were dozens of things to do.

The remoteness of Broken Hill attracts all kinds of interesting people and I forged friendships that were all the sweeter for being so unexpected. Among the group who made regular sorties to the desert for a creek bed barbecue were artists, administrators, doctors, university lecturers, researchers, a retired florist, a schoolteacher and an occupational therapist. Not quite what I was expecting.

The sense of community worked closer to home too. I'd normally cross the road to avoid a Harley-Davidson biker, especially one as imposing as Gary our next-door neighbour, but he and his wife, Ellen, were gentle, considerate people of unfailing kindness.

I learnt to cope with the spiders and locusts that were quickly followed by a plague of crickets then hordes of mice and thousands of small black beetle things. 'No idea what they are, love,' said the shop assistant in Big W as she swept them off the counter. 'We've all got 'em. They'll be gone soon.' We were all in it together.

Apart from the occasional workshop there was little to distract me from the task I'd set out to complete, and nowhere to run and hide when issues came up in the relationship with CC. It was simply a matter of working through them.

My pack of Tarot cards was gathering dust on top of the bookcase and I stopped looking for signs and symbols. Gradually, inexorably, I started to appreciate the beauty and sense of community that can be found everywhere you look in Broken Hill.

It was puddings that really brought it home.

chapter twenty-five

Steam rose from the bank of boiling coppers like a dragon exhaling its breath.

'How many have you got in there? Was that sixteen or seventeen?'

'Seventeen, due out at ten thirty.'

June lifted the lid, checked the water levels and then stirred the puddings bobbing in the copper. Her outline was swallowed by steam. Was it just me or would the thought of standing in front of a bank of boiling coppers all day (without air-conditioning) make most people check their diaries and find they were otherwise engaged? It was thirty-five degrees outside, at least forty-five inside, and I couldn't see anything in that steaming, sweaty kitchen. I certainly couldn't see the point of spending the best part of two weeks making 2000 Christmas puddings when there had to be quicker and *much* easier ways of raising money. I would normally be the first heading for the door but I didn't want to lose face in front of the Broken Hill Women's Auxiliary, most of whom looked to be in their sixties, seventies and eighties, so I stayed put. Words like resilience and fortitude didn't even come close.

'You'll need a hat,' said pudding convener Margaret, handing me a blue plastic hat.

'Mind your backs, another batch coming through,' said a voice behind me as an identical blue hat emerged from the steam, attached to someone pushing a supermarket trolley full of mounds of calico-wrapped parcels.

'Copper number nine,' said June, her disembodied voice rising from the mist.

Olwyn took pity on me. 'It's a bit hot in here, why don't you join the pleating team?' she said, steering me out of the kitchen and into the preparation room next door where trestle tables buckled under the weight of boxes of mixed fruit, cartons of butter and margarine, sacks of flour, crates of brandy and thousands of cartons of eggs. Six hundred metres of white calico had been washed, ironed and torn into nineteen-inch squares, each square waiting to be dusted with flour and then draped onto the worn metal scoop of an old-fashioned set of scales. Those scales wouldn't have looked out of place in a greengrocer's shop in the 1930s.

'What time's smoko?'

'About nine.'

'Coming through, mind your backs.'

I stepped out of the way of the trolley and took a seat next to a laughing woman in a blue hat (Jenny), who was clutching what looked to be a pair of pliers. She was sitting opposite another laughing woman in a blue hat (Val), who was pleating calico. I could have stood next to either of them in a supermarket queue and not known who they were; we all looked indistinguishable in our blue plastic hats. Team Pudding.

My first job as a novice was to take bent pieces of steel wire and bend them into a different shape (another novice further up the production line had bent them into the wrong shape, apparently). I was a fan of Kevin McCloud's *Grand Designs* and I could have sworn I'd seen those exact same lengths of wire being used by builders to hold concrete foundations together.

'What will you do with the wire?' I asked. Jenny showed me by twisting a piece around the top of a calico-wrapped pudding, grabbing the ends with what looked 'like a pair of pliers (but wasn't) and yanking hard.

Within minutes my fingers were tingling and blackened. Everywhere I looked, women in aprons and blue hats were hard at work. An immaculately attired woman who looked to be in her early seventies with impeccable make-up and a spotlessly clean pinny (Pam had been on pudding duty for forty-six years) was weighing and measuring ingredients for the next batch of puddings. A woman with a ready smile and thick black hair that filled her blue hat (Cynthia) was mixing fruit, while Julie was cracking eggs. When June wasn't stirring puddings, she was softening butter over a steaming bucket of boiling water to get the exact consistency for the temperamental industrial-sized mixer that Maxine was in charge of, and Annie was elbow-deep in pudding mix, squeezing the next batch of sticky goo through her fingers.

A softly spoken woman with crow's-feet radiating out from her smiling eyes (Marie) sat quietly in the corner dusting individual sheets of calico with flour so Val (keeper of the scales and mistress of weights and measures) could drape each sheet onto the metal scoop and plop a precise one-kilo dollop of pudding mix into the middle, time after time after time. Val had been standing at those scales for decades, Maxine had been on mixing duty for more than thirty years and Jenny had been yanking metal ties for just as long. Everywhere I looked it was the same story of loyal devotion.

'Where do you live?' I asked Jenny.

'Wiawera Station.'

'Is that far?'

'About an hour and a half out of town.'

Pudding production had started at seven that morning so Jenny must have been up well before dawn. It was the same for many of the women who lived on stations scattered across far western New South Wales.

Preparations had begun months before with label making, calico tearing (cutting the fabric didn't give the same effect), wire snipping and almond chopping. You know that sprinkle of spice that goes into a Christmas pudding? They needed four *kilos* of nutmeg alone, the same again of mixed spice, sixty litres of brandy, 740 kilos of dried fruit . . . the list went on and on. There were order forms to prepare and send, rosters of volunteers to organise, postage and packing to think about.

Pudding production was undoubtedly the crowning glory of the Broken Hill Women's Auxiliary's fundraising efforts for the RFDS and it was an awe-inspiring achievement, with over 2000 calico-wrapped puddings produced by hand in less than two weeks. But why? Why would a group of sensible mature-aged women put themselves through such arduous, back-breaking, labour-intensive, sweat-inducing work, year in year out? There had to be easier ways of raising money, surely? The demonstration of support for the RFDS through a sacrificial process of such epic proportions absolutely mystified me.

As the morning wore on agile hands swiftly removed each calico parcel from the scales. A line of women – Helen, Coral, Margaret, Sandy, Barbara, Jenny, Pauline, Lynne and so many more whose names were lost in a cloud of flour – shaped each ball of sticky pudding mix into a mound, sprayed it with water, then pleated the calico around the solid mass, deftly pulling and tweaking it into shape with experienced fingers. A steel tie was partly closed around the top, then more hands – sometimes Jack's, the only man who seemed to have made it onto the pudding production line – linked a heavy puller under the steel tie and yanked it tight.

The pudding passed down the line for more tweaking, patting and pulling before Val gave it a final check and plopped it into the bottom of the supermarket trolley. Pudding convener Margaret, an unflappable woman with endless slow-burn energy, wheeled it through to the kitchen to the waiting June, Julie and Sharon, whose excitable enthusiasm reminded me of a spaniel eager for a walk. There was a worrying moment when Sharon lowered a pudding into a copper of boiling water and mistakenly plunged her fingers into the broiling fatty swirl at the same time. She sat with her hand in a bucket of iced water to reduce the scald, and work continued regardless.

'Remember that year all the puddings went mouldy because of the rain?'

'What about that old tin shed we used to work in? That wasn't much fun when it hit forty degrees.'

'What about that beast of a mixer?'

There was a peal of laughter from Maxine who told me her face would get so splattered with pudding mix she couldn't see through her glasses to drive home. The sense of camaraderie was tangible and there was no telling any of us apart in the dense steam and blue plastic hats: we were all in it together.

The talk moved on to pipe work.

'Look at that automatic drainage, fantastic,' said June.

'Perilya installed waste pipes last year,' Olwyn explained. 'We have to empty the coppers at the end of each day and until those pipes were installed we used to catch the water in a bucket, then pour it down the sink.'

I imagined them catching gushing streams of boiling, fatty water in a fleet of buckets and ferrying them *Fantasia*-like across the room. It would have been sweaty, slippery, dangerous work.

There was no charge for the new pipes, not when it was for the Broken Hill Women's Auxiliary and the RFDS.

As each batch of puddings was lowered into the bubbling water, Margaret wrote the time on a soggy chart leaning against the wall. She made a note of the time the puddings were due out, the number of puddings in the copper and finally, in the all-important column at the end, the running total. It crept up as the day advanced – sixteen, thirty-three, forty-nine, sixty-six . . . it was a long way from the 2000-plus required.

Work stopped for smoko, the Australian equivalent of morning tea, and again for lunch when we escaped the steam and sat in the sunshine, nibbling on lemon shortbreads that someone had found time to make, although goodness knows when.

There was no slacking in between breaks. Olwyn kept track of orders as the temperature rose in the steaming kitchen and laughter mingled with the mist.

June was one of the younger helpers (somewhere in her mid-sixties, I guessed) and she had just been awarded the Order of Australia for leading groups of cyclists across remote parts of Australia to raise money for the Flying Doctor.

'You should come with us one day,' she said, standing at one of the coppers, wearing two pairs of rubber gloves. After three hours in boiling water, the butter-rich puddings couldn't be handled without a double protective layer.

'Where did you go last time?' I said, wary of my experience so far of cycling in the desert. I'm glad I asked. Their last trip was a seven-week ride of almost 4000 kilometres, from Broken Hill to Darwin.

'You're never too old for cycling,' she said, lifting out a soggy pudding and patting it with a towel before squeezing out the excess moisture and adding it to a growing pile stored in a baby's bath.

Another line of women (where did they all come from?) wiped the puddings dry with an assortment of towels and tea towels. They cleaned the pleats, pulled out the calico ears, checked the ties and patted the precious bundles into perfectly round balls (flat-bottomed puddings were frowned upon).

Having proved myself capable of bending bits of steel wire, I progressed later to pulling out the ears on the calico, and later still to wiping the cooked puddings as they came out of the steaming coppers. Months earlier someone had printed 2000 labels, placed each one inside a ziplock plastic bag, closed the bag, punched a hole through it, threaded a plastic-covered wire through the hole and twisted it ready to attach to a pudding. That was my next job. Once the labels were attached, the heavy puddings were carried next door in twos and threes, threaded onto butcher's hooks (homemade, of course) and then finally hung in the store-room to dry. The drying racks, made from sturdy metal poles over three metres long and lashed together with rope, reached from the floor to the ceiling. That was a lot of racks to fill.

By going-home time at three thirty in the afternoon on my first day of volunteering, we had made 270 puddings. Only another 1630 to go . . .

*

There was something about the extreme self-sacrifice of the participants that mystified me. Leaving aside the hundreds of hours spent on pudding production itself, there was all the prep work and cleaning up every day, sweeping floors, scraping off wet flour paste stuck to benchtops, washing and drying dozens of towels, then packing puddings to be sent to Sydney, Adelaide, Perth and beyond, some even overseas.

As a student I spent several months in Seville, in southern Spain, where I witnessed the religious fervour that hit town during

Semana Santa, the Holy Week just before Easter. Whole suburbs vied for the right to bear the weight of statues of the Virgin Mary that were paraded through the streets on huge floats, resting on the backs of the Catholic faithful. For hours on end the followers swayed through the narrow streets thronging with worshippers, offering themselves to God. That same martyrdom seemed to be at play in Broken Hill, only in this case the offering was to the RFDS. If I counted up the hours spent on pudding production, even with a conservative estimate of say twenty volunteers working eight hours a day, I quickly reached over a thousand hours. Add the preparation, the clean up and the post-production sales operation and that total could easily have doubled.

On the sweaty seventh day of pudding production I was on autopilot, pleating, prodding, cleaning and wiping. Jenny was sitting opposite, chatting with remarkable equanimity about the last major flood that swamped her remote property.

'We lost a horse, a cow, all the chooks and ducks and most of the sheep.'

'How many sheep was that?'

'Three thousand.'

'Didn't you have any warning?'

She laughed and shook her head. 'It got noisy all of a sudden.'

The normally sluggish creek that ran past their house was inundated by floodwater ten feet high that arrived without warning and roared through the property, destroying the sheep, the house, most of the outbuildings and all of the garden, including her treasured rosebushes.

'We eventually found the shearer's quarters sixteen kilometres downstream,' she said. 'They were forty foot up the side of a hill.'

More seriously Jenny's father, who had been staying with them while he recovered from a heart bypass operation, was also taken by the flood and swept off his feet. He ended up clinging to a pepper tree in the garden and had to be rescued by helicopter. There was worse to come. Far from being safe, Jenny's father ended up back in the floodwater when the helicopter that rescued him got caught in the swirling water as it tried to take off. It crash-landed, leaving the pilot Dave, Jenny's son Andy, and her unlucky father stranded. Two of Jenny's grandchildren – eight-year-old Ben and ten-year-old Keith – had already been airlifted to safety and they witnessed the crash from a nearby rise.

'They set off to get help,' said Jenny. That meant embarking on a long and difficult walk to Olary to raise the alarm, and it was another six hours before the stranded threesome were eventually rescued. It was a year before the family could move back in and even then they slept on the veranda for months while repair work continued.

'I vowed I'd never plant another rosebush,' said Jenny, and then she looked at me and smiled. 'I have, of course.'

I listened with growing incredulity to the litany of disasters she'd witnessed: the time a gaslight blew up in a local girl-guide camp, the time her son, Greg, knocked his teeth out and tore his nose off falling from his bike, and the day her husband, Keith, speared his arm on the branch of a mulga tree. Each time, the Flying Doctor was called. Jenny and Keith hosted a Flying Doctor clinic on their property once a month, in a purpose-built clinic that attracted patients from miles around. 'It was the least we could do after all the Flying Doctor has done for us,' said Jenny.

Everywhere I turned it was the same story. When a lad mustering sheep came off his motorbike and broke his back the Flying Doctor landed on a dirt strip, stabilised his injuries and flew him to the nearest major hospital. When a child needing regular chemotherapy couldn't get to hospital the Flying Doctor stepped in. When a stockman was bitten by a king brown, when a first-time mum went into premature labour or a girl got poked in the eye with a stick, when skin cancers, heart attacks, strokes, broken bones, dog bites, spider bites and car crashes happened in a remote area, the story was always the same. The hardship those women had endured was something far beyond anything I had ever experienced.

As the final day drew to a close I realised with quiet shame that I had missed the point. Yes, of course there were easier ways of raising money and faster ways of making Christmas puddings but there was a reverence in what we were doing, a sense of grace in the endlessly repetitive tasks and the challenge of facing another gruelling day and another eight hours of nurturing those blobs of unremarkable ingredients until they were transformed into something magical. Each pudding was given such close attention at every stage of production that some of that attention rubbed off. Each plump, cosseted, calico-wrapped parcel became a silent offering of thanks, a grateful acknowledgement of all that the Flying Doctor had done to help desperate families no one else could reach.

The last pudding was lifted out of the copper at 2.45 in the afternoon, to be squeezed and drained, dried and wiped, patted and pulled into shape. The wire was checked, the calico cleaned, the pleats smoothed, ears tugged, tag attached, tie twisted, hook threaded and the final pudding was hung on the rack to dry at ten past three. Seeing all those fat calico bundles, each a creamy white with pert rabbit ears protruding from tightly closed wire necks, I felt a sense of pride that I'd had a small part to play in that huge production. I gave one of the puddings a discreet pat on its round bottom before I left the storeroom.

I went home at the end of that final exhausting day clutching a calico-wrapped Christmas pudding, with instructions to hang it for two months and boil it for two hours on Christmas Day.

On the way home I stopped at the petrol station. I was still wearing an apron and had to explain what I'd been doing.

'I don't know why those ladies bother,' the attendant casually remarked. 'I always buy my Christmas pudding in a tin.'

A tin? *A tin?* God forbid. I could no longer accept that puddings be wrapped in anything other than calico nor boiled in anything other than coppers.

That Christmas we enjoyed every mouthful of our Broken Hill Women's Auxiliary pudding. We both knew how much loving attention had gone into each little bundle of joy.

chapter twenty-six

So what of you and CC, I hear you ask. Well, I'd thought not falling madly in love with him when we first met was a negative, but I grew to realise it was the best thing that could ever have happened. The warmth, tenderness, respect and love – yes, that was in there too – that I felt for CC grew stronger the longer I knew him. I was glad I hadn't lost my head and that for once my feet were firmly on the ground. I wasn't a jittery bag of jangled passion or a sinister stalking spinster, I was a grown-up (it took long enough but I got there in the end). I learnt to approach CC with kindness and reason instead of the tortured angst of misplaced passion and thwarted desire that had characterised most of my other relationships. When we disagreed on something I argued my case without worrying he would leave me or thinking our relationship was on the rocks. That said, there are degrees of disagreement and for a while there we were in the middle of an absolute humdinger.

We had decided to get a dog. We were too old for children and a dog was the next best thing. The question that nearly drove us apart was what sort of dog? CC knew what he wanted (a guard dog) and what he didn't want (a poodle) but other than a family

Jack Russell in childhood I'd never had a dog, so I was hesitating. I wanted a loyal companion and a faithful friend, an obedient dog that didn't shed too much hair, wouldn't destroy the garden, wouldn't eat the chickens and would come when called. I was searching for an unattainable ideal of the 'right' dog. I couldn't shake the romantic notion that the right dog would simply turn up one day; it would find us rather than the other way around. It was ridiculous, a throwback to the notion I used to have that the right man would simply turn up one day and my life would be sorted – no work involved, just an instant fix. CC *did* turn up but he was the wrong man, not my type at all, but then he turned out to be the right man so where did that leave me? In the Broken Hill library and back at the second-hand bookshop.

I armed myself with *What Dogs Want, A Dog of Your Own, Dogs for Dummies, Let's Have Healthy Dogs* and *Identifying Dog Breeds.* I downloaded copies of *Before You Get Your Puppy* and *After You Get Your Puppy* because what if we didn't get a rescue dog? What if we got a puppy instead? I bought dog beds in three different sizes and shifted them between my office, the laundry and the back door to find the perfect location. I bought three dog bowls and a range of chews and treats. CC already had a lead, there was a kennel in the garden from his last dog and I got quotes on putting up fencing to protect the veggie patch. I went back to the tip and scavenged for soft toys so the new member of our family would have something to play with and I bought a bright purple collar (all right, three – I wasn't sure what size I'd need). I was an expectant dog owner, a dog owner in waiting, and the only thing we didn't have was a dog. It was beginning to feel a bit like a phantom pregnancy.

Leaving aside the indecision about breeds, we couldn't agree on what dogs were *for*. In CC's world a dog should stand at least as tall as your knees and exhibit clear dog-like behaviour: living outdoors, guarding your property, chewing on the thighbone of an even larger animal and barking at intruders.

'Dogs don't like to be kept indoors, they feel trapped, it's cruel to keep a dog indoors,' CC declared.

'It doesn't say that in any of the books,' I muttered, feeling like CC had an unfair advantage as he'd had dogs all his life. His last was a blue heeler and from what I'd read, that was the Australian cattle dog equivalent of a German shepherd, the classic dog of choice for police forces and military units around the world. And in my humble opinion, only slightly less aggressive than a Rottweiler (courageous, loyal, fearless, confident and devoted, according to the books, which sounded more like the perfect attack animal than the ideal family pet).

I'd seen a litter of soft, floppy, dove-grey bundles at the RSPCA as I was driving past one day so I called in, picked one up and cuddled it.

'What is it?' I cooed.

'A rottie cross,' the vet cooed back.

A rose by any other name, I thought, and put the small dove-grey bundle down.

If a dog was any smaller than a blue heeler CC believed it should have certain physical attributes to compensate, like the strength and muscle of a Staffordshire bull terrier. 'A dog has to be able to defend itself,' he said. 'And if your dog gets into a fight you've got to back it up.'

Who said anything about fighting? I was thinking a dog might sit on the sofa with us. Dogs were part of the family where I came from. Gran had spaniels, my sister had West Highland whites, and other friends had a variety of street dogs: mutts with wagging tails, lolling tongues and curly coats that slept indoors, curled up against the Aga. Some even had their own armchairs. I remembered Nipper the Jack Russell loved nothing better than curling up on your lap and falling asleep while the television was on. CC and I had a long way to go to find a compromise.

It didn't help that every second dog in Broken Hill seemed to be a staffy, a rottie, an American pitt bull or a mix of all three. I saw them chained up in the back of utes, salivating and ready to attack with huge jaws and powerful shoulders. The *Barrier Daily Truth* carried regular reports of stray dogs roaming the back lanes and savaging innocent passers-by or randomly killing timid family pets. I didn't want a vicious beast, I wanted a dog I could cuddle.

'What about a spaniel?' I suggested.

'Its ears are too long; they get infected.'

'Golden retriever?'

'Too much hair.'

'Bichon Frisé?'

'White rat.'

In his own way, CC was as prejudiced as I was. He refused to consider anything with curly hair and floppy ears, which ruled out spoodles, cavoodles, labradoodles and all the other cute ooodle crossbreeds. 'They're not real dogs,' he said, definitively. Our conversations degenerated into mud-slinging arguments.

'What's your problem with bull terriers?'

'Those hairless white things with long snouts? They look like ugly thuggish brutes.'

'You shouldn't judge a dog on its looks.'

'Really? So how come you don't like poodles?'

'Poodles aren't real dogs.'

'Of course they are! Poodles don't shed, they're alert, loyal, easy to train and the French use them as police dogs, did you know that?' All that research I did was coming in handy.

'That's the French for you. What about a staffy?'

'I'd rather have a pig as a pet.'

*

Tabby was a tall lugubrious vet with a face like a bloodhound and an air of distracted exasperation, often quoted in the local paper urging owners to get their dogs microchipped. He ran the local pound on Rakow Street. When I found a stray beagle wandering along Williams Lane I took it to Tabby, expecting praise for my civic duty. He just sighed and shouted to someone hidden at the back of the surgery. 'That bloody beagle's back again.'

I felt bad about the pig comment so I had gone back to the pound to see if I could take a staffy home on trial. All I knew about the breed was what I'd read ('affectionate, bold, reliable, courageous'). I'd never even stroked a staffy. Maybe I was the one being prejudiced.

'Do you have any staffies?' I asked Tabby.

He sighed. 'Nothing but.' (In my humble opinion, that wasn't a good sign.) 'Have a look at the cages out the back. You can take your pick.'

'What do you think of the breed?' I asked, playing for time before venturing out to the back of the building where I could hear large beasts baying for blood.

Tabby shrugged. 'They're OK, as long as you can forget what they were originally bred for.'

'What was that?'

'Fighting.'

The cages contained an achingly sad line-up of misfits and ugly crossbreeds. Some threw themselves at the bars as I approached, others just lay on the ground, dejected and bored. Saddest of all were those that dropped to their haunches and sat as I approached, trying to do the right thing in the hope that I might open the cage and let them out. In the end I picked out a gentle female. She didn't jump up when I opened the cage, she just pressed against me and begged to be taken home. From certain angles she looked almost like a black Labrador. Almost.

'Have her for as long as you like,' said Tabby.

The timid staffy ('tenacious, muscular and descended from dog-fighting ancestors') sat on my lap as we drove away and I was nervous without knowing why; maybe it was the solidity of her muscle and the size of her jaw. I bought a kangaroo bone as a treat, a heavy piece of bone and gristle the size of a man's foot, and she took it onto the lawn when we got home. Four efficient monster crunches later it was all over. Everything – bone, meat, marrow and gristle – was gone.

CC was thrilled when he got home and he made a big fuss of Staffy, even letting her into the lounge room to sit by the sofa, but I was still nervous. 'She's only on trial,' I reminded him.

Next morning Staffy ('fearless, tough, stocky') sat beside me on the lawn while I weeded the vegetable patch. She seemed placid enough and paid no attention to the chooks noisily scratching behind the fence so I nipped inside to pick up a packet of basil seeds I'd left on the kitchen table. I couldn't have been gone more than two minutes, but that was long enough for Staffy ('can be aggressive to other dogs') to find Bertie the Bantam's nest hidden under the lavender bush, grab Bertie behind the back of the neck and kill her. Staffy carried out the attack silently and efficiently, just as silently and as efficiently as I drove her back to the pound ('surprisingly popular choice for pet owners'). It wasn't her fault as she was just doing what a lot of dogs might have done. It was my fault that I hadn't put Bertie somewhere safe, but that didn't help the staffy's cause.

I buried Bertie in the back garden, shedding guilty tears that I had failed to protect her. When CC found out he was almost as upset as I was. Bertie had been his favourite.

'Whatever breed of dog we get, it won't be a staffy,' I said grimly.

*

The six-week-old puppy was small enough to fit into the palm of my hand, a bundle of warm fur with a wet nose that curled up and nuzzled into the crook of my arm. I stroked the sleepy puppy and felt its fluttering heartbeat through my fingers.

I'd always had a soft spot for beagles ('amiable, intelligent, even-tempered') ever since I'd discovered they were the dog of choice for scientists in the 1950s, who shamelessly tried to find out if cigarette smoking was harmful by fitting the dogs with facemasks and forcing them to inhale tobacco smoke. Only a biddable beagle would have put up with such an atrocity. They had floppy ears that ruled them out, but their coat was short and they didn't shed, which ruled them back in. All the books said they didn't have an ounce of aggression in them.

The ad appeared in the *BDT* while CC was away on business, which looked like fate stepping in. (In my experience it always looks like fate stepping in; the trick is to figure out when it's fate stepping in and when it's you trying to justify an otherwise unjustifiable action; I hope you can see where I'm going with this.) 'Tri-colour beagle puppies, male and female, $300 each.' I took a unilateral decision and drove 120 kilometres to Menindee to see them.

'Is this one taken?' I asked. The breeder shook his head and I handed over a fifty-dollar deposit, ignoring the stark evidence in front of me: all the adult beagles on the breeder's property were either chained or caged ('clever escape artists, seldom come back when you call them'). Some people don't know how to build a proper fence. The breeder docked a millimetre of hair from the puppy's tail so he would know she'd been taken and I agreed to go back and pick her up in two weeks.

'We're getting a beagle,' I told the woman at the garden centre when I arrived back in Broken Hill.

'Great,' she said. 'Beagles are lovely dogs. You can't train them, though. They're led by the nose.'

I told the man in the paper shop we were getting a beagle and he said, 'What do you call a man with a lead in his hand and no dog on the end of it?'

'I don't know.'

'A beagle owner,' he replied, laughing.

I rang Tabby. 'What's your opinion of beagles?'

'Want to know the difference between a staffy and a beagle?' he said. 'A staffy won't see the fence standing in its way, it will plough straight through it. A beagle will go over it, under it or around it. It is the greatest escape artist ever.'

I called the breeder in Menindee and backed out of buying a beagle, forfeiting my fifty-dollar deposit. I was terrified of getting the wrong dog, much like I used to be terrified of making the wrong choice in relationships. Maybe it was just the idea of a dog I loved. Did I really want a boisterous, demanding, needy animal that couldn't be left alone for too long in case it might dig up the garden, chew the furniture or crap on the carpet? If CC had his way the dog would never come indoors, so what was the point of having one anyway? And what if it turned out to be an over-excitable ninja like my friend Sue's little Bichon Frisé? What if it turned out to be a chook killer? An escape artist? What if I found I didn't even like dogs? Maybe I should get a dog and call it Whatif. There was a slogan they often used on television in England in the run-up to Christmas: '*A dog is for life, not just for Christmas.*'

Two days before Christmas I was down on my knees, poking my fingers through the bars of a cage that contained two eager, eight-week-old Tenterfield terriers ('alert, loyal, bold, confident, fearless') with surprisingly sharp teeth. The RSPCA sat in a kind of no-man's-land between north and south Broken Hill, sandwiched between the railway line and the back of the slagheap on one side, and the Water Board on the other.

I was a regular visitor, waiting for a sign that I'd found the right dog. The Tenterfields reminded me of Nipper, the Jack Russell we'd had as children, and when I heard a new litter had come in I checked the 'Top Ten Dog Breeds for Families' website. Tenterfields were on the list.

'Would you let us take a puppy on trial over Christmas?' I asked the nurse, hedging my bets. Maybe I did just want a dog for Christmas.

'We wouldn't normally, but we're pretty full at the moment. Hang on, I'll ask the vet.'

I wandered across to a cage full of muscular puppies that looked like Great Danes crossed with Rottweilers. The timid beagle cross in there with them looked out of place. He pressed against the bars of the cage with soft paws, softer skin and huge brown pick-me-please eyes.

'You won't go wrong with him,' said the nurse, reappearing at my side as I stroked his head. 'He's a very gentle dog. I don't think I've heard him bark the whole time he's been here.'

'How old is he?'

'About three months. The last of a litter; he didn't get sold for some reason and he ended up here. The vet says it's OK by the way – you can take one of the dogs for Christmas.'

'What about this one? Could I take this one?'

She gave his head a rub. 'Yeah, I reckon you could take Benson.'

Benson. What a great name. Was this the one?

I sent CC a quick text. *Puppy on trial over Christmas, what do you think?* He replied, *Up to you.* My phone pinged again. *House-trained?* As if. *Not sure*, I pinged back.

CC wasn't exactly brimming with enthusiasm at the thought of spending our first Christmas together in the company of a stray dog, and a puppy at that, but he did at least agree to a trial.

'We're about to close now so why don't you come back tomorrow,' said the nurse. 'We'll be open until midday.' I went home via the tip to find the one thing missing from my arsenal of dog paraphernalia – a child gate for the laundry door so we could keep Benson contained, just in case.

The next morning, Christmas Eve, I strung lights and hung slices of dried oranges and lemons on a large pot plant pressed into service as an impromptu Christmas tree. The air-conditioning was on high, the shopping done, water bowls full and the child safety gate was in place. We were as ready as we would ever be. Given the holiday shutdown, we would be having Benson for four nights and five days, which should be plenty long enough to decide if he was the right dog . . . The right dog for us, that is. I had to keep remembering that *we* were getting a dog. Not just me.

The nurse at the RSPCA had a string of tinsel draped around her neck. 'Here you go,' she said, handing me a surprisingly heavy burden. Benson came equipped with enough food to see him through the shutdown period, like a dog on an all-inclusive package holiday. I cradled him in my arms and carried him out to the bright sunshine. He licked my hand and I was hopelessly in love before we'd left the car park.

CC was at work and wouldn't be back until late that afternoon so I had Benson all to myself, like an early Christmas present. I felt skittish, elated, nervous and excited. There was no going back now; the RSPCA was closed for Christmas. Benson would need a lot of looking after and I'd have to make sure I didn't neglect CC in the rush of enthusiasm for Benson. I could tell CC wasn't convinced about getting a puppy, especially one with floppy ears and a fair amount of beagle in the mix. But we had a puppy and I had a good feeling about him (a nervous, skittish, elated kind of good feeling, that is).

I carried Benson into the garden, made sure the chooks were safely penned and let him loose. He wagged his tail and pushed his nose into the dirt under the grapevine, where I'd hidden several stashes of dog biscuits in the hope of keeping him occupied over the next five days. It took less than twenty seconds for him to find and eat the lot. When he'd scoffed the biscuits he turned his attention to the back doormat and chewed a large chunk out of it. Then he headed inside, crapped on the kitchen floor, flopped onto his bed in the laundry and promptly fell asleep. What a dog.

CC came home unexpectedly early from work and I was keen to introduce him to Benson but he seemed distracted. 'I don't feel well,' he said, patting the sleeping dog's head. 'I'm going to lie down for a bit.'

'OK, give me a shout if you need anything.'

I'd been so stressed about getting a dog, so nervous about what would be required that I was on high alert, wondering if Benson would fit in, worried what CC would think. Now suddenly they were both asleep and the house was silent.

I squatted down by Benson's bed and took a closer look at him. He was a funny thing with his rippled head, like a squashed bull-mastiff crossed with a bull terrier (or maybe a staffy?). He had the ears of a beagle and the paws of a lion. Adorable. I stroked his sleeping body and marvelled at how quickly he seemed at home. Seconds later he woke up and wanted to play.

Some time later I tiptoed into the bedroom to check on CC and was horrified to find him passed out on the bathroom floor. I dropped to my knees beside him and put one hand on his clammy forehead and the other on his pulse. 'Where am I?' he mumbled, before vomiting litres of bile mixed with Gatorade.

'Passed out at work . . . where is everyone . . . what time is it?' He wasn't making any sense so I called an ambulance.

'Illness is a weakness,' he muttered as they lifted him onto a stretcher and carried him away. 'I'll follow in the car,' I shouted, heart thudding as CC lifted a weak hand that flopped back onto the white sheet like a fish gasping for water. I didn't want to let him out of my sight but I had to deal with a puppy (and whose silly idea was that?).

I picked Benson up and stepped over the child gate (which I couldn't work out how to open properly), put him in his bed with water and toys, locked up the house and drove to the hospital.

CC was on the emergency ward, hooked up to a drip.

'I forgot to take water,' he said, already looking a lot better. He'd gone cycling that morning before work, when it had been thirty-eight degrees. He'd taken his phone with the app that followed his route and recorded his time so he could tell if he was beating his personal best, but he'd forgotten to take water. After the ride he went straight to work, got caught up and didn't drink anything there either, so by lunchtime he was vomiting because of acute dehydration. He worked in a base full of doctors and nurses but he didn't want to bother them so he came home and collapsed.

I sat by CC's bedside, holding his hand, and the emergency doctor gave me a stern look as if somehow it had all been my fault. 'Couldn't you see his skin looked dehydrated?' he asked. I shook my head, holding CC's rather dry hand. I stayed with him while they gave him another infusion and carried out ECG checks and blood tests. Eventually they gave him the all clear and we went home. By then Benson had been shut in the laundry for over four hours but he didn't even whimper when he saw us. I'd been worried about how much looking after a dog would need and it turned out Benson could cope.

By Boxing Day CC was feeling much better and Benson had destroyed the welcome mat at the back door. He'd also pulled all the unripe tomatoes off every plant he could find. He'd sunk his teeth into the green balls then tossed them over his shoulder, looking up thrilled each time to find another one.

'Is he your ideal dog?' CC asked.

'We could do a lot worse.'

Benson had worked out how to worm his way under the wire enclosure around the rose garden (he was part beagle and we did make a poor job of the fence) but did he eat the chooks when he got in? No. Did he chase them? No. He was more interested in scoffing their food. True, he bounded through the vegetable patch chewing plants and digging holes, and there were echoes of chook mania when I warned him, time and again, to get *off* the garden, an order he blithely ignored, but so what? He was adorable. He didn't whine when we left him, he happily spent time outdoors on his own and once, when he could have been digging holes in the vegetable patch, he lay outside his kennel and chewed on an old piece of carpet instead. He slept in the laundry without any fuss and since that lone accident on the first day he never crapped or peed inside. In short, Benson was the best fun ever. I was totally in love with him. Besotted. Bewitched. Bewildered.

CC was doing his best to like him. 'He'll be hard to train,' he said, standing at the back door and watching Benson dig another hole in the garden.

'Possibly,' I conceded.

Benson was easily distracted. I could have his full attention, he'd be as alert as a pointer waiting for a ball, then his head would whip round and he'd start chasing a scent, his lanky body lagging behind a fat wet nose pressed to the ground. When that happened, nothing I did or said would deter him until he'd finished sniffing whatever trail he'd been following.

'He's not a great guard dog either. In fact he's not really a dog.'

'What do you mean?'

'He's a pet.'

'He's both!'

There was a look of disappointment on CC's face as he watched Benson flop around the lawn, tossing green tomatoes over his shoulder.

'Boof used to come running with me every morning, then he'd sit in his kennel and wait for me to come home at night,' he said. 'When the gasman tried to get round the back of the house one day, Boof trapped him in a corner of the garden and kept him there until the housekeeper arrived to rescue him. Good old Boof,' he said wistfully.

Boof was a blue heeler and I shuddered at the thought of an aggressive dog snarling at unsuspecting visitors. 'Cattle dogs need lots of exercise and you don't run every morning anymore,' I said.

'Fair enough, but you still need a guard dog. What's the point in having a dog if it's not going to guard your house?'

'Companionship? Fun?'

CC looked at me as if I was speaking a foreign language. We both knew that Benson's floppy ears and soulful eyes would never deter a would-be intruder but so what? Wasn't that what burglar alarms were for?

We talked late into the night. The RSPCA opened again the following day and that's when we either had to take Benson back or agree to keep him. We fell asleep without any decision being made.

chapter twenty-seven

CC closed a gap in the curtains to banish the needle of sunlight that threatened to light up the whole room, then he came back to bed.

'Did you feed him?' I mumbled.

'Later,' he mumbled back.

Sleep descended again and I dreamt of large dogs barking aggressively at the back door and then woke to find it wasn't a dream. I could hear a low growl that wasn't remotely wimpy or yappy and it was followed by a deep baritone bark. Benson was letting us know he wanted to be fed. I woke CC to tell him the good news.

'Benson can bark!' I exclaimed. 'He can repel intruders and scare off burglars. He can keep the house safe!'

CC pushed a fist into his crumpled pillow and turned over. 'Great. What happens when they spot his wagging tail?'

I ignored his grumpy response and got up to feed the adorable Benson. There was no point continuing our late-night discussion; Benson was staying. He could bark! I made up a celebratory break-fast tray of muesli, orange juice, toast and fresh coffee and wafted

it under CC's nose before heading outside with the paper. At eight
o'clock it was already well into the high thirties and the only cool
spot was under the shade of the pergola, now covered in thick vines
that drooped under the weight of ripening grapes. I ignored what
looked like a new gap in the chook fence and averted my eyes from
the crater-sized holes in the vegetable patch. Benson was staying.

CC poured coffee and I turned to the classified ads in the
local paper, a habit after so much time spent searching for the
right dog. 'Seven-year-old female red heeler cross, friendly and
free to a good home.' I closed the paper and pushed it aside.

A small voice inside me knew a red heeler cattle dog was
more the kind of dog CC would like ('protective, brave, obedient,
energetic, cautious, loyal, faithful') and Benson was still on trial.
I could have taken him back to the RSPCA and we could have
trialled the red heeler to get a comparison, but why? What if the
red heeler had bad habits? What if it had an aggressive streak?
What if it shed hair? My friends in Sydney had a red heeler,
a gorgeous dog that shed hair faster than you can shear a sheep.
Benson hadn't shed a single hair since he'd arrived. What if we
took Benson back and while we were trialling the red heeler
someone else came along, saw how adorable and sweet and loving
Benson was and we ended up losing him? What if the red heeler
was no good? We might end up with no dog at all. We would just
have to accept that Benson was not that far off perfect . . . in my
eyes anyway. I resolved to throw the paper away and not show it
to CC. The decision was made: we were keeping Benson.

*

'What number did he say?'

'That must be it, look.'

A man in a singlet, sporting several days of stubble, raised
his hand as we pulled up outside a house towards the end of

a street in South Broken Hill, a patch of desert just visible in the distance. A ute sat on the driveway and a large red dog was pacing the sparse front lawn, its head as high as the man's shorts. With its thickset body it looked more like an ageing Labrador than a red heeler, although the pointy ears gave it away. It was panting in the heat and lumbered off with its tail between its legs as we approached, shuffling in a way that suggested rheumatism or arthritis. Bad hips, anyway.

'Her name's Maggie,' the guy said, reaching out a hand. 'Come round the back, I've been waiting for you to arrive so I could feed her.'

Why did I tell CC about the ad? I should have kept quiet, hidden the paper and he'd never have known. Did I want to find out how he would react to the thought of a different dog? Maybe I wanted to prove that no dog could be better than Benson, or maybe there was a niggle of doubt in my mind too. Whatever the reason, I had told CC about the red heeler ad and he was on the phone straightaway. 'There's no harm having a look,' he said. So there we were, having a look.

The backyard was as barren as the front and the dog stumbled along after the man in shorts, shuffling sideways any time we tried to approach to stroke her. 'She's an outdoor dog,' the man said. 'Never been indoors.'

'That's good,' CC said, his voice animated, upbeat. I shot him a warning look. I thought we'd agreed, after much heated debate, that any dog of ours would come indoors. 'What's she like with chooks?' he asked.

'No idea, she's never had anything to do with them.' The man in shorts handed me a large bowl of food. 'Here, you feed her,' he said. I took the bowl of food and the red heeler approached warily, then shuffled sideways and backed off.

'Hang on.' The man stood in front of the nervous dog. 'Maggie, sit.' She sat. 'Give me your paw.' She held up her paw and he shook it. 'Now give me your other paw.' She obediently held up her other paw and he shook that one too. 'Good girl.' He turned to me. 'Now you can feed her,' he said. I put the food down and the dog didn't move, just sat and waited. 'She won't eat until you tell her she can,' he said.

'Go ahead, Maggie,' I said. She pushed her nose into the bowl and devoured the food as if she hadn't been fed in days. CC was impressed (and if I'm honest, so was I).

'Dad got Maggie from the RSPCA,' the man said. 'Had her since she was a pup. He's gone into the War Vets' Home on Thomas Street.'

'So he can't take the dog,' said CC.

'Right. Loves that dog, he does.'

'Had many enquiries?'

'You're the only one. Hang on a sec, I'll see if there's a lead in the shed.' He wandered off and Maggie shuffled from side to side, nervously wanting to approach, but wary about doing so. She eventually settled down on the grass and watched us from a distance. 'We didn't say anything about taking her on trial,' I whispered. 'What are we going to do?'

'We'll have to see what she's like with the chooks. If she chases chooks there's no point even thinking about it.'

'What, check now?'

'Why not?'

'Because we've still got Benson! We can't have two dogs on trial at the same time.'

'We'll put Benson inside while Maggie's in the garden. We'll know straightaway if she's going to chase the chooks.'

'She looks a lot older than seven,' I hissed as the man came back holding a length of rope. 'Sorry, I'm not sure where her lead is,' he said, tying the rope to her collar and handing me the other end.

I offered the rope to CC. 'Why don't you take her?' I said.

He shook his head. 'No, she'll be happier with you. I'll drive.'

The lumpy red dog looked at me with suspicion and didn't move. 'Come on,' I said, with as much enthusiasm as I could muster. She stayed put. 'Magsy, come on,' urged the man in shorts and Maggie lumbered to her feet, following dutifully as we trooped out towards the car. I moved in a dream, clutching an old piece of rope with a dog attached to the other end, wondering how this was happening. It was all going too fast. I'd only wanted to go and have a look; I didn't think we'd be going home with her.

We opened the back door of CC's treasured new Subaru and I scooted across, holding fast to the frayed length of rope. The man in shorts encouraged Maggie to follow. 'She loves going for a drive,' he said. 'Come on Magsy, hup!' The red dog turned her head to look back at the open ute she was clearly used to travelling in, then turned to me, sitting primly in the back of a Subaru with leather upholstery and tinted windows. No contest. In the end, the man in shorts hoisted her up and she scrabbled in beside me. Suddenly the back seat was full of dog, a big bulky mass of agitated dog, heavy and unhappy, with me on the end of a rope tied to her collar. She was so big she could barely turn around. What if her fear turned to anger at being cooped up in the back of a strange car? I was nervous about reaching across to comfort her in case she turned on me. Her slack jaws hung open at the same height as my face and she was panting in distress, her tongue hanging out. I pictured rabid fangs sinking into the flesh of my arm and a powerful head shaking from side to side as a strange dog tried to rip my arm out of its socket.

'Open the window,' said CC.

I nervously reached across, pressed the button and Maggie was transformed from a potential killer into a family pet. She poked her head out of the open window, her face turned to the wind, and sniffed joyfully at the breeze. I took a deep breath and only then realised how shallow my breathing had been. Clumps of red hair came out in handfuls when I reached across to pat her greasy coat and my fingers were quickly smeared with dirt.

'She's filthy.'

'Nothing a good wash won't cure.'

We were home in ten minutes and Maggie jumped down from the car, leaving behind an alarming amount of dirt and oily hair on the back seat. 'Don't worry, we can clean it up,' CC said. Finding dirt on the back seat of his brand new car was the equivalent of me realising I'd spilt wine on my laptop, then remembering it had been weeks since the last backup. (Let me tell you, I didn't laugh.) I put Benson inside, snuggling his warm body that already smelt so familiar, and CC led Maggie into the garden.

I felt a bit like the chooks must have felt when Bertie was thrust into their cage. I didn't *want* another dog – we already *had* one. I walked into the centre of the lawn, subconsciously claiming my territory, and Maggie followed. She sat at my feet, then looked up with eyes full of trust. There was something so obvious in her expression it made my heart jump. She was asking to stay, appealing to me. I reached down to stroke her and she sank to the grass and rolled over. Ten minutes later we were still there, Maggie lying on her back, me rubbing her tummy.

'Leave her alone, see what she does,' said CC, calmly sitting under the pergola reading the paper. I sat down next to him and Maggie followed, then lay at my feet. 'She's taken to you,' he said.

I got up and walked onto the lawn. 'Maggie,' I called. She came straightaway, lay down and thumped her tail on the grass.

My heart constricted and I felt like crying. I thought the decision had been made. We were keeping Benson, the boisterous but practically perfect puppy in every way, and now there was Maggie, the placid, calm hair-shedding red heeler.

'What shall we do?' I asked, desperate for CC to make the decision.

'It's up to you.'

'But what do you think?'

'Maggie's the better dog.'

'What do you mean, better?'

He put down his paper and we ran through the pros and cons, contrasting the youth and energy of Benson the beagle with the placid temperament of an older dog. Maggie came when she was called and did what she was told. No one else wanted her and if we didn't take her, who would? Something told me to make the decision quickly so I let my instincts take over and I opened my mouth to speak, not knowing what would come out, not letting reason get in the way.

'We'll take Benson back,' I said, my voice wavering.

'Sure?' CC asked.

I nodded, not trusting myself to say anything else. The fact that CC didn't try to talk me out of it told me Benson was never going to be the right dog for us. Sure, CC would have accepted Benson if I'd insisted, but we both had to be happy with the dog we adopted.

'I'll take him back,' he said. 'You stay with Maggie.'

He wanted to spare me the unhappy task because he knew how hard I would find it but I couldn't let him do that. I chose Benson and I had to take him back.

'Seriously, I'm happy to do it,' he said and I shook my head, feeling tears prickle behind my eyes. If I said anything else I knew I would start crying.

I went inside and Benson put his paws up at the child gate across the laundry door, looking at me with the same trust I saw in Maggie's eyes. I wanted to reach out and hold him tight and never let him go. I stroked his soft coat, smoothed his long velvet ears and kissed the top of his head, then I picked him up and carried him out to the car. He sat on my lap the whole way, not struggling or protesting, and I drove one-handed, the other hand resting on the soft, warm skin of his back, sensing his youth and gentle nature. By the time we pulled into the yard of the RSPCA I was weeping openly.

I carried Benson in and the receptionist looked up from her paperwork. Her smile didn't last long. 'I'm bringing Benson back,' I said, my voice choked with emotion. 'We had him on trial over Christmas and it didn't work out.'

She drew the microphone towards her without taking her eyes off me. 'Reject in front reception,' she said coldly, then went back to her paperwork. A door opened and the veterinary nurse who introduced me to Benson appeared. She knelt down beside us and Benson nestled his head into her lap, pressing against her as she stroked his soft ears. 'Was there something wrong with him?'

'No,' I said, shedding more tears. 'There was nothing wrong with him. He's a lovely dog, he learnt to sit really quickly and I think he's house-trained now, he didn't chase the chooks and he'll make a great pet for the right person.' I could barely get the words out. 'He wasn't right for us, that's all. He's just not the right dog for us.'

'Never mind,' she said. 'At least we know he's OK. We'll find a good home for him, don't worry.'

She picked Benson up and I rested my hand on his soft puppy head one last time, then I walked back out to the car, gulping back sobs. I'd done the right thing. Benson had been on trial over Christmas, he wasn't permanent and it didn't work out – wasn't that what a trial was for? A dog had to be right for both of us and

Benson wasn't. I kept thinking about what CC had said, only half in jest, about Benson not being a proper dog, and I cried some more. He was a proper dog in my eyes.

I got home, sat on the sofa and howled. I couldn't stop weeping and I wasn't sure why. No one told me it would be this hard. I had no idea you could fall head over heels in love with a dog and the feeling of loss was so intense it reminded me of other times when I've walked away from someone I loved, knowing the relationship wasn't right and yet longing to be with them at the same time.

'You've made the right decision,' said CC, coming to sit down next to me and patting my arm.

'I know.'

'We went through the pros and cons,' he reminded me.

'I know, but loving Benson wasn't on the list. I loved him,' I said, choking back the tears, my eyes streaming and my nose running. 'I loved him,' I wailed. CC looked alarmed. The sane, logical woman who left twenty minutes ago now couldn't stop crying.

'Have you made the wrong decision?'

'No! I can't change my mind now, I can't! We've got Maggie and I have to accept that. I'm just upset, that's all. I'll learn to like her.' What was I saying? I couldn't even bring myself to say I might learn to love her.

'Frosty, if you've made the wrong decision there's no shame in reversing it.'

I shook my head, my nose was blocked by now, and the tears kept coming. 'I'm just grieving for Benson,' I said, and the sound of his name set off a renewed fit of crying.

CC scanned my face to try to understand. 'Let's sleep on it,' he said. 'If you wake up tomorrow and you still feel the same way, we'll go and get Benson back.'

I went to bed barely able to breath through a blocked nose, thinking all the time about Benson. He was such a loveable, adorable dog; why did I give him away? What was I doing swapping the beautiful Benson for a scruffy, smelly, arthritic dog who shed hair and wanted to sleep outdoors?

chapter twenty-eight

My waking thought was of Benson, alone in a cage with a concrete floor. The word 'reject' rang in my ears, a stinging indictment of failure.

I dressed without enthusiasm and went to join CC under the pergola. Maggie thumped her tail as I walked past. A slight breeze rustled the leaves on the lemon eucalypt as the early morning sun filtered through the grapevine, the chooks were happily scratching in the rose garden and the damp grass tickled my bare feet. It was a perfect summer morning but for one thing. Benson, the adorable and practically perfect three-month-old puppy, had been banished from our lives.

CC looked up from the paper. 'You seem a bit calmer this morning,' he said. I promptly burst into tears and slumped onto a garden chair.

'Frosty, this is silly. If you feel that strongly about Benson, we can go and get him back. I just think he'll give you a lot of trouble in the garden, that's all.'

'No-oh! I gave Benson up and I don't deserve to have him back.' Fuelled by guilt and self-pity, I didn't know what I wanted anymore. I sounded like a petulant child.

'Stop it,' said CC, refusing to take part in the drama. He was the calm eye of the storm. 'I'll explain to Maggie's owners that we made a mistake. It's easily rectified.'

'But you don't want Benson,' I howled, forcing the problem onto him. 'You never wanted Benson. You said Benson wasn't a proper dog!'

'He's not,' said CC in reasonable, measured tones. 'And it's not that I don't want him. I just think he'll be a lot of trouble for you.'

'See? You said he'd be trouble for *me*, you didn't say us. You don't want him.'

'Are you saying it's my fault?' He looked shocked and I stared at the floor, my bottom lip quivering. 'Did you send Benson back because of me? Is that why you got Maggie,' he persisted. 'Because of me?'

'I got her because she'll be a better dog for us.' I mumbled, sounding sulky and unconvinced.

'Then why are you still crying?'

Why *was* I still crying? Nobody made me take Benson back; it had been my decision, just like it had been my choice to point out there was an ad in the paper for a red heeler. Gut instinct made me take Benson back. I didn't always listen to my instincts but when I did they'd always been proved reliable. Now I was so upset I couldn't think straight. Why did I want to give up an adorable puppy? I loved him yet I took him back. Why? I didn't understand what was happening and I didn't trust myself to talk it through either; there was a danger I would blame CC (who was I kidding, it was an odds-on certainty).

'Like I said before, it's up to you,' he said, turning to the financial section. 'I'm happy to do a swap if you want to.'

'You don't want Benson, though, do you?'

He sighed. 'I've told you I don't mind. I think Maggie's the better dog but if you want Benson back, we can go and get him.'

When you fall in love you don't consider better or worse, you just go with the flow and follow your instincts; isn't that how it's meant to go? It was something I had never trusted myself to do since that first doomed love affair at fifteen and the catalogue of disasters that followed. I fell in love with Benson yet my instinct told me to take him back, so that's what I did. But why was I talking about falling in love with a dog? What was wrong with me? It was tempting to go and get Benson back but I knew what would happen if I did. There would always be an unspoken 'I told you so' any time Benson escaped, chewed the furniture or crapped on the carpet. And I couldn't keep changing my mind. How could I compound my error (if that's what it was) by taking another dog back to the pound? Who else would take an elderly, arthritic, overweight red heeler? I hadn't suggested we take Maggie on trial, I had just said let's keep her. Instinct. The slight breeze that helped mitigate that morning's heat had disappeared and the air felt sultry and heavy. My sweaty legs were stuck to the white plastic chair and I stared at half an inch of murky liquid swirling in the bottom of my coffee cup.

'Well, here's my plan,' said CC, patiently folding his paper and getting up from the table. 'I'm going to do some figure work on the computer, then I'm going to finish my filing. When I've done that we need to make some decisions.' What a reasonable approach; how sensible and grown-up compared to the moody middle-aged brat sitting opposite with a red nose and blotchy face.

CC went in and Maggie watched him go from a shady spot under the tree, ears pricked, then she turned her head towards me. I looked away. Had I made a complete mess of the whole dog business after so much research and agonising over what breed to get? I tried to make sense of what had happened, searching for clues. I'd spent months preparing to get a dog and we'd had endless late-night discussions about dog breeds, dog behaviour, where a dog would sleep, what place a dog had in a family, the pros and cons of getting one now or waiting until CC retired, the pros and cons of getting one at all. We had navigated our way through a minefield of differences and somehow found compromises, something I never could have done in previous relationships (few of them lasted long enough for there to be much talking). After all that, I picked out Benson on my own. Sure I sent CC a text to check he didn't mind having a dog on trial over Christmas but I didn't involve him in the choice of dog. I chose Benson, just like I chose the staffy that killed Bertie and the unsuitable beagle puppy in Menindee. Maggie was the first dog we had gone to see together. Is that what made my instincts kick in?

*

I rummaged through torn sheets, light bulbs, batteries, boxes of tissues, cans of flyspray, bike helmets, mousetraps, inner tubes, extension cords and vacuum-cleaner bags, searching for the dog brush I knew I'd seen in the cupboard in the laundry. I found it hidden under a pile of plastic carrier bags, its wooden handle cracked with age.

Maggie wagged her tail as I knelt on the grass and her coat shed dirty clumps of slippery hair, which were taken by the wind and blown about the garden. The soothing, rhythmic brushing calmed me as much as it did Maggie and she rolled on her back, wriggling in the grass. As I brushed, her true colour slowly revealed itself, a rich golden ochre, the colour of desert sand. She was a paler version of the red earth that surrounded Broken Hill itself.

'She could do with a bath,' CC said, appearing beside me with a plastic baby bath in his hands.

'Where did you get that?'

'It used to be Boof's. I kept it in the shed, just in case.'

He put the bath on the lawn in the shade of the gum tree and I kept brushing while CC fetched boiling water, a bucket and a bottle of dog shampoo, another treasure unearthed from the cupboard in the laundry. After pouring boiling water into the bath he topped it up with cold from the hose, testing the temperature as carefully as if Maggie was a newborn. This was a side of him I hadn't seen before. He brought out a lead in case Maggie struggled but we needn't have worried – she was as docile as a koala when we lifted her bulky weight into the bath.

'There we go, old girl,' CC said, with a tenderness that took me by surprise. Maggie stood in the bath, quietly compliant as we doused her grubby coat in warm water. She didn't move or struggle as we lathered shampoo into her coat, working away at the ingrained dirt. More clumps of hair came loose in soggy bundles that floated on the murky surface as we worked together, quietly soothing Maggie with murmured words of encouragement. After a final rinse from a bucket of warm water, she clambered out of the bath and shook herself, with as much vigour as an elderly lady could muster. CC laid a hand on top of her head.

'She'll dry off in the sun,' he said, his fondness for her evident in every gesture.

I took a towel to rub Maggie dry and she leant against my body, pressing her weight into me. Washed and brushed, she wasn't as overweight as I'd thought. Her large pointed ears were darker than the rest of her coat and the patch of white fur at her throat was more noticeable now that she was clean. It matched her white socks and feet. The other thing I hadn't noticed before was a tiny white tip on the end of her long, sweeping tail. I stroked the top of her head and realised she was a good-looking dog.

I spent the next hour gardening while CC was inside on his computer. When I looked up Maggie was never far away. Sometimes I could sense her watching me, sometimes I forgot she was there but always if I called her, Maggie was at my side in an instant. When the heat got too intense I sat down under the shade of the tree and stroked her warm coat. It was smooth and fresh smelling after the bath. Did I really want Benson back? I had asked to take him on trial and I'd sent him back at the end of that trial. Now here we were with Maggie, the red heeler cross who didn't appear to have any of the famed red heeler aggression, nor any of the frenetic activity so prevalent in the kelpie she was supposedly crossed with. I had thought there was a touch of Labrador in her but now I wasn't so sure – with her thin face and tall pointed ears she looked quite alien. I'd never met a dog like Maggie before, certainly not one that was so placid and happy to take so much stroking and cuddling, without once trying to struggle free. She was a lovely creature.

CC's desk was positioned under the window, which gave him a view of the whole garden. When I went in to see him later and ask if he'd like a cup of tea I found him staring out of the window.

'She adores you,' he said, looking at Maggie stretched out on the grass. 'You can tell by the way she follows you around. Benson was a playful puppy. He may have been a lot of fun and you may have loved him but he didn't love you, not in the way Maggie does.'

It was a long and surprisingly emotional speech for CC who rarely revealed the depth of his feelings. It must have taken him by surprise because he put his head down and made out he was concentrating on the line of figures in front of him, but I knew better. I knew exactly what he was trying to tell me and it felt like someone had taken a metal spoon and scooped out my insides.

In that moment I understood just how much my infatuation with A3 had hurt him.

'I want to keep her,' I said, my throat constricting. 'I want to keep Maggie.'

CC nodded. His eyes were full of tears.

'I'm glad,' he said.

'And don't worry, I'll get over Benson. I will definitely grow to love Maggie,' I said, smiling now through my own tears.

The next day, New Year's Eve, I took Maggie to the RSPCA to sign the official change of ownership papers. While we were there, it made sense to ask the vet to give her a quick health check. Far from being unnerved by the busy surgery Maggie trotted calmly into the consulting room.

The vet bent down to stroke her head. 'Hello Maggie, how are you?' Maggie thumped her tail. There was something in the familiarity of their greeting that made me wonder if the vet knew her. 'I do,' he said in answer to my question. 'Maggie's been coming here since she was a puppy, haven't you?' he said.

'Six or seven years then?' I said.

The vet laughed. 'Maggie's older than that.'

He took a moment to check her record on his computer. 'Here we go, she's nine or ten, we're not exactly sure.' I nodded. I didn't blame the owner for fudging her age; he just wanted to make sure someone would adopt her.

'She's a gorgeous girl, aren't you?' Maggie looked at the vet with trusting eyes. 'I've never met a nicer dingo,' he said.

The air in the surgery felt charged. If I'd been a dog, believe me, my ears would have been pricked and pointing forwards. 'A what?' I said quietly.

'A dingo,' he repeated. 'She's got a bit of kelpie in her but she's mostly dingo.'

*

Maggie padded up to CC when we got home and he scratched her behind one of her exceptionally large ears. She flopped to the floor. We were the proud owners of an adopted dingo. ('Grandma, what big ears you've got!')

'Everything all right at the RSPCA?'

'She's not a red heeler,' I said.

'Isn't she?' CC kept scratching and Maggie thumped her tail.

'Maggie,' I said, pausing for dramatic effect, 'is a dingo!'

CC looked remarkably unfazed by the news. 'We had a dingo once when I worked at Arkaroola, in the Flinders Ranges. Lovely dog, it was.' He smiled at the memory and that's when I suspected he had known all along we were adopting a dingo. When challenged, he shrugged. 'I knew she wasn't a red heeler,' was all he would admit.

I googled dingo and multiple images of Maggie popped up on screen, all with the same ears, face, white paws and white-tipped tail. It turned out dingoes aren't even dogs, they're a separate subspecies – *canis lupus dingo* – ancient wild animals, according to Wikipedia, more akin to a grey wolf than a domestic dog. I read everything I could find, including Dreamtime stories that told of a close relationship between Aboriginal people and dingoes. Some Aboriginal languages gave dingoes living with them one name (Walaku) and those that lived in the wild another (Ngurakin). Whatever you called them, it was worrying to discover that you weren't allowed to own a dingo as a pet in western New South Wales, an area that included Broken Hill. They were feral animals; vertebrate pests; according to the Department of Primary Industries. Australia's famous dog fence, the world's longest barrier at 5500 kilometres, was built to keep them out of grazing and pastoral land. The Wild Dog Destruction Board did exactly what it said, employing dozens of people to maintain the dog fence. According to one report, they paid ten dollars for each dingo scalp and farmers were allowed to shoot them on sight to prevent attacks on livestock. Thankfully the papers we'd signed had Maggie listed as a kelpie cross.

It was dark by the time I switched off the computer. I pushed back my chair and Maggie lumbered to her feet from where she'd been snoozing under the desk. I could have handed her back and claimed we'd been misled, I could have admitted she was a dingo and told the previous owner we weren't allowed to keep her, but the thought of Maggie being put down made my stomach lurch. I reached down to give her a hug and she rested her head on my knees, then flopped to the floor.

Far from being an outdoor dog, our domesticated dingo came into the house at every opportunity. She was mild-mannered, timid and could sometimes be encouraged to play with a ball. She did all the usual things you'd expect a dog to do – buried her bone in the vegetable patch, shed enough hair to stuff a sofa and stole the bacon I was planning to cook for breakfast – but really all Maggie wanted to do was lie down and be stroked. Tickle her under the chin and she would flop to the floor, offering her belly for a rub. She loved hugs, hated being left alone and would rather sleep than go for a walk. She was obedient, friendly and a delightful companion, wary of large men but a gentle pushover with children. That said, there was no denying she was a dingo. When one of the chooks escaped from the enclosure and fluttered around the garden in a mad panic, Maggie couldn't help but pounce. I found her moments later with a surprised look on her face and a mouthful of feathers. Where once there were four, now there were only three.

CC wanted Maggie to sleep outdoors and I wanted her to sleep inside. There was a time when such intractable positions would have been a deal-breaker, proof of irreconcilable differences that marked the end of any fledgling relationship. Not any more. I'd learnt to negotiate, learnt to accept I couldn't always get my own way, and so we reached a compromise. If the temperature dipped below double digits Maggie slept inside. On balmy nights she slept outside.

As a child CC used to trap dingoes and sell the pelts, adding to his family's meagre income in William Creek. When he discovered the dingoes were willing to chew their own legs off in an attempt to get away, he put strychnine on the traps. 'I couldn't bear the thought of them dying a lingering death,' he said. Maybe that explained his tenderness towards Maggie now, retribution for all the dingoes he'd trapped and skinned as a child. He's a softie at heart. The first Christmas after his wife left, CC had laid a place for Boof at the dining-room table and they ate Christmas dinner together, he and his blue heeler sitting opposite one another on padded pink plush velour.

The irony of the situation – that the dog we ended up with wasn't a dog at all but a dingo – didn't escape either of us and I shamelessly used it to my advantage. 'You said a dog couldn't come indoors. Maggie's not a dog, she's a dingo,' I would say, pushing the back door wide open and watching Maggie trot past. She would head for my office where she would clamber onto the battered sofa and stretch out in luxurious comfort, arching her back when I sat next to her in the hope I might tickle her tummy.

Benson quickly found another home with a young family, just like the RSPCA said he would, and I quickly got over losing him. He was a reminder of all those past relationships, good and bad, that never moved beyond the puppy stage. Much as I had hated handing him back, I'd known it had to be done.

Maggie may have been a dingo but she was definitely the right dog for us.

chapter twenty-nine

So here we are, no longer him and me. We. CC sent me a Valentine's Day card and scratched out the word 'love'. *I like you*, he wrote. *Friends like you are hard to find*, I responded. There's no rush, although at the risk of sounding like a middle-aged, loved-up babe from Broken Hill, CC is the best thing that's ever happened to me, by an outback country mile. He's the yin to my yang. He's even dealt with PK, the nickname Frosty enough of a nod in her direction to acknowledge her existence, yet keep her in check. She's happy with the choice of CC as mate; we're well matched. I might have an edge in cultural awareness but he has far more native cunning, offset by a streak of decency that runs through his core like the writing in a stick of Blackpool rock. We make each other laugh.

We've been noodling for opals in White Cliffs, attended a two-day gymkhana at Innamincka Station, a cricket match in the middle of the Strzelecki Desert and even met royalty (nothing new for CC but I was in a lather of excitement, let me tell you). Their Royal Highnesses Prince Charles and the Duchess of Cornwall flew to Longreach to name a new RFDS aircraft and CC was

MC (sorry, couldn't resist). He wore an Akubra hat pushed back on his head like a pro, affording a glimpse of the nine-year-old who'd lived in William Creek, then run off to muster brumbies.

There was an ex-patient there that day, Jim Nunn, who told the royal couple about his life-or-death rescue by the Flying Doctor after an accident with an angry bull in Queensland. After the ceremony Jim came up to me. CC was busy talking to VIPs and Jim nodded in his direction. 'Has he ever lived in William Creek?' he asked.

'Yes!' I said. 'How did you know?'

'I knew he was too smart to stick around there too long,' said Jim. It turned out Jim was one of the stockmen who had taken CC brumby mustering all those years ago. They talked after the ceremony and it was the first time they had met in almost sixty years. Living in outback Australia is full of surprises.

Crown Princess Mary of Denmark, that unknown Tasmanian who met her Danish prince at the Slip Inn on Sussex Street, also came to Broken Hill to launch a new breast care service for the RFDS. She was guest of honour at a glittering lunch held in the hangar and I was on the top table, a nerve-racking occasion almost ruined when I went to pick up my knife and fork before Her Royal Highness had lifted hers. 'Don't,' whispered CC, saving me, and him, from acute embarrassment. That came later, when HRH got up to leave and we all stood up to say goodbye. The glasses perched on top of my head hadn't been cleaned for a while and I didn't want to miss seeing her plane take off so I whipped them off, grabbed the bottom of my shirt and cleaned them. It was an automatic gesture, something I do several times a day because I always wipe them on my shirt. On this occasion though I wasn't wearing a shirt. In honour of the royal visit, I was wearing a dress. The saving grace was that Crown Princess Mary had her back to me. She was shaking hands with Her

Excellency Professor Marie Bashir, Governor of New South Wales and Patron of the RFDS, who along with the rest of the assembled dignitaries in the hangar that day had risen to say goodbye. If any of them had been looking my way (and I do hope they weren't), they would have been afforded the briefest flash of clean white underwear. I didn't even know I'd done it. After lunch dentist Lyn Mayne came up to me and said, 'I wish I'd had a camera. That was priceless.'

I don't belong in a princess's world, in spite of the endless diet of fairytales I had consumed as a child. Now I know there's no such thing as the perfect mate or the ideal husband, just another person with flaws and failings like the rest of us. A person you can love.

Among the many wonderful things Peter Ustinov wrote was this: 'I am at my happiest with imperfect happiness. Perfection has no personality.'

I was worried that because I hadn't *fallen* in love with CC it meant we had no future. A lifetime of intense emotion had immured me to the quieter feelings of joy and pleasure, the warmth of a caress, the reliability of a trusted partner. I'd grown accustomed to sorrow, loneliness and disappointment; the familiarity and intensity of such feelings had been oddly comforting. Over the years I'd clung to them, nursing old hurts, reliving old disappointments, enjoying the nostalgia of looking back on something that hadn't worked, revisiting the past and aching over lost love. I'd spent years carrying a sick feeling of dread and emptiness around like an old familiar, nursing the desperate last shreds of hope that lost love might be resurrected.

I'm glad I didn't fall in love with CC. That plummet through space invariably turned me into a helpless loon, a needy, nervous, anxiety-ridden shadow, eager and desperate for approval one minute, bullish and sullen the next (there are those who might be tempted to suggest that describes my normal behaviour but I beg to differ – falling in love did that to me). *Not* falling in love with CC was the best thing that could ever have happened. He saw the best, and the worst, of the real me and I saw a man I liked and admired, a man I respected. The longer I spent with him, the more I liked him. There are those who can handle love at first sight, and if you're one of them, congratulations. I'm not suggesting a 'sleep with someone you like and see what happens' approach will suit everyone, but it suited me. I like having my feet firmly on the ground.

So if I don't belong in a fairytale princess world, where do I belong? I think it must be with CC. He fell off his bicycle not long after we met, a competitive race across a desert track that ended abruptly with him flying over the handlebars and breaking several vertebrae in his back, effectively ending any future tennis, running or mountain biking. He's left with swimming, so we swim together. The fifty-metre open-air heated swimming pool is one of the many things I love about Broken Hill.

Of course, embracing CC means letting go of the notion that I could jump on a plane, fly to Paris and fall in love with a Frenchman smoking Gauloises and drinking pastis in a basement jazz bar (then no doubt wandering lonely along the Champs-Élysées after I discover he's having an affair with a student thirty years younger). It means letting go of the idea that I could audition for the Royal Shakespeare Company, land a lead role in a production of *Macbeth* and join a six-month tour to the Indian subcontinent where I might fall in love with a maharajah (who in all probability would turn out to be an imposter from Peckham with no money and three ex-wives). Pick any unlikely scenario, any fantastical notion and it's a possibility denied if I jump in the river with CC, who of course represents the biggest adventure I could ever embark on.

When love turned up unexpectedly at fifteen, the feeling was so intense I couldn't resist; it was the kind of passionate, burning desire poets write about. Instead of sharing the pain of that disastrous first love affair – with my Mum, my sisters or any of my girlfriends – I locked it away. *Give sorrow words*. I couldn't. The self-destructive behaviour that followed only added to the tally of disasters as the years went by until eventually I grew to mistrust love, and falling in love. Still, at least I can take heart from studies that have shown that passionate phase only lasts about six months, then your hormones go back to normal and you wake up one morning wondering what you're doing with the fallible, complex, entirely human person lying in bed next to you. If you're lucky, you'll still love that person.

This morning, emptying the kitchen bin behind the back door, I understood that phrase, 'seek and ye shall find'. It was a phrase that had always got under my skin. How could it be that easy? What if I was the kind of person who didn't know what she was looking for until she found it? Seek what? Find what? The expression irritated me, largely because it contained a nugget of wisdom I couldn't grasp, until this morning. Tying the top of the plastic bin liner I realised it meant I would find what I was looking for. So if I expected to find a selfish, bullying coward who treated me badly, I would; if I looked for a lost soul with nothing but heartache in his pockets and hurt in his eyes, that's what I would find.

And with another blinding flash of insight (maybe I should try doing the ironing one day as well) came another revelation. You can turn that around. Expect to meet someone good, decent, kind and considerate and you will. Seek and ye shall find.

Last year I planted Lynne's gift of strawberry plants and I was disappointed at the meagre crop of misshapen, tight little berries the plants produced. I thought about digging them up and moving them, thought about buying more plants, a different variety, better stock, heavier croppers and did none of it, partly because I couldn't be bothered to uproot the plants and dig over a new bed, and partly because of a faint hope that they might do better the following year. This summer I picked a bumper harvest of ripe, succulent fruit, a crop we savoured each morning, bowls full of ripe berries warmed by the sun. And after weeks of continual harvest, when I'd picked the plants clean, I left the woodlice, slugs, ants and birds to have their fill of whatever I'd missed. We went away for two weeks, set the watering system to automatic and came back to find the plants had thrown out more shoots with more berries, bigger and juicier than before, and in another week or so the harvest will begin again. Sometimes it's worth waiting and hanging in there to see what might happen.

CC asked me the other day what emotion I thought was stronger: love or hate? I'd always thought love was stronger than hate, based on what I'd read and heard from others. Now I know it's true. Hate feeds on itself and turns inward like a canker; love looks out. The more you love, the more that love spreads, infecting everyone it touches with light and joy.

Many years ago my grandmother was in service as an under-house parlour maid at Thornbury Castle in Gloucestershire. She walked with the man courting her through the historic gardens, following ancient paths that Henry VIII and Anne Boleyn once trod. Her suitor stopped at an ivy-clad wall and got down on one knee to propose. 'You see the way that ivy clings to the wall?' he said. 'That's how closely I'm going to cling to you.' Decades later, Gran showed me the spot when we visited the castle, tears in her eyes as she recounted the story. I couldn't imagine anyone saying something so beautiful to me.

CC has topped it.

On a short trip to Darwin for work we extended our stay for a couple of days and took an afternoon walk beside a marina. I noticed a man with a weathered face and sunburnt arms sitting alone in a bar, nursing a glass of beer, and I pointed him out to CC. 'He looks sad,' I said.

'Maybe his wife has died,' CC replied. 'Maybe they used to come here for a drink and now he comes back each day, knowing she'll never turn up. If I lost you, I would lay a place for you at dinner every night,' he said quietly. It was one of those unexpected flashes of emotion that sometimes surfaced when I least expected it.

Is that when I fell in love with CC? Who knows? I don't know that I ever did really *fall* in love, but I do know I love him. The looks, the smiles, the caresses, the laughter, the spread sheets and the cooked breakfasts, the swimming and the Sunday roasts, have all added up. The sum total of the past four years has led somewhere completely unexpected. Love has never involved friendship for me. Fire, yes: burning, raging fire that eventually burnt itself out. Love was dangerous, illicit, scary, unsettling, threatening, passionate and something to be avoided. I don't know if I have ever loved someone in a way that stood any real chance of lasting. I kept expecting love to turn up like a lightning flash; I didn't realise it could melt your heart like a blanket of snow disappearing on the first warm day of spring.

My dear old dad died last year and I went back to England for the funeral, leaving CC in Broken Hill with Maggie and a workload that couldn't be put off. I was planning to read the eulogy but as the day approached, I wobbled, worried I would burst into tears and ruin it. CC supported me from a different time zone and another continent. 'You have a job to do,' he said on the phone. 'Do the job and make your dad proud.' Just before the funeral he sent me a text message. *I love you. I am standing next to you. My strength is your strength. You will stand tall.* And I did.

I've been in Broken Hill almost four years now and another winter is drawing to a close. Sitting on the sofa with CC, rugged up, log fire lit, glass of sauvignon blanc in hand, I think of that quote from Shakespeare: 'There is a tide in the affairs of man, which taken at the flood leads on to fortune.' I can't remember the rest, something about life being spent in the shallows if you don't seize the moment. I've been puddling around in the shallow end for long enough. It's time to jump.

I love an Aussie bloke who can't spell, whose main interest is sport, whose idea of a gourmet meal is steak and peas, followed by yoghurt mixed with a liberal helping of protein powder, and whose dress sense is . . . getting better. When he wears jeans and a pale blue shirt he looks gorgeous, with his silver grey hair and tall, slim frame. Other women glance at him as we walk along.

We make an odd sort of couple here in Broken Hill, with a dwindling clutch of chooks and Maggie, the domesticated dingo: Captain Considerate, the carnivorous, share-trading, sports-mad liberal and Miss Prissy Knickers, ex-stalker, left-wing, tree-hugging vegetarian.

It must be love.

epilogue

The humidity is at eighty per cent, the back of my neck is burning and the sand feels gritty under my fingers. It's two days after Christmas and we're lying on Shark Beach, surrounded by a sprawl of excitable Sydneysiders.

CC looks as alarmed as I feel at the sensory overload of brightly coloured beach towels, red-and-white-striped sun umbrellas, swaying shelters, deck chairs, runners, joggers, walkers, swimmers and sunbathers. Fragments of humanity fill the beach, surrounding us with a jigsaw of pregnant stomachs, long legs, dimpled cellulite, crawling babies, bikinis, seagulls, six-packs, bald heads, tight shorts, trendy underpants, tattoos, body piercings, teenagers, grannies, beer bellies, sunburnt arms, pale legs and naked children.

There's a game of cricket underway behind us, the fielders positioned between picnic blankets spread on the grass under the trees and somehow, implausibly, two people are playing ping-pong in front of us, standing waist deep in the water. Beyond the shark netting, passenger ferries plough through the choppy waves, overtaking yachts and pleasure cruisers, avoiding windsurfers and dinghies. Children laugh, gulls screech, seaplanes take off from nearby Rose Bay and the occasional A380 roars into the blue sky above us, two small specks lying side by side on a small patch of warm sand.

The sign at the entrance to Nielsen Park said 'No dogs'. It's just as well we didn't bring Maggie – even if she had been allowed in she wouldn't have enjoyed the frenetic activity on this beach. We took her for a walk through Birchgrove Oval yesterday, venturing along the wooden jetty that reaches into the harbour, and the shifting patterns of light on the surface of so much water spooked her. She pricked up her ears, turned around and trotted smartly back to the park. So we left her at home today.

Home? Yes, home. You see, just as the final chapter of this book was being written CC heard his job was moving to Sydney. After decades in Broken Hill the corporate office of the Royal Flying Doctor Service South Eastern Section was relocating, and CC had to move with it. So we packed up our belongings, loaded Maggie into the back of the car and drove twelve hundred kilometres towards the coast to our new home in Sydney.

We live in beautiful Birchgrove now, my favourite suburb, in a lovely house with a wrought iron balcony and a spreading frangipani tree in the back yard. I have close friends living nearby and Kate and James live just around the corner. Of course the irony is that I miss Broken Hill. I miss the space, the silence and the quiet sense of community I found there.

Opening the lid of one of the boxes soon after we arrived, I discovered a small spider, no bigger than my little fingernail, with a tell-tale red stripe along its back. Far from filling me with dread, the sight of that tiny redback brought a warm glow of nostalgia for the outback community I grew to love.

Maggie will take a while to get used to living in Sydney, as we all will, so CC and I have made a pact. If we can't settle, we'll pack up the car, ship our belongings and drive back over the Blue Mountains. We'll follow the wide Mitchell Highway through Bathurst, Orange and Dubbo, turn left at Nyngan and keep going for another six hours until we reach the hot and dusty place we once felt privileged to call home.

acknowledgements

I am enormously grateful to Pippa and Laura at Curtis Brown
for believing I could write this book, to Ingrid Ohlsson at
Macmillan who astonished me by commissioning it and to editor
Sam Sainsbury, whose insightful comments helped guide and
shape the story. Deonie Fiford's thoughtful editing made a huge
improvement to the original manuscript and I also thank Kate
and Lisa for their helpful feedback and eagle-eyed proofreading.

A three-week residency at Varuna gave me a glimmer of hope
that I might one day manage to write a book and I also want
to thank Rae Luckie for a series of inspirational workshops at
Broken Hill library. The Bristol Writers group kick-started my
desire to write and residential workshops at the Arvon Foundation
in England reinforced it.

I'd like to thank the people I met in Broken Hill who so
generously welcomed me into the community and all the dedic-
ated staff who work for the RFDS, some of whom I'm now
privileged to call friends.

I owe a huge debt of gratitude to my three sisters, Wendy,
Elizabeth and Rachel, and their partners, Jef, Don and Ray

acknowledgements

(aka George), for their constant love and encouragement. I also want to thank my nieces and nephews, Charlotte, Emma, Thomas, Jessica and Daniel, for showing me how easy love can be.

To all my girlfriends in England and Australia, especially Kate, Helen, Louise, Cathy and Andrea, who have patiently suffered through what must have seemed at times like a never-ending series of crises over men (which of course it was). Your loving friendship has been and remains a source of abiding strength and joy. And thank you to all the As for what you tried to teach me. It was my failing, not yours.

Writing this memoir has been a deeply personal exercise and I have inevitably intruded into the lives of others. I thank those who allowed me to include their names in this book and I apologise to those I was unable to track down. I trust the innocent have been suitably protected by name changes.

My greatest thanks go to CC, who stands by my side with loving patience and unswerving kindness. His support and encouragement kept me going as this manuscript progressed.

Thank you CC, for showing me the true meaning of love and for allowing me to share our story.

Fiona Higgins
Love in the Age of Drought

When Fiona meets Stuart at a conference in Melbourne she isn't looking for a relationship, let alone the upheaval of falling for a cotton farmer from South-East Queensland. But then life never quite goes according to plan . . .

When Stuart sends Fiona a pair of crusty old boots and a declaration of his feelings sixteen days into their relationship, it's the start of a love story that endures – in spite of distance, the strain of Stuart's farm entering its fourth year of drought, and Fiona's issues with commitment.

Something's got to give, and eventually Fiona puts everything on the line – her career, her Sydney life, her future – and moves to Stuart's farm. Nearest township? Jandowae, population 750.

Here, Fiona encounters an Australia she's never really known, replete with snakes on the doorstep, frogs in the toilet and the perils of the bush telegraph. Gradually, she begins to fall in love with rural life, but as Stuart struggles to balance environmental and commercial realities she realises that farming isn't quite as simple as she'd imagined. Ultimately, Fiona has to learn to cope with the devastating impact of the drought that grips the countryside, and what it means for Stuart, the farm and their future together.

Love in the Age of Drought is a delightful fish-out-of-water story about the city–country culture clash overcome by the course of true love. Written with heart and humour, it's also a moving portrait of country Australia's capacity for survival and renewal amid a drought that won't be broken.

Sheryl McCorry
Diamonds and Dust

Sheryl McCorry grew up in Arnhem Land carrying crocodiles to
school for show and tell. When she was 18, Broome beckoned,
and it was there that – only hours after being railroaded into
marriage by a fast-talking Yank – she locked eyes with Bob
McCorry, a drover and buffalo shooter. When her marriage
ended after only a few months, they began a romance that
would last a lifetime and take them to the Kimberley's harshest
frontiers.

As the only woman in a team of stockmen, Sheryl soon learned
how to run rogue bulls and to outsmart the neighbours in the
toughest game of all – mustering cattle. The playing field was
a million acres of unfenced, unmarked boundaries, But Sheryl
soon saw that to survive in the outback a woman needed
goals. Hers was to become the first woman in the Kimberley
to run two million-acre cattle stations. But it was to come at an
unimaginable cost.

Inspiring and unforgettable, *Diamonds and Dust* is a classic
story of a woman finding her destiny in the further reaches of
the outback.

Sara Henderson
From Strength to Strength

Sara Henderson's bestselling autobiography has touched
the hearts of thousands of people all over Australia. As
tough, spirited, warm and funny as the woman herself, *From
Strength to Strength* is the inspirational story of one woman's
extraordinary courage and determination.

In 1959 Sara met American war hero and shipping magnate,
Charles Henderson III, and so began what she calls the world's
most demanding, humiliating and challenging obstacle course
any human could be expected to endure.

Three years after their marriage, Charles presented Sara with
her new home – a tin shack in a million acres of red dust. Bullo
River. After twenty years of back-breaking work on this remote
Northern Australian cattle station, Charlie's death revealed that
Sara had not only been left with a floundering property, but also
with a heart-breaking mountain of debt.

With very little to lose, Sara and her daughters Marlee
and Danielle, took up the challenge of rebuilding Bullo
River . . . with such tremendous results that in 1991 Sara was
named the Bulletin/Qantas Businesswoman of the Year.

'Everyone has a book in them, they say, but not everyone has
the kind of story Sara Henderson tells, and tells well'

THE BULLETIN